BIBLICAL RESEARCH INSTITUTE
STUDIES IN ADVENTIST ECCLESIO

TOWARD A THEOLOGY OF THE

REMNANT

AN ADVENTIST ECCLESIOLOGICAL PERSPECTIVE

ÁNGEL MANUEL RODRÍGUEZ, EDITOR

Biblical Research Institute
Silver Spring, MD 20904

2009

Copyright © 2009, by the Biblical Research Institute
General Conference of Seventh-day Adventists
Silver Spring, MD 20904

Texts or quotations credited to ASV are from the *American Standard Version*.

Texts or quotations credited to KJV are from the *King James Version*.

Texts or quotations credited to NASB are from the *NEW AMERICAN STANDARD BIBLE®*, Copyright © 1960, 1962, 1963, 1968, 1971, 1972, 1973, 1975, 1977, 1995 by The Lockman Foundation. Used by permission.

Texts or quotations credited to NEV are from the *New English Bible* © Oxford University Press and Cambridge University Press, 1961, 170. Used by permission.

Texts or quotations credited to NIV are from the *HOLY BIBLE, NEW INTERNATIONAL VERSION*. Copyright © 1973, 1978, 1984 International Bible Society. Used by permission of Zondervan bible Publishers.

Texts or quotations credited to NKJV are from the *New King James Version®*. Copyright © 1982 by Thomas Nelson, Inc. Used by permission. All rights reserved.

Texts or quotations credited to NRSV are from the *New Revised Standard Version of the Bible*, copyright © 1989 by the National Council of the Churches of Christ in the USA. Used by permission. All rights reserved.

Texts or quotations credited to REB are from the *Revised English Bible* © Oxford University Press and Cambridge University Press 1989. Used by permission.

Texts or quotations credited to RSV are from the *Revised Standard Version of the Bible*, copyright © 1952 [2nd edition, 1971] by the Division of Christian Education of the National Council of the Churches of Christ in the United States of America. Used by permission. All rights reserved.

Printed in the U.S.A. by the
Review and Herald Publishing Association
Hagerstown, MD 21740

ISBN 978-0-925675-18-7

Editor
Ángel Manuel Rodríguez

BRI Staff

Marlene Bacchus	Gerhard Pfandl
Kwabena Donkor	Ekkehardt Mueller
Brenda Flemmer	Clinton Wahlen

BRICOM Members 2005-2010

Niels-Erik Andreasen	Bill Knott
Radisa Antic	Robert E. Lemon
Roberto Badenas	Larry Lichtenwalter
John T. Baldwin	John K. McVay
Matthew A. Bediako	Jerry Moon
Ivan T. Blazen	Daegeuk Nam
Lael O. Caesar	Brempong Owusu-Antwi
Jaime Castrejón	Jon K. Paulien
Gordon E. Christo	Jan Paulsen
Gerard Damsteegt	Paul B. Petersen
Jo Ann M. Davidson	John Reeve
Richard M. Davidson	Teresa Reeve
Ganoune Diop	Richard Rice
Larry R. Evans	Nikolaus Satelmajer
William Fagal	Tom Shepherd
Denis Fortin	Galina Stele
Eugene Hsu	Alberto Timm
Gerry D. Karst	Woodrow Whidden
Gregory A. King	Ted N. C. Wilson
Miroslav M. Kiš	Randall W. Younker
Gerald Klingbeil	E. Edward Zinke

Gratefully dedicated to

NEAL C. WILSON

In recognition of
his leadership in the formulation of the
Statement of Fundamental Beliefs of the church,
his commitment to the message, mission, and unity of
God's remnant people, and his positive spiritual and administrative
influence on the world church.

Neal C. Wilson and his wife Elinor Wilson. Pastor Neal C. Wilson served the Adventist Church for fifty-one years in many capacities. Among them, as President of the North American Division for twelve years and President of the General Conference for an additional twelve years. In 1980, during his tenure in this latter capacity, the Statement of Fundamental Beliefs of the church was revised and expanded at a General Conference Session in Dallas, TX.

The members of the Biblical
Research Institute Committee

Contents

Dedication	v
Preface	ix
Abbreviations	xi
General Introduction	17

Chapter I
The Remnant in the Old Testament — *Tarsee Li* — 23

Chapter II
The Remnant in Non-Canonical Jewish Apocalyptic Works and in Qumran — *Leslie N. Pollard* — 43

Chapter III
The Remnant in the Gospels — *Clinton Wahlen* — 61

Chapter IV
The Remnant in Pauline Thought — *Leslie N. Pollard* — 77

Chapter V
The Remnant in the Book of Revelation — *Richard P. Lehmann* — 85

Chapter VI
The Remnant and God's Commandments: Revelation 12:17 — *Johannes Kovar* — 113

Chapter VII
Sabbath Theology in the Book of Revelation — *Mathilde Frey* — 127

Chapter VIII
Identifying Marks of the End-Time Remnant in the Book of Revelation — *Gerhard Pfandl* — 139

Chapter IX
The Remnant in Contemporary Adventist Theology — *Frank M. Hasel* 159

Chapter X
The Remnant People of God in the Writings of Ellen G. White — *Ángel Manuel Rodríguez* 181

Chapter XI
Concluding Essay: God's End-Time Remnant and the Christian Church — *Ángel Manuel Rodríguez* 201

Appendix
The "Testimony of Jesus" in the Writings of Ellen G. White — *Ángel Manuel Rodríguez* 227

Scriptural Index 245

Thematic Index 249

Preface

This volume is dedicated to exploring the concept of the remnant and its contribution to an Adventist understanding of the nature of the church. The chapters seek to uncover the biblical roots of the concept, its richness, its role within salvation history, and its relevance for the Christian world today. Particular attention is given to the Adventist appropriation of the concept. This book provides an introduction to the understanding and significance of the end-time remnant as an Adventist theological self-definition. It addresses the very identity of the Seventh-day Adventist Church, an identity that occasionally needs to be examined and reaffirmed.

In a sense the book follows a historical trajectory in the study of the concept of the remnant, but the main emphasis is on its significance. It begins with a study of the remnant in the Old Testament, written by Dr. Tarsee Li, followed by three articles examining the concept of the remnant in Jewish writings (Dr. Leslie Pollard), in the Gospels (Dr. Clinton Wahlen), and in Paul (Dr. Leslie Pollard). Several articles address aspects of the concept in the book of Revelation. In one of them, written by Dr. Richard Lehmann, the presence and meaning of the concept is explored. We also find a study of the theology of the Sabbath in Revelation (Dr. Mathilde Frey) and another on the role of the commandments of God in Revelation (Dr. Johannes Kovar). Dr. Gerhard Pfandl discusses the distinctive marks or characteristics of the end-time remnant in Revelation. Of the two remaining studies, one explores the remnant in the writings of Ellen G. White (Dr. Ángel M. Rodríguez); the other looks at the contemporary discussion of the remnant among Adventists (Dr. Frank Hasel). The concluding essay attempts to synthesize the main theological aspects from the various contributors while also pushing the discussion forward by introducing the biblical concept of the remnant as fundamental to an Adventist ecclesiological self-understanding. An appendix is included which explores the usage of the phrase "testimony of Jesus" in the writings of Ellen G. White (Dr. Ángel Manuel Rodríguez). The reader will find some repetitions throughout the volume. These were unavoidable in order for each writer to clearly develop his/her argument. Throughout the volume, the term "ecclesiology" is employed to refer to the study of the biblical doctrine of the church. Since we are planning to publish other volumes on the subject of ecclesiology, we have included a general introduction to the series in this volume.

I would like to thank the writers for their contributions to this book and for their commitment to this project. I also acknowledge the valuable guidance and input provided by the members of the Biblical Research Institute Committee during the discussion of each of the papers now included in this volume. I am particularly indebted to my colleagues at the Biblical Research Institute—Kwabena Donkor, Ekkehardt Mueller, Gerhard Pfandl, and Clinton Wahlen—who made significant observations/suggestions in the process of editing the book. The editorial and technical contributions of Brenda Flemmer, my Administrative Assistant, and Marlene Bacchus, our Desktop Publishing Specialist, are greatly appreciated. We hope and pray that what has been accomplished will be useful for the church as it fulfills its God-given mission.

Ángel Manuel Rodríguez
Director
Biblical Research Institute

Abbreviations

2 Bar.	2 Baruch
AASS	Asia Adventist Seminary Studies
ABD	*Anchor Bible Dictionary*, D. N. Freedman, ed.
AdvA	*Adventist Affirm*
AdvBibComm	*Seventh-day Adventist Bible Commentary*, Francis D. Nichols, ed.
AdvChManual	*Seventh-day Adventist Church Manual* (17th ed.)
AdvEnc	*Seventh-day Adventist Encyclopedia*
AdvR	*Adventist Review*
ANET	*Ancient Near Eastern Texts Relating to the Old Testament*, J. B. Pritchard, ed.
Apoc. Abr.	Apocalypse of Abraham
ASTI	*Annual of the Swedish Theological Institute*
AUSS	*Andrews University Seminary Studies*
BDTh	*Baker Dictionary of Theology*, Everett F. Harrison, ed.
Bib	*Biblica*
BibInt	*Biblical Interpretation*
BJRL	*Bulletin of the John Rylands Library*
BR	*Biblical Research*
BSac	*Bibliotheca Sacra*
BT	*Bible Translator*
BTB	*Biblical Theology Bulletin*
CBQ	*Catholic Biblical Quarterly*
CD	Cairo Genizah Damascus Document
CH	*Church History*
DBS	*Dictionnarie de la Bible Supplément*, L. Pirot, A. Robert, H. Cazelles, and A. Feuillet, eds.
DEB	*Dictionnaire encyclopédique de la Bible*
DJG	*Dictionary of Jesus and the Gospels*, J. B. Green, S. McKnight, and I. H. Marshall, eds.
DPL	*Dictionary of Paul and His Letters*, G. F. Hawthorne, R. P. Martin, and D. G. Reid, eds.
DSS	Dead Sea Scrolls
EDNT	*Exegetical Dictionary of the New Testament*, H. Balz and G. Schneider, eds.
EDSS	*Encyclopedia of the Dead Sea Scrolls*, Lawrence H. Schiffman and James C. VanderKam, eds.
et al.	and others (Latin, *et alii*)

EvMisQ	Evangelical Mission Quarterly
ExpTim	Expository Times
FoiVie	Foi et Vie
Gen. Rab.	Genesis Rabbah
Heb.	Hebrew Language
IDBSup	Interpreter's Dictionary of the Bible: Supplementary Volume, K. Crim, ed.
Int	Interpretation
ISBE	International Standard Bible Encyclopedia, G. W. Bromiley, ed.
ISJR	Iowa State Journal of Research
ITQ	Irish Theological Quarterly
JAAS	Journal of Asia Adventist Seminary
JAMS	Journal of Adventist Mission Studies
JATS	Journal of the Adventist Theological Society
JBL	Journal of Biblical Literature
JCThR	Journal of Christian Theological Research
JETS	Journal of the Evangelical Theological Society
JHS	Journal of Hellenic Studies
JJS	Journal of Jewish Studies
JSNT	Journal for the Study of the New Testament
JSOT	Journal for the Study of the Old Testament
JTS	Journal of Theological Studies
Jub.	Jubilees
JW	Josephus, Jewish Wars
Kgdms	Kingdoms (LXX)
LCL	Loeb Classic Library
LXX	Septuagint (Greek Version of Old Testament)
LW	Luther's Works
1-4 Macc	Maccabees
Mig	On the Migration of Abraham
Mos	Moses
MT	Masoretic Text
n.	Footnote
NBD	New Bible Dictionary, D. Guthrie and J. A. Motyer, eds.
NDBTh	New Dictionary of Biblical Theology, T. D. Alexander, B. S. Rosner, D. A. Carson, and G. Goldworthy, eds.
NIDB	New Interpreter's Dictionary of the Bible, K. D. Sakenfeld, ed.
NIDNTTE	New International Dictionary of New Testament Theology and Exegisis, C. Brown, ed.

NIDOTTE	*New International Dictionary of Old Testament Theology and Exegesis,* W. A. VanGemeren, ed.
NovT	*Novum Testamentum*
NT	New Testament
NTS	*New Testament Studies*
OT	Old Testament
OTP	*Old Testament Pseudepigrapha,* James H. Charlesworth, ed.
PH	Pamphlets
PT	*Present Truth*
QG	*Questions and Answers on Genesis*
RB	*Revue Biblique*
RH	*Review and Herald*
RPP	*Religion Past and Present,* H. D. Betz, D. S. Browning, B. Janowsici, e. Jüngel, eds.
RevQ	*Revue de Qumran*
RevScRel	*Revue des sciences religieuses*
SBL	Society of Biblical Literature
SJT	*Scottish Journal of Theology*
ST	*Signs of the Times*
StTh	*Studia Theologica*
SwJT	*Southwestern Journal of Theology*
TDNT	*Theological Dictionary of the New Testament,* G. Kittel and G. Friedrich, eds.
TDOT	*Theological Dictionary of the Old Testament,* G. J. Botterweck, H. Ringgren, and H. J. Falory, eds.
TestJud	*Testament of Judah*
TestLevi	*Testament of Levi*
Tg. Neof.	*Targum Neofiti*
Tg. Ong.	*Targum Ongelos*
ThBl	*Theologische Blätter*
TLOT	*Theological Lexicon of the Old Testament,* E. Jenni and C. Westermann, eds.
TWOT	*Theological Wordbook of the Old Testament,* R. L. Harris, G. L. Archer, Jr., and B. K. Waltke, eds.
v.	verse
VT	*Vetus Testamentum*
vv.	verses
Wis.	Wisdom
ZNW	*Zeitschrift für die neutestamentliche Wissenschaft*
ZPEB	*Zondervan Pictorial Encyclopedia of the Bible,* M. C. Tenney, ed.
ZST	*Zeitschrift für systematische Theologie*

Bible Translations/Versions

ASV	American Standard Version
AV	Authorized Version
KJV	King James Version
NASB	New American Standard Bible
NEB	New English Bible
NIV	New International Version
NKJV	New King James Version
NRSV	New Revised Standard Version
REB	Revised English Bible
RSV	Revised Standard Version

Hebrew Alphabet

א	= ʾ	ח	= $ḥ$	פ	= p
ב	= b	ט	= $ṭ$	פ	= p
ב	= b	י	= y	צ	= $ṣ$
ג	= g	כ	= k	ק	= q
ג	= g	כ	= k	ר	= r
ד	= d	ל	= l	ש	= $ś$
ד	= d	מ	= m	ש	= $š$
ה	= h	נ	= n	ת	= t
ו	= w	ס	= s	ת	= $ṯ$
ז	= z	ע	= ʿ		

Masoretic Vowel Pointings

ֲ	= a	ִי	= $î$
ָ	= $ā$	ׂ	= $ō$
ֲ	= $ᵃ$	ֳ	= o
ֶ	= e	וֹ	= $ô$
ֵ	= $ē$	ֻ	= u
ֵי, ֶי	= $ê$	וּ	= $û$
ִ	= i		

Greek Alphabet

α	= a	ζ	= z	λ	= l	π	= p	φ	= ph
β	= b	η	= $ē$	μ	= m	ρ	= r	χ	= ch
γ	= g	θ	= th	ν	= n	σ,ς	= s	ψ	= ps
δ	= d	ι	= i	ξ	= x	τ	= t	ω	= $ō$
ε	= e	κ	= k	ο	= o	υ	= u	ʽ	= h

Abbreviations

Qumran Documents

1Q14	*Pesher Micah*
1Q20	*Genesis Apocryphon*
1Q27	*Mysteries*
1QH^a	*Hodayot^a* (Thanksgiving Hymns)
1QM	*War Scroll*
1QpHab	*Pesher on Habakkuk*
1QS	*Rule of the Community*
1QSa	*Rule of the Congregation*
1QSb	*Rule of Benedictions*
4Q161	*Isaiah Pesher^a*
4Q162	*Isaiah Pesher^b*
4Q163	*Isaiah Pesher^c*
4Q183	*Historical Work*
4Q196	*Tobit^a*
4Q206	*Enoch^e*
4Q208	*Astronomical Enoch^a*
4Q209	*Astronomical Enoch^b*
4Q252	*Genesis Pesher^a*
4Q368	*Apocryphon Pentateuch*
4Q390	*Pseudo-Moses^e*
4Q424	*Sapiential Text*
4Q427	*Hadayot^a*
4Q537	*Testament of Jacob*
4Q556	*Book of Giants^e*
4Q558	*Vision^b*
4Q561	*Physiognomy Horoscope*
4Q563	*Aramaic E*
4QFlor	*Florilegium*
11Q10	*Targum of Job*
11Q19	*Temple Scroll^a*

GENERAL INTRODUCTION

For several years the Biblical Research Institute of the General Conference (BRI) has been working in conjunction with the Biblical Research Institute Committee (BRICOM) on a series of studies exploring different aspects of an Adventist doctrine of the church. This volume and others will provide materials that will be useful to pastors and theologians as they seek to gain a better understanding of the Adventist movement and as they attempt to develop an Adventist ecclesiology. The beginning of the twenty-first century may be a good historical moment for the church to look at itself and reaffirm its self-understanding and its mission. The volumes to be published will address topics such as church ordinances, church authority, the ministry, liturgy, the mission of the church, the church and the Spirit, and the church and Scripture.

This is not the first time that BRI has attempted to study the doctrine of the church. On May 12, 1982, BRICOM voted to undertake a series of studies in ecclesiology. It was not until 1988 that a list of subjects was compiled and the writers selected. The project did not develop as quickly as intended, mainly because BRICOM had to spend most of its time and resources addressing other pressing theological issues of interest to the world church. These issues finally overshadowed the ecclesiology project to the point that it was never finished. Some of the papers reached the stage of semi-final editing, but hardly any of them became ready for publication. Most of them are now outdated. But since they are part of the history of Adventist ecclesiology, a number of the most important papers are being made available through the BRI website (www.adventistbiblicalresearch.org). This new ecclesiology project is progressing well, and we will make the material available in printed form as soon as it is ready for publication.

By way of introduction to this series, I reflect on what I consider to be some of the key elements in the formulation of an Adventist ecclesiology. I will specifically emphasize the need for such an ecclesiology and its contribution toward a clearer expression of the identity of the Adventist movement. I will also suggest that in our discussions on ecclesiology, we should identify some of the most important elements of the biblical faith that should be taken into consideration and that should be part of our theological journey.

I. Need for an Adventist Ecclesiology

The church is by nature a dynamic social and spiritual institution. Therefore, it is and should constantly be on the move as a community of spiritual pilgrims. Such dynamism should not exclude the need for serious theological reflection on its very nature and the implication for the mission and life of the church itself. In doing this, the church may be revitalized toward the fulfillment of its mission.

Need to Remain Relevant

The Adventist movement is still relatively young and faces constant challenges of growth and development. Probably one of the most important challenges it confronts is maintaining its vitality and relevance in a world that has changed significantly since the inception of the movement. Relevance implies that the presence of the church is vital because it satisfies a significant need within society and in the life of its members. Keeping the church relevant requires, among other things, constant reflection on its identity, nature, and mission. For instance, changes in liturgy should be preceded by a serious analysis of the nature of Christian worship that will help to enrich the worship experience of believers. If the church becomes irrelevant, it will slowly fade away from social consciousness, significantly weakening its influence.

Need to Preserve Unity

The unity of the end-time people of God takes us directly into the essence of the church, into the mystery of its union with the Risen Lord from whom it derives its life. The phenomenal growth of the Adventist movement should provide an occasion to strengthen that unity. The natural tendency in a religious movement characterized by ethnic, national, and cultural diversity is toward further diversification. To preserve the unity that characterizes us, it is important to continue to reaffirm the biblical elements that constitute our bond of unity in Christ. I would suggest that the key elements are located in our ecclesiology. We need almost constantly to reaffirm the importance and need of that unity through analysis and reflection within the context of our diversity. Adventists are a people with a distinctive body of beliefs, a particular lifestyle, and a biblical worldview. These elements, together with the church's worldwide organization, characterize Adventism around the world and directly contribute to its unity. An Adventist ecclesiology will explore the significance of that union in a world increasingly characterized by fragmentation.

Need to Interact Properly with Others

A clearly enunciated Adventist ecclesiology will be helpful in properly interacting with other Christian communities and with non-Christian religions. As the Adventist movement continues to grow, it will become more and more influential around the world. We can easily anticipate an increase in the need to engage in conversations with other Christian communities and with religious leaders from other world religions. The church should be ready to express in a clear and persuasive form its identity and mission, its reason for existence. Such expression should be characterized by clear theological and biblical thinking. This will be of central value to the community of believers and to other audiences and could be helpful in eliminating prejudice and stereotypes.

II. Central Theological Elements in an Adventist Ecclesiology

Let us be clear that we are not pioneers in the development of an Adventist ecclesiology. The Adventist church is already here: it has a clear self-understanding, a unique identity, and a specific mission. Adventists believe that "the church is the community of believers who confess Jesus Christ as Lord and Savior."[1] This community gathers together through the call of the Lord "for worship, for fellowship, for instruction in the Word, for the celebration of the Lord's Supper, for service to all mankind, and for the worldwide proclamation of the gospel."[2] The origin and authority of the church are found and grounded in Christ, as He has revealed Himself in Scripture. The church is the body of Christ, "a community of faith of which Christ Himself is the head."[3] He has entrusted authority to the church, and it resides in the community of believers as a whole. It is the task of ecclesiology to explore the nature and extent of that authority and how it operates within the church. Based on the New Testament, Adventists have understood that the community of faith delegates some of its authority to elected individuals, e.g., the ministry within the church, to facilitate the work of the body of Christ.

In our task we should take into consideration our history as a church and our mission and message. This means that we should take with us some non-negotiable aspects of biblical theology as understood by the Adventist movement. I will mention a few of them.

---

[1]"Fundamental Beliefs of Seventh-day Adventists," in *2008 Yearbook: Seventh-day Adventist Church* (Silver Spring, MD: General Conference Corporation, 2008), p. 6.

[2]Ibid.

[3]Ibid.

Eschatological Outlook

It has been correctly said that Adventism is an apocalyptic movement and that as such it will play a particular role within the closing chapters of the cosmic conflict. This means that our self-perception is strongly related to our eschatological expectations. Any attempt to free our ecclesiology from its eschatological moorings will have to redefine the first or ignore the second. Such displacement will not be able to produce an ecclesiology that is Adventist in thinking, orientation, and worldview. It appears to me that the role of the church within the cosmic conflict and its particular role in the final confrontation are of paramount importance in our ecclesiology.

Soteriological Outlook

Our ecclesiology should be firmly grounded in the conviction that the church is the result of the incarnation, ministry, death, resurrection, ascension, and mediation of Christ. This theological conviction will influence the way we develop our understanding of the church, its identity, its message, and its function. This may well be one of the areas where we could make a contribution to Christian theology. We also hold that there is a deep-rooted connection between the church and the role of Christ as our Mediator in the heavenly temple. In fact, the church received, so to speak, its "breath of life" from God as a result of Christ's mediation before the Father (John 14:16; Acts 2:33). Our ecclesiology should examine the biblical witness to that connection and make room for the high-priestly work of Christ and the role of the Spirit within the church. This will have an impact on our theology of the ministry and even in our understanding of the ordinances.

Gospel Outlook

The gospel is the truth proclaimed by the church. Paul describes "the church of the living God" as "the pillar and foundation of the truth" (1 Tim 3:15). In Adventist thinking, as well as in Scripture, truth plays a fundamental role in the cosmic conflict and is directly related to this central issues. The search for truth and its proclamation make a direct contribution to our self-understanding, that is to say, to our ecclesiology. With respect to biblical truth, Adventists have seen themselves as restoring truths that have been "cast to the ground" (Dan 8:12; cf. Isa 58:12), truths that have been rejected or ignored by other Christian communities. From that perspective, Adventism is a reform movement within the Christian world. Since the message that is proclaimed is in direct continuity with apostolic truth (apostolicity), it is indispensable to reestablish it before the return of Christ. In fact, our mission is fueled by the seriousness with which we have taken biblical truth and its relevance for the last days. Since the message and the responsibility of the church are of universal significance, we are persuaded that the church is also universal (catholic). This concern with biblical truth is at the very core of our ecclesiology, and we should not dislodge the one from the other.

Missiological Outlook

It took some time for our pioneers to realize that the Adventist movement had a mission to the whole world. This had a significant impact on the understanding of the nature of the Adventist church. A clear message was to be proclaimed by a unified community of believers to every people, nation, and tongue. That message transcends ethnicity, gender, race, and national distinctions. This missiological outlook has contributed in a direct way to the unity of the church and to the development of an ecclesiastical organization of world proportions. An Adventist ecclesiology should incorporate in its formulation that central missiological concern at the close of the cosmic conflict. Therefore, the church is not simply to be defined through the concept of *koinonia* ("communion"), important as it is, but also by the fulfillment of the gospel commission as a witnessing community.

Remnant Outlook

Adventist ecclesiology cannot ignore the fact that from its beginnings, the Adventist movement saw itself as the remnant mentioned in Rev 12:17. This concept proved to be valuable in that it placed the movement within the flow of prophetic history, it served to define its nature vis-à-vis the rest of the Christian world, and it determined its missiology. In other words we are dealing here with an essential aspect of the nature of the Adventist faith and existence that cannot be ignored in an Adventist ecclesiology. I would suggest that an Adventist ecclesiology is fundamentally a remnant ecclesiology. It is precisely this aspect that makes it challenging, interesting, biblical, and unique. Our theological task is to develop it, properly integrating the biblical material and keeping in mind that we are part of the larger Christian community.

III. Conclusion

The church will always need to reflect on itself and its connection with the Living Lord. This cannot be disjoined from the dynamism of its mission but should be considered an essential component of it. The church is an active entity at the service of its Lord and of humanity. It needs to remain relevant in the culture in which it exists, but in doing this the church should not abandon or modify its identity, message, or mission. Otherwise, it would be transformed into little more than a social movement procuring the betterment of human society and the individual, hardly interested in their redemption from the enslavement of sin and guilt through Christ or in their commitment to Him as Lord in the cosmic conflict. The church will always remain a mystery because of the mystery of its union with the Lord, a mystery in which we all participate as part of His body.

Ángel Manuel Rodríguez
Editor

CHAPTER I

THE REMNANT IN THE OLD TESTAMENT

Tarsee Li
Associate Professor
Oakwood University
Huntsville, AL

The remnant motif has been treated almost exhaustively in a number of studies.[1] In what follows I will summarize some of the relevant conclusions of those previous studies concerning the origin and meaning of the remnant motif. Next I will offer some brief comments on the nature of the faithful remnant that both summarize and build on those previous studies. The third section of this study fills an important gap, in that most of the studies on the Old Testament remnant motif have focused primarily on pre-exilic texts. I will explore the relationship between the remnant motif and the self-identity of the post-exilic community. Finally, I will highlight some parallels relevant to a Seventh-day Adventist ecclesiology.

I. The Origin and Meaning of the Remnant Motif

Origin of the Concept

The simplest definition of the remnant may be "what is left of a community after it undergoes a catastrophe."[2] However, as we will see, such a simple definition fails to capture the full extent of its theological relevance and significance. Although there is no scholarly consensus on the origin of

---

[1] An extensive survey and discussion of earlier literature may be found in Gerhard F. Hasel, *The Remnant: History and Theology of the Remnant Idea from Genesis to Isaiah*, 3rd ed. (Berrien Springs, MI: Andrews University Press, 1980). Other important articles written by him on the remnant include, "*Pālāṭ*," *TDOT*, vol. 11, pp. 551-567; "Remnant," *IDBSup*, pp. 735-736; and "Remnant," *ISBE*, vol. 4, pp. 130-134. A number of studies on various aspects of the remnant motif in the Old Testament have also appeared since then, but Hasel's treatment remains the "authoritative study" on the remnant (Eugene H. Merrill, "A Theology of Ezekiel and Daniel," in *A Biblical Theology of the Old Testament*, Roy B. Zuck, ed. [Chicago, IL: Moody Press, 1991], p. 377, note 21). We will closely follow him in our discussion.

[2] Lester V. Meyer, "Remnant," *ABD*, vol. 5, p. 669.

the remnant motif, I would suggest that the best possibility was offered by Gerhard F. Hasel. He traces the presence of the remnant motif in the ancient Near East beginning with the Sumerian texts and ending with materials from the time of Isaiah. According to Hasel, the origin of the motif predated the biblical materials. The "common denominator" of all the usages of the motif is "the life-and-death problem, i.e., man's existential concern."[3] Mortal threats "raise the immediate question of whether life will be wiped out or whether a remnant will survive to preserve human existence."[4] Thus, the remnant motif did not arise as part of a particular biblical context and was "originally not eschatological."[5]

Hence, the use of the remnant motif in extra-biblical and biblical materials indicates that it arose out of man's existential concern for the preservation of human life.[6] In the Hebrew Bible the remnant motif was from the start incorporated into salvation history and became gradually employed to express the future expectations of the Yahwistic faith. The remnant and the possibility of a future are so deeply connected that "where there is no 'remnant,' there is no longer a future."[7] The motif received for the first time a distinctly eschatological emphasis in Amos. Isaiah of Jerusalem solidified the eschatological usage. The eschatological or holy remnant, purified by divine purging, was for Isaiah an object of faith and a future reality. This element of the Isaianic remnant motif proved to be of great importance for later prophecy and the further development of Israelite eschatology.[8]

The remnant motif can be found throughout the Old Testament, either explicitly or implicitly,[9] but it is most prominent in the prophetic books. For instance, it has been argued that the entire book of Micah is struc-

---

[3]Hasel, *Theology of the Remnant*, p. 383.

[4]*Idem*, "Remnant," *ISBE*, vol. 4, p. 132.

[5]*Idem*, *Theology of the Remnant*, p. 402.

[6]*Idem*, "Remnant," *IDBSup*, p. 735; see also, F. Dreyfus, "Reste d'Israël," *DBS*, vol. 10, p. 418.

[7]Rolf Rendtorff, *Canonical Hebrew Bible: A Theology of the Old Testament* (Leiden: Deo, 2005), p. 706. See also Hasel, "Remnant," *IDBSup*, p. 736, where he writes, "The remnant theme is an essential part of biblical hope and eschatology."

[8]Hasel, *Theology of the Remnant*, p. 402.

[9]Héctor E. Urrutia argues that the message of the final eschatological remnant is prefigured in the Wisdom literature ("El mensaje del remanente final en los libros sapienciales," in *Pensar la iglesia hoy*, Gerald A. Klingbeil, Martin Klingbeil, and Miguel Ángel Núñez, eds. [Libertador San Martin, Entre Rios: Editorial Universidad Adventista del Plata, 2002], pp. 71-92).

tured around the theme of God's promises to the remnant.[10] As already mentioned, "Amos is the first Hebrew writer to connect the remnant motif with eschatology,"[11] and this motif becomes even more prominent "in the Isaianic pericopes than in the earlier parts of the Hebrew Bible."[12]

Biblical Remnant Terminology

The terminology of the Old Testament remnant motif is represented by six Hebrew roots: š'r ("be left over, remain"), plṭ ("escape"), mlṭ ("escape"), ytr ("remain over, be left over"), śrd ("run away from;" śārîd, "survivor"), and 'aḥ°rît ("posterity, remnant").[13] The word 'aḥ°rît is more often used in a context of total destruction (e.g., Amos 4:1-3),[14] but the others are more frequently employed in a positive context, e.g., "the escape . . . from a mortal threat."[15] In the LXX, these Hebrew roots are most frequently translated into Greek words formed from leimma/leipō ("remnant, remainder/leave behind").[16] The presence of one of these words does not automatically mean that the remnant motif is present (e.g., 1 Sam 20:29).[17] Conversely, the remnant motif can also be implicitly present even where remnant terminology is not used (e.g., Cain in Gen 4:1-15). Furthermore, the remnant motif may also occur in a negative sense, i.e., in passages that state the absence or destruction of a remnant, as in Joel 2:3: "A fire consumes before it [the locust swarm] and a flame burns

---

[10]Kenneth H. Cuffey, "Remnant, Redactor, and Biblical Theologian: A Comparative Study of Coherence in Micah and the Twelve," in *Reading and Hearing the Book of the Twelve*, James D. Nogalski and Marvin A. Sweeney, eds. (Atlanta, GA: Society of Biblical Literature, 2000), pp. 185-208. It has also been suggested that the book of Obadiah focuses on the concept of the remnant; see Merling Alomía, "El motivo del remanente en Abdías," *Theologika* 11 (1996): 8-35; and that it is of fundamental importance in the literary structure of Zephaniah (Bernard Renaud, "Le livre de Sophonie: Le thème de YHWH structurant de la synthèse redactionnelle," *RevScRel* 60 [1986]: 1-33; see also Greg A. King, "The Remnant in Zephaniah," *BSac* 151 [1994]: 414-427).

[11]Hasel, *Theology of the Remnant*, p. 394; see also his "Remnant," *ISBE*, vol. 4, p. 133.

[12]Hasel, *Theology of the Remnant*, p. 394.

[13]Hasel, "Remnant," *ISBE*, vol. 4, pp. 130-131; also idem, *Theology of the Remnant*, pp. 386-388.

[14]See Horst Seebass, "'Aḥ°rîth," *TDOT*, vol. 1, pp. 209-210.

[15]Hasel, "Remnant," *ISBE*, vol. 4, p. 131. Individual authors may use these words in slightly different ways. For example, Kenneth D. Mulzac claims that śārîd is used in the book of Jeremiah in the context of total destruction ("Śrd as a Remnant Term in the Context of Judgment in the Book of Jeremiah," *AASS* 7 [2004]: 39-58).

[16]V. Herntrich and G. Schrenk, "Leimma," *TDNT*, vol. 4, pp. 194-198.

[17]Another possible instance where a word for "remnant" is used without any reference to the theological motif is in Neh 7:72 (š°'ērît; 7:71 MT).

behind it. The land is like the garden of Eden before it, but a desolate wilderness behind it, having not even a survivor [$p^e l\hat{e}\d{t}\bar{a}h$]."[18]

Remnant Types

According to Hasel, the remnant motif is applied to three types of groups, which he names *historical, faithful*, and *eschatological*.[19] The *historical* remnant consists of any group that escaped a catastrophe that threatened its survival. This aspect of the remnant motif is applicable regardless of the group's faith or commitment to God. An example of the historical remnant occurs in the first implicit reference to a remnant in the Bible, namely Gen 4:1-15, "which left only Cain as the progenitor of the human race."[20] Likewise, the remnant of the Canaanites, who later became a source of trouble for Israel, is also an historical remnant (Num 33:55; Judg 3:1).[21]

The second type of remnant, the *faithful* remnant, may be characterized as a community that exhibits genuine spirituality and a true faith relationship with God; His promises for the future rest on this remnant. An example of a faithful remnant can be found in the very first explicit reference to the remnant recorded in Gen 7:23, where "Noah and his family represented a righteous remnant."[22] The third group, the *eschatological* remnant, consists of the faithful ones who go through the cleansing judgments and apocalyptic woes of the end time and are victorious. They receive from the Lord the everlasting kingdom.[23] Joel refers to this remnant when he writes, "The sun will be turned into darkness and the moon into blood before the great and awesome day of the Lord comes. And it will come about that whoever calls on the name of the Lord will be delivered [mlt]; for on Mount Zion and in Jerusalem there will be those who escape [$p^e l\hat{e}\d{t}\bar{a}h$], as the Lord has said, even among the survivors [$\acute{s}\bar{a}r\hat{i}d$] whom the Lord calls" (2:31-32 [3:4-5 MT], NASB).[24]

---

[18] My own translation.

[19] Hasel, "Remnant," *ISBE*, vol. 4, p. 130. See also Hans K. LaRondelle, "The Remnant and the Three Angel's Message," in *Handbook of Seventh-day Adventist Theology*, Raoul Dederen, ed. (Hagerstown, MD: Review and Herald, 2000), pp. 860-863.

[20] Hasel, "Remnant," *ISBE*, vol. 4, p. 132.

[21] Ibid.

[22] Ibid.

[23] As can be seen from the explanation, although the term "eschatology" has a broad range of applications, it is here used in a purely chronological sense, i.e., the end of an era.

[24] Bible quotations are from NRSV unless otherwise indicated.

The Remnant in the Old Testament

This threefold grouping of the remnant "must not be pressed too hard, for the distinction between the groups is sometimes blurred in the biblical portrayal."[25] For one thing, there is an overlap in the groupings, i.e., the faithful remnant is also an historical remnant, and the eschatological remnant is also a faithful remnant. In addition, the pre-exilic prophecies about the return from captivity sometimes blur the distinction between the faithful and the eschatological remnant. This overlapping will be discussed in more detail below. Even the terms "historical," "faithful" and "eschatological" should not be understood as precise definitions, but only as approximate labels. Nevertheless, though Hasel's threefold grouping and its terminology are a bit imprecise and may not be completely adequate, I find it useful for our discussion.

II. Presence and Nature of the Faithful Remnant

Having summarized some relevant conclusions of previous studies on the origin and meaning of the remnant motif, I turn now to a more detailed, though not exhaustive, discussion on the nature of a faithful remnant community. In the Old Testament, a faithful remnant community consists of those who survive a catastrophe (whether physical or spiritual), who are the recipients of God's grace and thus heirs of the covenant promises, and who have a specific mission related to the preservation of the true knowledge of God and His worship. Below is a discussion of some issues relevant to the concept.

Remnant as a Faithful Community

Generally in the Old Testament, a remnant community is clearly identifiable. The exception seems to be in cases of national apostasy when the life of God's faithful ones is threatened, making it necessary for them to hide from the public eye. In those cases the emphasis seems to be placed on the individual rather than on the community. Possibly the best example of this aspect of the remnant is found 1 Kgs 19, where Elijah says, "I only am left [*ytr*]" (v. 14), and God responds by assuring him that he is not alone (v. 18). That is, Elijah and 7,000 others are faithful remnant individuals. He is the only one who is clearly identified by others as a faithful servant of the Lord. He and the 7,000 are part of a larger group or a community, the majority of which has become unfaithful and cannot be identified as such with God's remnant. In fact, "for the first

---

[25]King, "Remnant," p. 427.

time in the Old Testament, a distinction is made within corporeal Israel, a distinction based on religious fidelity and leading to a new Israel bound to Yahweh."[26]

However, when the faithful remnant motif is applied to a community, whether a family or a nation, others are able to identify it. Such a community may include some unfaithful individuals, for it is only at the eschatological Day of the Lord that the remnant will only consist of the faithful ones.[27] This is suggested by Malachi:

> Then those who revered the LORD spoke with one another. The LORD took note and listened, and a book of remembrance was written before him of those who revered the LORD and thought on his name. They shall be mine, says the LORD of hosts, my special possession on the day when I act, and I will spare them as parents spare their children who serve them. Then once more you shall see the difference between the righteous and the wicked, between one who serves God and one who does not serve him. See, the day is coming, burning like an oven, when all the arrogant and all evildoers will be stubble; the day that comes shall burn them up, says the LORD of hosts, so that it will leave them neither root nor branch. But for you who revere my name, the sun of righteousness shall rise, with healing in its wings. You shall go out leaping like calves from the stall. And you shall tread down the wicked, for they will be ashes under the soles of your feet, on the day when I act, says the LORD of hosts. (Mal 3:16-4:3 [3:16-21 MT]).

The context of the passage indicates that people were complaining that God treated the faithful and the unfaithful alike (3:13-15). God responded in the passage cited by promising that He was going to separate the two groups (visibly, 3:18) on the day of the Lord, i.e., the "day when I act" (3:17), the day "burning like an oven" (4:1).[28]

Meanwhile, the faithful remnant communities in the Old Testament often included members who were not completely faithful. For example, although Noah and his family were a faithful remnant that survived the flood (Gen 6:9; 7:23), Ham later uncovered Noah's "nakedness" (9:20-27). Also, in Gen 19, Abraham's intercession for God to spare Sodom for

---

[26]Hasel, "*Pālaṭ*," p. 563.

[27]So also in the New Testament; e.g., Matt 13:24-30, 37-43; 25:1-4, 31-33.

[28]Although the word "remnant" is not used in this passage in Malachi, the motif is implicit, since those who "revere" God's name emerge victorious on the day of the Lord's final judgment.

the sake of the "righteous" and Lot's hospitality to the strangers indicate that Lot and his family were a faithful remnant that escaped Sodom.[29] Yet, Lot's wife looked back and was turned into a pillar of salt (v. 26), and Lot's daughters gave birth to sons fathered by Lot (vv. 30-38).

Therefore, since a faithful remnant community may include elements of unfaithfulness, one must go beyond the narrow context of the particular passage in which remnant terminology is used to the larger context of the book, or even the entire canon, to determine whether a surviving community in the Bible is a faithful remnant or simply an historical remnant. For example, although the preservation of Jacob's family through Joseph in Egypt was not ascribed to their faith or commitment (Gen 45:7), the context provided by the book of Genesis makes it clear that they were the recipients of the divine promises made to faithful Abraham. That is, Abraham's descendants through Jacob constitute a faithful remnant, though the family members were not always faithful to God. The Joseph cycle demonstrates a "connection between the remnant motif and the election tradition."[30]

A Remnant of Grace

The label "faithful remnant" does not point to self-achievement. Rather, as Hasel demonstrates, the faithful remnant is a remnant of grace. For example, though both Noah and Lot were "righteous" (Gen 6:9; 18:23-32), their righteousness was not meritorious, but they were the recipients of God's "grace" and "mercy" (Gen 6:8; 19:16, 19). Thus, "the salvation of a remnant is not due to merit on the part of the remaining survivors but to the grace of Yahweh."[31] Although a community may be characterized as faithful, their remnant status is not granted to them on the basis of their faithfulness, but on the basis of God's grace. Similarly, the term "perhaps" in Amos 5:15 suggests that the salvation of the remnant is not guaranteed by their fulfillment of specific conditions but by God's grace:[32] "Hate evil, love good, and establish justice in the gate! Perhaps the LORD God of hosts may be gracious to the remnant of Joseph" (Amos 5:15). Though the people are invited to return to God, their

---

[29]Hasel, *Theology of the Remnant*, pp. 147-152.

[30]Ibid., p. 158.

[31]Ibid., p. 152.

[32]Ibid., p. 206. The same is implied, though in different words, in expressions such as "who knows?" (Joel 2:14; Jonah 3:9) or "if" (Dan 4:27 [v. 24, MT]). Although such expressions primarily express the hope that God will be merciful, they also allude to God's sovereignty, i.e., God responds because He chooses to, not because He is obligated to.

repentance and conversion do not merit God's grace. The deliverance of the remnant is an act of divine grace. Still, as King points out, "A faithful remnant community is characterized by certain qualities. For instance, the remnant people in Zephaniah are fully committed to the Lord and are righteous and ethical in their social interaction."[33]

Furthermore, although a faithful remnant community owes its status to the reception of God's grace and mercy, it is not an unconditional status. Human action cannot substitute for divine action, nor can divine grace substitute for human faithfulness.[34] God's grace does not preclude the call to faithfulness on the part of its recipients.

Need for a Remnant

Hasel argues that the expression "remnant of Joseph" originated from a commonly held belief that Israel as a whole and as an earthly entity would be the "remnant of Joseph" that survives the Day of Yahweh and the destruction of the surrounding nations, and that Amos took this expression and gave it a new meaning, applying it to a future eschatological entity (Amos 5:14-15; cf. Gen 45:7).[35] That is, the "mass of Israelites who refused to return to Yahweh would perish in the judgment to come upon the nation, but a remnant, those who returned to Yahweh, would 'perhaps' be spared."[36] This perspective is also echoed in E. Merrill's following observation:

> It was a fact that the people of the Lord always tended to fall away from Him except for a small minority, the remnant, who would remain faithful to their covenant responsibilities. In other words, there was always an Israel within Israel, the true kernel surrounded by the husk of an external national entity. The saving purposes and promises of Yahweh could not, therefore, find fulfillment in the nation as such but only in that godly core that He preserved through the ages.[37]

---

[33]King, "Remnant," p. 417.

[34]Although it is beyond the scope of this article, which is limited to the Old Testament, more can be said concerning human action vis-à-vis divine action in the light of the New Testament. Jesus' statement that many are called but few are chosen (Matt 22:14) is relevant to the remnant motif in the New Testament. Thus, the fact that Jesus' parables mention those who decline a royal invitation (e.g., 22:1-14; Luke 14:16-24) suggests that part of the human responsibility consists of an openness to accept God's grace.

[35]Hasel, *Theology of the Remnant*, pp. 199-205.

[36]Ibid., p. 203.

[37]Eugene H. Merrill, "A Theology of Ezra-Nehemiah and Esther," in *Biblical Theology*

In fact, there is an historical pattern in the Old Testament motif of the faithful remnant. We find that after the Lord chooses a faithful remnant out of a larger group, this faithful remnant later tends to depart from the Lord to such an extent that the Lord chooses a new faithful remnant from that group, thus initiating the cycle again.[38] Originally the seed of Abraham, Isaac, and Jacob, i.e., all 12 tribes, were recipients of the divine promises, and thus the faithful remnant. Nevertheless, the "LORD was very angry with Israel, and he removed them from His sight; none was left [š'r] except the tribe of Judah" (2 Kgs 17:18). However, v. 19 makes it clear that Judah was not entirely faithful to the Lord. Finally, because of Judah's unfaithfulness, Jerusalem was also destroyed, and a remnant was taken away to Babylon (2 Kgs 25:11). From these exiles, a remnant returned to rebuild the nation and form the post-exilic community of Judah.

Remnant as a Status and a Mission

Being a faithful remnant involves both a status and a mission. In terms of status, it is important to underscore the fact that a faithful remnant community is composed of those who are the heirs of the divine election promises. Thus, a community does not by itself become a faithful remnant. Rather, it is chosen by grace and constituted into the concrete expression of the people of God for a particular reason. For example, the fact that Naomi "survives" [š'r] the rest of her family is not ascribed to any faithfulness on her part (Ruth 1:3, 5), but neither is she unfaithful. On the other hand, the terminology of the remnant is not even applied to Ruth, who does exhibit a faithful character. As it turns out, they both together shared God's blessing in the birth of an heir (Ruth 4:14-17), who through his descendants had a special role in the future of the people of Israel, the heirs of the covenant promises (vv. 18-22). Thus, the story emphasizes God's grace, rather than the faithfulness of the recipients of His grace.

On the other hand, remnant status also involves a mission. The mission may entail different details due to differing historical circumstances, such as Noah's mission to build an ark to preserve human and animal life, or

---

of the Old Testament, p. 194. Though Merrill's statement above seems to be more an echo of Rom 9 than a reading of the Old Testament alone, it does reflect the history of the Old Testament remnant.

[38]This phenomenon is analyzed by Norbert Lohfink, "Kleiner werdende Konvente und das biblische Prinzip der kleinen Zahl," *Die Beiden Türme* 37 (2001): 66-81. I do not mean to imply here that this cycle must be repeated in perpetuity. It appears that the remnant as an eschatological phenomenon will in the end be the final recipient of God's saving grace.

the post-exilic community's mission to rebuild God's temple, etc. However, there is a common thread shared by all. In the Old Testament the mission of the remnant involved the preservation of faith in God. Thus, when God chose Abraham and blessed him, Abraham's mission was to lead his family through example and word to faithfulness to the Lord (Gen 18:19; 12:3).

The sharing of the knowledge of God by Israel was to reach universal dimensions and would take place through God's remnant people. They would witness to the nations:

> For I know their works and their thoughts, and I am coming to gather all nations and tongues; and they shall come and shall see my glory, and I will set a sign among them. From them I will send survivors [pelêṭîm] to the nations, to Tarshish, Put, and Lud—which draw the bow—to Tubal and Javan, to the coastlands far away that have not heard of my fame or seen my glory; and they shall declare my glory among the nations. They shall bring all your kindred from all the nations as an offering to the Lord, on horses, and in chariots, and in litters, and on mules, and on dromedaries, to my holy mountain Jerusalem, says the LORD, just as the Israelites bring a grain offering in a clean vessel to the house of the LORD. (Isa 66:18-20)

One could contrast God's Old Testament promise to bring the other nations to Jerusalem (e.g., Zech 14:16-19) with Jesus' New Testament commission for Christians to go out into the world (e.g., Matt 28:18-20). However, this distinction should not be overstressed, since both concepts are found in both Testaments, although there is a difference in emphasis.

The Remnant as a Specific Community

The ecclesiological phrase "visible/invisible church" is not traditionally utilized in the study of the Old Testament. The ecclesiological use of the term "invisible" has commonly been understood as expressing the idea that only God knows the true believers who will finally be saved.[39] They are, so to speak, "invisible" or unknown to humans, though not to God. It is difficult to apply that terminology to the remnant. An invisible community is practically a contradiction in terms, because a community presupposes more than simply a group or a category. A community presupposes that each member knows at least one other member, and that they inten-

---

[39]See Raoul Dederen, "The Church," in *Handbook of Seventh-day Adventist Theology*, pp. 545-546.

tionally collaborate in some way to achieve common objectives. Whereas it may be possible to consider individuals as "invisible remnants," e.g., the 7,000 faithful in Elijah's time (1 Kgs 19:18),[40] there are no examples of remnant communities in the Old Testament (or in the Bible) that were not in some way identifiable as such. The incident just quoted from 1 Kgs 19 is a good example: "Whoever escapes [*mlṭ*] from the sword of Hazael, Jehu shall kill; and whoever escapes [*mlṭ*] from the sword of Jehu, Elisha shall kill. Yet I will leave [*š'r*] seven thousand in Israel, all the knees that have not bowed to Baal, and every mouth that has not kissed him" (1 Kgs 19:17-18, NRSV).

In the context of the above passage, Elijah is told to anoint Hazael, Jehu, and Elisha. Then comes the announcement of judgment ("the sword"), followed by the promise that 7,000 will survive.[41] Prior to this, those who had neither bowed the knee to nor kissed Baal may have been scattered and "invisible." But, at the end of the judgment, they become "a remnant" community because they survive a catastrophe, in this case, God's judgment. They are a community of the faithful who escape divine judgment and can be identified as such by others.

One more illustration may be helpful. In Isa 65, God promises to spare a remnant from a rebellious nation: "As the wine is found in the cluster, and one says, 'Do not destroy it, for there is a benefit in it,' so I will act on behalf of my servants in order not to destroy all of them" (Isa 65:8). Yet concerning this spared remnant, we are further told: "They will build houses and inhabit them; they will also plant vineyards and eat their fruit" (v. 21). Notwithstanding the possibility that the group mentioned in the passage may (or may not) have consisted of scattered individuals before God's judgment, as they emerge from the judgment, they are a clearly identifiable community. Therefore, in Isa 65, the spared remnant (in this case, the eschatological remnant) consists of a visible community, rather than a scattered "invisible" remnant.

---

[40]If Walter Brueggemann is right, another example of an invisible individual remnant may be the young girl of 2 Kgs 5:2-3 ("A Brief Moment for a One-Person Remnant (2 Kings 5:2-3)," *BTB* 31 [2001]: 53-59).

[41]Although the KJV translates it in the past ("I have left"), the Hebrew construction (often called a "Perfect Consecutive") is better translated as a future ("I will leave"). Though the mention of their faithfulness (e.g., not bowing to Baal) may have reference to the past, the fulfillment of the promise that they would survive the sword was still to come.

III. The Remnant and the Post-exilic Community

Since most previous studies of the Old Testament remnant motif focus primarily on pre-exilic texts, I will spend some time exploring the relationship between the remnant motif and the self-identity of the post-exilic community. It has been argued that Jeremiah applies the term "remnant" not to the survivors who remained in the land of Judah but to those who were taken captive and who would be the recipients of the new covenant and undergo the new Exodus.[42] Therefore, those who returned from the exile constitute the faithful remnant (Jer 31:7-9), the recipients of the Lord's new covenant (vv. 31-34), the "carriers of the ancient covenant blessings."[43]

Nevertheless, as already mentioned, the pre-exilic prophets did not always clearly distinguish between the faithful remnant who would return from captivity and the eschatological remnant. For example, Isaiah's description of the return of the exiles in Isa 11 occurs in the context of an eschatological restoration:

> The wolf shall live with the lamb, the leopard shall lie down with the kid, the calf and the lion and the fatling together, and a little child shall lead them. The cow and the bear shall graze, their young shall lie down together; and the lion shall eat straw like the ox. The nursing child shall play over the hole of the asp, and the weaned child shall put its hand on the adder's den. They will not hurt or destroy on all my holy mountain; for the earth will be full of the knowledge of the Lord as the waters cover the sea. (Isa 11:6-9)

It is in the context of the above eschatological promise that we find the promise of the return of the captives:

> On that day the root of Jesse shall stand as a signal to the peoples; the nations shall inquire of him, and his dwelling shall be glorious. On that day the Lord will extend his hand yet a second time to recover the remnant [šeʾār] that is left [šʾr] of his people, from Assyria, from

---

[42]Kenneth D. Mulzac, "The Remnant and the New Covenant in the Book of Jeremiah," *AUSS* 34 (1996): 239-248. This, of course, does not preclude the application of the remnant motif negatively to those who remained in the land (see Ezek 14:21-22). However, it is the remnant led into captivity who received the promises of restoration (Ezek 6:8-10; 11:14-21).

[43]Hasel, "Remnant," *ISBE*, vol. 4, p. 133.

Egypt, from Pathros, from Ethiopia, from Elam, from Shinar, from Hamath, and from the coastlands of the sea. He will raise a signal for the nations, and will assemble the outcasts of Israel, and gather the dispersed of Judah from the four corners of the earth. The jealousy of Ephraim shall depart, the hostility of Judah shall be cut off; Ephraim shall not be jealous of Judah, and Judah shall not be hostile towards Ephraim. (Isa 11:10-13)

Thus, in the prophecies of the pre-exilic prophets, it is sometimes hard to distinguish between the faithful remnant who would return from captivity and the eschatological remnant. Therefore, the post-exilic experience of the Jewish people helped to further refine this important Old Testament motif by highlighting more clearly the distinction between the faithful and the eschatological remnants.[44] In what follows, it will be suggested that even though the post-exilic community consisted of a faithful remnant that emerged as a fulfillment of prophecy, it was also a community that did not claim to be the eschatological remnant.

Returnees as the Remnant

After the time allotted for their captivity, the Jewish captives were told to escape from Babylon (Zech 2:7 [2:11 MT; *mlṭ*]), and the term "remnant" is applied to the post-exilic community that returned (Ezra 1:4, *š'r*; 9:8, 13-15; possibly also in Hag 1:12, 14; 2:2).[45] It is also clear from the context of those passages that the post-exilic community is more than just an historical remnant; it is also a faithful remnant:

> "Thus says King Cyrus of Persia: . . . Any of those among you who are of his people—may their God be with them!—are now permitted to go up to Jerusalem in Judah, and rebuild the house of the Lord, the God of Israel—he is the God who is in Jerusalem; and let all survivors [*š'r*], in whatever place they reside, be assisted by the people of their place with silver and gold, with goods and with animals, besides free-

---

[44]Although the eschatological tenor of the pre-exilic remnant prophecies is partially due to the conditional nature of prophecy (as argued in "The Role of Israel in Old Testament Prophecy," in *AdvBibComm*, vol. 4, pp. 25-38; see also Richard M. Davidson, "Interpreting Old Testament Prophecy," in *Understanding Scripture: An Adventist Approach* George W. Reid, ed. [Silver Spring, MD: Biblical Research Institute, 2005], pp. 192-200), Old Testament theology allows for progressive revelation.

[45]The term is also applied to those who survived the Assyrian invasion (2 Chron 30:6 *pᵉlêṭāh*, *š'r*; see also Isa 10:20-23; 11:11, 16).

will offerings for the house of God in Jerusalem." The heads of the families of Judah and Benjamin, and the priests and the Levites—everyone whose spirit God had stirred—got ready to go up and rebuild the house of the Lord in Jerusalem. (Ezra 1:2-5)

Then Zerubbabel son of Shealtiel, and Joshua son of Jehozadak, the high priest, with all the remnant [*šeʾērît*] of the people, obeyed the voice of the Lord their God, and the words of the prophet Haggai, as the Lord their God had sent him; and the people feared the Lord. Then Haggai, the messenger of the Lord, spoke to the people with the Lord's message, saying, I am with you, says the Lord. (Hag 1:12-13)

The returnees are the ones who were moved by God's Spirit to return and rebuild God's temple in Jerusalem (Ezra 1:5), i.e., not all returned, but only a remnant. In their work of rebuilding, they were encouraged by God's prophets (Ezra 5:1-2) and received God's blessing (Hag 2:19). Moreover, the genealogical lists establish a linkage between God's promises to Abraham and the post-exilic community (e.g., Ezra 2:1-70; 8:1-14; Neh 7:5-65; 1 Chron 1–9).[46]

In fact, the application of the faithful remnant motif to the post-exilic community is clear even from passages that do not explicitly use remnant terminology. For example:

Remember the word that you commanded your servant Moses, "If you are unfaithful, I will scatter you among the peoples; but if you return to me and keep my commandments and do them, though your outcasts are under the farthest skies, I will gather them from there and bring them to the place at which I have chosen to establish my name." They are your servants and your people, whom you redeemed by your great power and your strong hand. (Neh 1:8-10)

Nehemiah is citing God's promise in Deut 3:1-4 to restore those who would return to Him, and applying them to the post-exilic community. Thus, for Nehemiah, the post-exilic community (i.e., "they" in v. 10 above) was clearly a "faithful," though not perfect, community.[47]

---

[46]The fact that those whose priestly lineage could not be demonstrated were barred from serving as priests (Ezra 2:62) also shows how they were concerned about maintaining spiritual purity.

[47]See, for instance, M. W. Elliot, "Remnant," *NDBTh*, p. 724.

The Eschatological Remnant Community

However, although the remnant motif is applied to the post-exilic community, the post-exilic prophets also made reference to a future remnant, an eschatological remnant (Zech 8:6, 11-12, $\check{s}^{e}$'ērît; 13:8, ytr; 14:2, yeter; Joel 2:32 [3:5 MT],[48] plṭ, mlṭ, śārîd).

> In the whole land, says the LORD, two-thirds shall be cut off and perish, and one-third shall be left alive [ytr]. And I will put this third into the fire, refine them as one refines silver, and test them as gold is tested. They will call on my name, and I will answer them. I will say, "They are my people"; and they will say, "The LORD is our God." (Zech 13:8-9)

Zechariah also included those who were left from the other nations (14:16, ytr) among those who will worship the Lord (cf. 1:11 [1:15 MT]; 8:22-23), thus hinting at the fact that the eschatological remnant will include individuals from outside the nation of Israel:[49] "And it shall come to pass that everyone who is left [ytr] of all the nations which came against Jerusalem shall go up from year to year to worship the King, the LORD of hosts, and to keep the Feast of Tabernacles" (Zech 14:16, NKJV). Thus, although the post-exilic prophets saw their community as the historical and faithful remnant, they did not see themselves as the final eschatological remnant.

This future remnant expectation is present not only in the post-exilic prophets but also in the post-exilic historical writings. Though explicit references to eschatology are absent from Ezra, Nehemiah, and Chronicles,[50] this is probably due to their genre which is primarily historical rather than prophetic in nature.[51] One can also detect a distinction in

---

[48]The date of the book of Joel is disputed. I provisionally consider it post-exilic.

[49]Zechariah is not unique in ascribing this inclusiveness to the eschatological remnant. It was also voiced by pre-exilic prophets (cf. Isa 14:1-2). See Hasel, "Pālaṭ," p. 565; and Rendtorff, Theology, pp. 709, 711.

[50]Although I do not accept Leopold Zunz's 1832 hypothesis that Chronicles and Ezra-Nehemiah constituted one single composition of the Chronicler's History, they both contribute to our understanding of the post-exilic community's self-identity in the light of each work's theological perspective of the community's history. On the other hand, William J. Dumbrell ("The Purpose of the Books of Chronicles," JETS 27 [2004]: 257-266) has argued that both Chronicles and Ezra-Nehemiah share a common theology.

[51]It is granted that their presentation of history is theological in nature. Nevertheless, see Isaac Kalimi's defense of the label "historian" for the author of Chronicles ("Was the Chronicler a Historian?" in The Chronicler as a Historian, M. Patrick Graham, Kenneth G.

perspective between Chronicles and Ezra-Nehemiah, insofar as Ezra-Nehemiah presents a community whose very survival is at stake, whereas Chronicles portrays the past as a promulgation of a vision for the present and the future.[52]

It has been argued against those who deny the presence of eschatological expectation in these historical books that Ezra-Nehemiah "allow for a continuing hope that prophecy may be completely fulfilled, while deliberately avoiding the claim that this has already occurred."[53] Among the evidences cited for dissatisfaction with their situation are the lamentation of the elders at the laying of the foundations of the temple (Ezra 3:11-13) and the reemergence of the problem of mixed marriages placed at the end of both Ezra and Nehemiah, with its associated threat of national slavery (Ezra 9 and Neh 9), which has been linked to their bondage to Persia.[54] Conversely, allusions have been found in Ezra to Jer 31 and to Isa, including Ezra's appropriation of the remnant motif in 9:13 (Isa 10:20-21) and 9:14 (Jer 31:7).[55] The conclusion has been drawn that Ezra interprets the promises not as totally fulfilled but in the process of fulfillment.

Such an assessment of the data is certainly correct, but I would suggest that it could be further refined by distinguishing the faithful remnant from the eschatological remnant. That is to say, although the post-exilic community did not see itself as the eschatological remnant, it certainly saw itself as the faithful remnant. Besides the temporal distinction between the two types of remnant, there is also a qualitative distinction between them, i.e., a faithful remnant community could contain unfaithful individuals, whereas the eschatological remnant would be composed only of faithful individuals; it is a purified remnant:

> After all that has come upon us for our evil deeds and for our great guilt, seeing that you, our God, have punished us less than our iniquities deserved and have given us such a remnant [$p^e l\hat{e}\underline{t}\bar{a}h$] as this, shall we break your commandments again and intermarry with the peo-

---

Hoglund, and Steven L. McKenzie, eds. [Sheffield: Sheffield Academic Press, 1997], pp. 73-89). See also Sara Japhet, "Chronicles, Book of," *RPP*, vol. 2, p. 655.

[52] Gary N. Knoppers, *I Chronicles 1-9: A New Translation with Introduction and Commentary* (New York: Doubleday, 2004), p. 84.

[53] J. G. McConville, "Ezra-Nehemiah and the Fulfilment of Prophecy," *VT* 36 (1986): 223.

[54] Ibid., pp. 210-213.

[55] Ibid., pp. 214-222.

ples who practice these abominations? Would you not be angry with us until you destroy us without remnant [$šeʼērît$] or survivor [$pelêṭāh$]? (Ezra 9:13-14)

In the above passage, Ezra refers to the post-exilic community as a "remnant" whose persistent problem of intermarriage placed their remnant status in jeopardy and raised the threat of extinction. Then again, the need to struggle to maintain their faithfulness would be a moot issue if the community were not the "faithful remnant." As for Chronicles, those from the northern kingdom who were willing to return to the Lord and to come to worship at the sanctuary were welcomed (2 Chron 30:7-8). Individuals from Asher, Manasseh, and Zebulun accepted Hezekiah's invitation (v. 11).[56] In fact, it has been argued that this welcoming attitude was extended to all foreigners,[57] further revealing the inclusive nature of the remnant. Chronicles does not deny that there were faithful individuals among the northern Israelites (e.g., 2 Chron 34:9). But the lineage of the faithful remnant was not continued through them. Therefore, for Chronicles, the post-exilic community of Judah had both an exclusive and an inclusive self-identity. They were exclusive in the sense that they saw themselves as the sole heirs of the long lineage of the faithful. On the other hand, they were also inclusive in two senses—first, the existence of spiritual forefathers meant that their status was not unique in world history, and second, they were open to welcoming others who willingly joined the Lord.

In summary, the remnant motif in the post-exilic writings appears in both prophetic (i.e., post-exilic prophets) and historical contexts (Ezra-Nehemiah and Chronicles). Individual writers differ on the emphasis given to the remnant motif and on its application to the then-current faithful remnant community or the still-to-come eschatological remnant. Nevertheless, both prophetic and historical post-exilic texts indicate that the post-exilic community considered itself to be the faithful remnant who, with God's providential blessing, returned from Babylonian captivity and was in the process of rebuilding the nation, but that they did not consider themselves to be, or at least are not described as, the eschatological remnant.[58]

---

[56]Ralph W. Klein, "Chronicles, Book of 1, 2," *ABD*, vol. 1, p. 1001.

[57]James D. Newsome, Jr., "Toward a New Understanding of the Chronicler and His Purposes," *JBL* 94 (1975): 206-207.

[58]The foregoing describes the remnant self-understanding of the post-exilic community according to the perspective of the extant canonical writings. I acknowledge

This distinction between the faithful and the eschatological remnants is helpful and relevant in another sense. Whereas the eschatological remnant is of necessity inclusive in that it is not only composed solely of the faithful but consists of all the faithful at the end of time, the faithful remnant, in contrast, features a tension between exclusivism and non-exclusivism, a tension that is exhibited in the post-exilic community's remnant self-understanding. On the one hand, as the exclusive heirs of God's faithful heritage, they struggle to remain faithful. On the other hand, they realize that other individuals might be willing to join them in submission to God. At the same time they are looking forward to an eschatological remnant that would even include others outside their nation.

IV. Parallels Relevant for Adventist Ecclesiology

In many respects, the self-identity of the post-exilic community of Judah is similar to the Seventh-day Adventist self-identity. Both the post-exilic community and the Adventist movement see themselves as remnant communities that came into existence in fulfillment of prophecy. Just as the post-exilic community consisted of the faithful remnant who returned from Babylonian captivity, so Adventists see themselves as having come out of spiritual Babylon and as heirs of a long lineage of the faithful from all ages. Nevertheless, just as the post-exilic community included individuals that were not fully faithful to God, so Adventists recognize that not all members of the Adventist church are faithful. This recognition also indicates that although Adventists see themselves as the historical and faithful remnant of the time of the end, they are not—at least not yet—the fullness of the eschatological remnant.[59] That is, just as the post-exilic Jewish community anticipated the visible revelation of an eschatological remnant which would include others who were not yet part of the community, so Adventists also anticipate the day when spiri-

---

that each individual member of the community may have had a unique perspective. Thus, some speak of "multiple voices" or "a majority and a minority opinion," etc., concerning Israel's self-identity—Bruce C. Birch, Walter Brueggemann, Terence E. Frethem, and David L. Petersen, *A Theological Introduction to the Old Testament* (2nd ed., Nashville, TN: Abingdon Press, 2005), p. 429. Nevertheless, there is no evidence for a "voice" that contradicted the perspective that the returnees from the exile considered themselves the faithful, but not the eschatological, remnant.

[59]The distinction between the faithful remnant of the time of the end and the eschatological remnant parallels the distinction between the "time of the end" (the last era or period of time in history) and the "end of time" (the very end of historical time).

tual Babylon will be completely fallen and the eschatological remnant will fully emerge.

Likewise, just as the post-exilic remnant community had a mission to the nations, so do Adventists. Participation in and incorporation into the post-exilic community was extended to all the nations. Adventists consider it their mission to reach out to every nation and people with the message of salvation within an end-time context. They acknowledge that they have spiritual forefathers[60] and that there are faithful individuals outside their community who will be part of the eschatological remnant.

Obviously, Adventists are not like the post-exilic community of Judah in all respects—nor should we be. Besides, the New Testament brings to light aspects of the remnant motif that go beyond what is available in the Old Testament alone. That, however, is beyond the scope of this study. Nevertheless, the remnant self-identity of the post-exilic community does shed light on the delicate balance between our appropriation of the remnant motif and the alleged exclusivism of such a claim.

---

[60]LaRondelle has aptly applied the term "remnant" to the faithful forefathers of Adventism: "Throughout Christian history different groups have arisen, in a sense remnant groups, with a burden to draw Christians of their day back to a more scriptural faith. While some have insisted that their faith was not entirely new, they held the Bible as their prime authority and longed to call the believers back to it. Although Seventh-day Adventists differ from these groups in various respects regarding doctrine and practice, they have in common with them the image of the remnant in the sense of bringing their contemporaries to a faith closer to the Scriptures" (LaRondelle, "Remnant," p. 880).

CHAPTER II

THE REMNANT IN NON-CANONICAL JEWISH APOCALYPTIC WORKS AND IN QUMRAN

Leslie N. Pollard
Vice President
Loma Linda University
Loma Linda, CA

The concept of the remnant continued to develop outside the Old Testament but remained under its influence. And, while the literature of the intertestamental period is exceedingly difficult to systematize, concepts of the remnant significantly contrast with the idea of the remnant found in the Old Testament. Understanding that historical shift could be helpful in the study of the New Testament concept. We will pay particular attention to two types of literature. The first is Jewish apocalyptic literature. The remnant motif became extremely important in apocalyptic writings, probably because of the close connection between the remnant and Old Testament eschatology. The future-oriented faith of Israel, climaxing in the unfolding and fulfillment of the divine purpose through an eschatological remnant, found fertile soil in that literature. The second type of literature that we will sample are the documents from Qumran, which provide an exciting view of how the concept was understood and applied within a passionately sectarian setting.

I. The Remnant in Jewish Apocalyptic Works

Scholars have acknowledged the contribution of Jewish apocalyptic literature to a better understanding of apocalyptic thought in the New Testament.[1] The authors of these writings frequently consider Israel to

---

[1] See, for instance, James H. Charlesworth, ed., *Old Testament Pseudepigrapha*, vol. 1 (New York: Doubleday, 1983); J. J. Collins and J. H. Charlesworth, eds., *Mysteries and Revelations: Apocalyptic Studies Since the Uppsala Colloquium* (Sheffield: JSOT Press, 1991); J. J. Collins, *The Apocalyptic Imagination: An Introduction to the Jewish Matrix of Christianity* (New York: Crossroad, 1998); Stephen Cook, *Prophecy and Apocalypticism: The Post-Exilic Social Setting* (Minneapolis, MN: Fortress Press, 1995); Paul D. Hanson,

be under divine judgment on account of apostasy (cf. *4 Ezra* 1:4-9; 2:1-14; 7:72-74; *2 Bar.* 1:4, 5; 62:4-5; 77:2-10; *Jub.* 1:7-14, etc.). Within this context of judgment, the prospect for the salvation of a remnant is available. However, in this literature, the remnant concept undergoes a transformation from its Old Testament heritage. Unlike in the Old Testament, the composition of the remnant community is restricted by a number of narrowed and exclusive claims. Contrary to the universalism anticipated in the Old Testament, the remnant concept in Jewish apocalyptic sources occasionally discloses anti-gentile elements (e.g., *1 Enoch* 5:1-9; *Apoc. Abr.* 29:1–32:6; *Wis.* 3:9; 4:15).[2] Only the "righteous" remnant of Israel will enjoy the blessings of life after the final terror (e.g., *1 Enoch* 45:5-6).[3]

The books, from which this survey of the remnant concept in Jewish apocalyptic literature is illustrated, are *1 Enoch*, *Jubilees*, *4 Ezra*, and *2 Apocalypse of Baruch*. Other works within the corpus of Jewish apocalyptic materials are cited as needed for further evidences of remnant understanding.

Remnant in *1 Enoch*

The book of *1 Enoch*[4] offers at least the following six perspectives on the concept of the remnant that reflect both continuity and discontinuity with the Old Testament concept of the remnant.

(1) *The remnant will be protected in the judgment*. *1 Enoch* opens with a promise to the remnant that is reminiscent of the Old Testament (1:1-3).[5] It describes the blessing upon the "elect" and "righteous" ones

---

Visionaries and Their Apocalypses (Philadelphia, PA: Fortress Press, 1983); and Phillip Vielhauer, "Apocalyptic in Early Christianity," in *New Testament Apocrypha*, vol. 2, Wilhelm Schneemelcher, ed. (Philadelphia, PA: Westminster Press, 1989), pp. 587-594.

[2]See D. S. Russell, *Method and Message of Jewish Apocalyptic* (Philadelphia, PA: Westminster, 1964), pp. 297-298. Generally Gentiles have no hope of salvation. See *1 Enoch* 50:2-5; 90:30, 33, 35; 91:14; *2 Bar.* 40:1-3; 68:5; 72:2-6; *4 Ezra* 7:36-38.

[3]See H. E. Ryle and M. R. James, *PSALMOI SOLOMŌNTOS: Psalms of the Pharisees Commonly Called the Psalms of Solomon* (Cambridge: Cambridge University Press, 1891), pp. 73, 81.

[4]*1 Enoch* is usually dated from the beginning of the pre-Maccabean period and probably completed no later than the first part of the second century A.D. It is widely considered a composite work, representing numerous periods and authors. All English quotations of Jewish apocalyptic literature, unless otherwise noted, are from the *OTP*, vols. 1 and 2.

[5]Scholars generally agree that the opening and closing chapters of *1 Enoch* are Christian additions to the work. But even these sections reflect the remnant thinking present in the general milieu of the first century A.D.

"who would be present on the day of tribulation at the time of the removal of the ungodly ones" (1:1). Then comes a promise to these righteous survivors of God's judgment:

> And there shall be a judgment upon all, (including) the righteous. And to all the righteous He will grant peace, He will preserve the elect, and kindness shall be upon them. They shall all belong to God and they shall prosper and be blessed; and the light of God shall shine unto them. Behold, he will arrive with ten million of the holy ones in order to execute judgment upon all. He will destroy wicked ones and censure all flesh on account of everything that they have done, that which the sinners and the wicked ones committed against him. (vv. 8-9)

Here, *1 Enoch* reflects the most fundamental view of the remnant concept. The remnant have been elected by God, are protected by Him, survive the divine judgment, and enjoy last-day existence. Their survival implies vindication before God in the face of oppression by the enemy.[6]

(2) *The wicked antagonize the remnant.* In *1 Enoch* the wicked perform acts of uncleanness (10:20), are hardhearted (5:4), blaspheme God (27:2), oppress the just (94:6), and persecute the righteous (94:7). Because of their disobedience to God, the wicked will ultimately perish (107:1).

(3) *The Elect One will dwell with the remnant.* In *1 Enoch* 45 the remnant are mentioned in the context of the work of the Elect One and the transformation of the earth:

> On that day, I shall cause my Elect One to dwell among them, I shall transform heaven and make it a blessing of light forever. I shall (also) transform the earth and make it a blessing and cause my Elect One to dwell in her. Then those who have committed sin and crime shall not set foot in her. (*1 Enoch* 45:4-5)

---

[6]In Dan 7:21-22, a similar vindication is represented. There the saints, under the tyranny of the little horn power, are vindicated in the judgment. This apocalyptic motif of judgment as punishment of the wicked and, simultaneously, vindication of the righteous, is implicit in this Enoch passage. For more on the Daniel passage, see Gerhard F. Hasel, "The Identity of 'The Saints of the Most High' in Daniel 7," *Bib* 56 (1975): 173-192; Gerhard Pfandl, *Daniel: The Seer of Babylon* (Hagerstown, MD: Review and Herald, 2004), p. 72. For support of the vindication-of-the-saints view of Dan 7:21 that includes a brief discussion of the alternative view, see Arthur Ferch, "The Judgment Scene in Daniel 7," in *The Sanctuary and the Atonement: Biblical, Historical, and Theological Studies*, A. V. Wallenkampf and W. Richard Lesher, eds. (Washington, DC: Review and Herald, 1981), pp. 166-167.

The survival of the remnant is dependent on receiving divine mercy. This passage emphasizes the contrasting destinies of the remnant and the disobedient.

(4) *"Seed" theology is closely associated with the remnant idea.*[7] In some sections of *1 Enoch*, "seed" theology plays a crucial role. This is partially grounded in the Old Testament where Jer 2:21; 31:27; and Isa 57:4 divide persons into "good" and "bad" seed. In *1 Enoch* 65:12, the concept of the remnant is used interchangeably with "seed" theology. God promised Noah, "I shall strengthen your seed (*zera^c*) before me forever and ever as well as the seeds of those who dwell with you; I shall not put it to trial . . . but it shall be blessed and multiply on the earth" (*1 Enoch* 67:3). The "seed" as a divine gift guarantees that the human community will exist after the cleansing of the cosmos through God's judgment.[8]

(5) *The remnant embodies the survival of godly humankind.* In 83:7-9, the writer introduces the exhortation from Enoch's grandfather, Mahalalel, saying: "How terrifying a thing have you seen, my son [Methuselah]! You have seen in your dream a powerful vision—all the sins of the whole world as it was sinking into the abyss and being destroyed with great destruction. Now, my son, rise and pray to the Lord of Glory, for you are a man of faith, so that a remnant shall remain upon the earth and that the whole earth shall not be blotted out." This exhortation to pray implies that the future of humanity will be embodied in a remnant.

(6) *The remnant expresses exclusiveness.* 1 Enoch contrasts the remnant with "the whole earth" (83:8). The righteous are those who follow God's precepts and who stand over and against the wicked.[9] The faithful persecuted by the Gentiles are considered to be God's remnant. Thus in

---

[7]Walter C. Kaiser, "*Zera^c*," *TWOT*, vol. 1, p. 252, points to four basic semantic categories that *zera^c* refers to: (1) the time of sowing; (2) the seed that is scattered; (3) the biological category of the seed as male semen; and (4) the seed as offspring in a genealogical line of specified patriarchs or matriarchs. "Seed" also functions as a synonym for the righteous in *1 Enoch*.

[8]Siegfried Schultz, "*Sperma, speirō, spora*," *TDNT*, vol. 7, p. 537, points also to the Greeks who used *sperma* to refer to the divine offspring. Cf. LXX Gen 3:15. For a more extensive discussion on seed theology, see Mark A. Elliot, *Survivors of Israel: A Reconsideration of the Theology of Pre-Christian Judaism* (Grand Rapids, MI: Eerdmans, 2000), pp. 314-328.

[9]*1 Enoch* contrasts in clear terms the righteous from the wicked: (1) the righteous are the "elect" (1:3, 8; 5:8; 25:5; 93:1, 5, 10); (2) the wicked will be destroyed, while the righteous will prosper (1:8-9); (3) the righteous are regarded as the eschatological elect (93:10); (4) the righteous remnant is the seed of Noah who will escape catastrophe (10:3, 7; 67:1-8).

100:5, destruction and judgment are promised to fall upon sinners. However, the promise to the remnant is:

> In those days, the angels shall descend into the secret places. They shall gather together into one place all those who gave aid to sin. And the Most High will arise on that day of judgment in order to execute a great judgment upon all the sinners. [But] He will set a guard of holy angels over all the righteous and holy ones, and they shall keep them as the apple of the eye until all evil and sin are brought to an end. (vv. 4-5)

The remnant in this context will survive through God's protection via His holy angels.[10]

In summary, in *1 Enoch* we find a remnant concept that nationalizes covenant loyalty. Membership in the eschatological remnant is signaled by implication. National Israelites who demonstrate covenant loyalty will be members of the eschatological remnant. We can detect some elements of continuity with the Old Testament, but the inclusiveness found there is absent in *1 Enoch*.

Remnant in *Jubilees*

Jubilees presents a triumphalistic vision of a nationalistic remnant[11] according to which anyone who does not belong to the covenant through circumcision belongs to "the children of destruction" (15:26). Three distinct perspectives are associated with the remnant idea in *Jubilees*:

(1) *The remnant people separate themselves from the Gentiles.* The reader is commanded: "Separate yourself from the gentiles, and do not eat with them, and do not perform deeds like theirs. Because their deeds are defiled, and all of their ways are contaminated, and despicable, and abominable" (22:16). In *Jubilees*, the division between Israel and the Gentile nations is, in fact, the division between good and evil. Non-Israelites are declared "Philistines" who should be cursed (24:28). It has been correctly pointed out that "the cursing of the Philistines is not part of the

---

[10]This notion of the holy angels as watchers over the righteous is reminiscent of the Old Testament. See Ps 91:10; Dan 4:13, 17, 23.

[11]*Jubilees* is a midrash on salvation history from the creation of the world to the exodus from Egypt and the Sinai event. It is an alleged account of matters revealed to Moses while on Mount Sinai for 40 days. Although the author borrows heavily from other sections of the Old Testament, the work is based primarily on Genesis and Exodus. Most scholars place *Jubilees* during the Maccabean period.

biblical tradition. It reflects the writer's attitude with respect to the contemporary inhabitants of the area regarded as Philistia."[12]

(2) *The faithful remnant is an instrument of destruction.* Similar to the destruction of the Philistines, the Gentiles are to be purged from Palestine: "And they [God's servants] will drive out their enemies, and the righteous ones will see and give praise" (23:30b). *Jubilees* records the doom of the other nations: "And no remnant will be left to them, nor one who escapes on the day of the wrath of judgment" (24:30). The assertion that "no remnant" will be left to them anticipates the day when the Gentiles will cease to exist, rather than being included in the remnant community. The clear message is that "no Canaanites will be spared on the day of judgment."[13]

(3) *The remnant exists as God's elect.* Though the term "remnant" occurs twice in *Jubilees* (20:5; 24:30), its status is implicitly connected to the election of Israel. God chose Israel above the other nations (2:19-21; 15:11, 32). Whether that survival comes through a "second seed" (4:7) or through Noah (5:5), Israel will always exist. As Yahweh's chosen, Israel will be impervious to destruction on the day of judgment.[14]

To summarize, in *Jubilees* the remnant are those Israelites who will survive, witness, and, most important, rejoice over the final annihilation of their Gentile oppressors. The nationalistic view of the remnant is strongly emphasized and promoted.

Remnant in *4 Ezra*[15]

Scholarly consensus holds that *4 Ezra* was written in the wake of the unsuccessful Jewish revolt against the Romans and the destruction of the Second Temple in A.D. 70. From the literary point of view, its author is responding to a catastrophic occurrence—the Babylonian invasion (i.e.,

---

[12]O. S. Wintermute, "Jubilees: A New Translation and Introduction," in *OTP*, vol. 2, p. 47.

[13]Gene L. Davenport, *The Eschatology of the Book of Jubilees* (Leiden: E. J. Brill, 1971), p. 54.

[14]As Martha Himmelfarb, "Jubilees and Sectarianism" in *Enoch and Qumran Origins: New Light on a Forgotten Connection,* Gabriele Boccaccini, ed., (Grand Rapids: Eerdmans, 2005), pp. 129-131 points out, by insisting not on merit but on an ancestral/hereditary definition for membership in Israel, *Jubilees* is, from another standpoint, "radically inclusive" (p. 130), though her late dating of the work to the time of John Hyrcanus (134-104 B.C.) is more speculative.

[15]For a discussion on how early Adventists appropriated passages from the Apocrypha, see Denis Fortin, "Sixty Books or Eighty-One: Did Ellen G. White Recommend the Apocrypha?" *AdvR*, March 28, 2002, pp. 9-12.

the destruction of Jerusalem). Through a series of dialogues between the pseudonymous Ezra and the angel, we can detect a struggle that oscillates between theodicy and eschatology.[16] While God chose Israel, He did not remove the evil heart, thus the Torah could not overcome Israel's condition. Curiously, God chose to punish Israel with the equally wicked Babylonians (3:26-36). Ezra's main problem is with the Gentiles. It is here that eschatology (4:22-25) provides the answers to the dilemma he faces.

In *4 Ezra*, the remnant motif is set against the eschatological backdrop of the concept of the two ages, in which there is a two-part schematization of history: the present age will be destroyed to be followed by the messianic age (e.g., 6:7-10, 34; 7:12-13, 29-31; 8:1, 46). The remnant are both the historically faithful who, like Noah, survived a catastrophe (3:8-11) and the final eschatological generation of the faithful "few" who will live through the messianic woes of the end-time (6:25; 7:27; 9:7-8; 13:16, 19). One could say that in *4 Ezra*, "salvation lies not only in the future of the covenant people but also in the destiny of the individual."[17] It is in this setting that the following seven aspects of the remnant appear in *4 Ezra*.

(1) *The remnant are the "few" who live righteously*. 4 Ezra 8:3 says, "Many have been created, but few will be saved." *4 Ezra's* motif of the saved few is grounded in the Flood narrative. Noah is the first character in the Old Testament to be called "righteous" (Gen 6:9). We read, "As death came upon Adam, so the flood upon them. But you left one of them, Noah with his household, and all the righteous who have descended from him" (3:8-11). Here Noah appears as the typological progenitor of the righteous in Hebrew sacred history. In many places in Jewish literature, Noah personifies the remnant ideal (e.g., *1 Enoch* 106:18-19; *4 Ezra* 3:11; Ecclesiasticus 44:17) and points to the fact that the righteous are in the minority (cf. 7:50-51; 8:1- 2). In this discussion, Noah as a remnant progenitor represents the continuation of the righteous line of those who worship God.

However, after tracing out the activity of God in history (3:5-36), the angel, Uriel, assures Ezra that the evil and injustice of the present age will soon end (4:26), but, as with the Flood, it will happen "in its time."[18]

---

[16]For a useful discussion of theodicy in relation to *4 Ezra* and *2 Bar.*, see Tom W. Willet, *Eschatology in the Theodicies of 2 Baruch and 4 Ezra* (Sheffield: JSOT, 1989), pp. 11-33, 65-72, 95-112, 124-125.

[17]Collins, *Apocalyptic Imagination*, p. 221. Collins is referring to *2 Baruch*, but it equally applies to *4 Ezra*, which *he views as* closely related to it in time and perspective.

[18]Michael E. Stone, *Commentary on Fourth Ezra* (Minneapolis, MN: Fortress, 1990), p. 69, says this "implies the predestinarian view of fixed times" (cf. 4:33-34; 5:49; 6:5-6; 7:74).

As Ezra probes for exactly when the injustice will end, he is told it will be "when the number of those like yourselves is completed" (4:36). Only God knows the final number, but it will certainly be few (7:48, 60). This witness to Ezra's life takes on eschatological significance since Ezra is reminded that his age "is hastening swiftly to its end" (4:26). He is promised that wickedness will increase until the end (5:1-4), but the righteous will be protected.

(2) *The remnant motif is connected to theodicy.* Ezra consistently correlates theodicy to eschatology (cf. 6:59; 7:26-34). The promise of a future existence for the faithful is held out as the corrective to the injustice that the community feels. The remnant motif functions as an assurance that when the judgments from the Most High fall, the chosen servants of God will be preserved.

(3) *The remnant will exist in a world transformed by final judgment and salvation.* The remnant idea also appears in the second vision of Ezra. Section 2 of the book of Ezra continues the two-age eschatology (6:2). The questions, "What will be the dividing of times?" or "When will be the end of the first age and beginning of the age that follows?" prepare the reader for another rehearsal of the signs of the end of the present age expressed in terms of cosmic and social distress (6:21-24).

4 Ezra 6:27-28 makes clear that the righteous will populate the earth because all the "earth's inhabitants shall be changed and converted to a different spirit" and "faithfulness shall flourish, and corruption shall be overcome, and the truth . . . shall be revealed" (v. 28). It is not clear whether the remnant will be the active agents in the transformation of the world or its passive recipients.

(4) *Remnant status assures physical survival.* In the fullest eschatological picture presented by Ezra, the remnant is mentioned as a group who physically survives the eschatological judgment. In 7:26-37, the hidden land will be revealed, every "delivered" soul will see the wonders, the Messiah will be revealed along with those with Him, and those who remain will "rejoice with him" for 400 years. Then the Messiah will die, and His human cohorts will die with Him, while the world will return to primeval silence. "Those who remain" are the remnant. They appear in the answer to Ezra's question as to why they are dispossessed (6:59). Ezra is informed that the remnant will inherit the land only after it has been purged of sin and wickedness.

(5) *The remnant idea is closely connected to the land.* The remnant motif is territorialized in 12:33-34. As an explicit remnant passage, 12:33-34 is found in the interpretation of the Eagle Vision (12:4-39). In the setting of judgment, reproof, and the final destruction of the wicked, the land-connected promise is: "But he will deliver in mercy the remnant of

my people, those who have been saved throughout my borders, and he will make them joyful until the end comes, the day of judgment, of which I spoke to you at the beginning" (v. 34). In this particular case the remnant are those in the land who will experience joy and celebration until the end comes. In the Old Testament, the deliverance promised to the remnant is evidence of divine favor (cf. Exod 15–16; Deut 8, 27-28).

(6) *The remnant will experience eschatological deliverance.* Another reference to the remnant is found in the interpretation of the Man from the Sea (13:25-26). This man is "my Son" (vv. 32, 37). He is the one "whom the Most High has been keeping for many ages" (v. 26). He "will deliver his creation" and "will direct those who are left."

(7) *Protection of the remnant and keeping the commandments of God.* Phillip Esler observed the close connection between law and eschatology in *4 Ezra*. He pointed out that "salvation in the next world is dependent upon compliance with the Law in this one."[19] In the Christian appendix to *4 Ezra*,[20] the connection of obedience to the remnant idea in Ezra appears in the context of the final predictions of warfare, doom, and persecution (15:1–16:73). The text reads: "'Hear, my chosen people,' says the Lord. 'Behold, the days of tribulation are at hand, and I will deliver you from them. Do not fear or doubt, for God is your guide, you who keep my commandments and precepts,' says the Lord God" (16:74-77). The remnant promise functions as a climax to the terrors described in the book.

In summary, in *4 Ezra* the remnant are those who survive the messianic woes and the great final war of the Redeemer (12:34; 13:26). They are a small minority (7:47-48; 7:60; 8:1-3; 9:21-22) who keep the commandments of God. The repeated emphasis in connection with the remnant idea serve to emphasize the notion of divine protection. In *4 Ezra*, to be among the remnant is to see the vengeance of God visited upon one's alien conquerors. No reconciliation is anticipated. Deliverance and vindication ultimately belong to the remnant who remain within the land.

Remnant in *2 Baruch*

2 Baruch so closely resembles *4 Ezra* that some scholars have debated whether *2 Bar.* is dependent on *4 Ezra*.[21] It was probably written

---

[19]Phillip F. Esler, "The Social Function of 4 Ezra," *JSNT* 53 (1994): 118.

[20]See Bruce Metzger, "The Fourth Book of Ezra: A New Translation and Introduction," in *OTP*, vol. 1, p. 522.

[21]Gwendolyn B. Sayler, *Have the Promises Failed? A Literary Analysis of 2 Baruch* (Chico, CA: Scholars Press, 1984), pp. 103-118; A. F. J. Klijn, "2 (Syriac Apocalypse of) Baruch," in *OTP*, vol. 1, pp. 616-617; George W. E. Nickelsburg, *Jewish*

after A.D. 70. An examination of the remnant motif in *2 Bar.* discloses the following three perspectives concerning it:

(1) *The remnant and good works.* Remnant status seems to be earned by storing up good works (14:12).[22] Later we read, "For behold the days are coming, and the books will be opened in which are written the sins of all those who have sinned, and moreover, also the treasuries in which are brought together the righteousness of all those who have proven themselves to be righteous" (24:1). The remnant is an eschatological group who will survive to enjoy a share in the messianic kingdom.

(2) *The remnant and the land.* Those performing the desired works must also be occupiers of the physical land of Israel. Occupation of the land is a pre-condition for receiving protection. It is in this context that the first reference to the remnant appears in *2 Bar.*: "And He answered and said to me: 'That which will happen at that time bears upon the whole earth. Therefore, all who live will notice it. For at that time I shall only protect those found in this land at that time'" (29:2). The remnant promise of protection is explicitly limited to those *in the land*. It is repeatedly expressed that the land will be protected during the tribulations to come (29:2; 40:2; 71:1). In harmony with the Old Testament promises of the renewal of the land, this land is undoubtedly the land of Israel.

It should be noted that in *2 Bar.* the Lord provides for the remnant in times of distress (29:5-8). Even the former objects of superstitious fear, Leviathan and Behemoth, will be a source of nourishment for the remnant. The remnant are told that these two great monsters will be food for "all who are left" (v. 5). Protection and provision converge to assure the readers that they will not be left to come to ruin again. This is an important aspect of remnant theology in *2 Bar.* The Torah is associated with the

---

Literature Between the Bible and the Mishnah (Philadelphia, PA: Fortress, 1981), p. 287; Collins, *Apocalyptic Imagination*, pp. 213, 222-224.

[22] *2 Bar.* 14:12. The idea that there are heavenly treasuries is a common notion in the apocalyptic literature of this period. *1 Enoch* 17:3 asserts that God has munitions stored up for the eschatological war. Conversely, there is a parallel notion that humans may escape punishment emanating from God's storehouse by storing up good works with God. *Psalms of Solomon* 9:5 states, "The one who does what is right saves up life for himself with the Lord and the one who does what is wrong causes his own life to be destroyed." Here the idea is that one who does righteousness is saving life for the future realm. Thus deeds of righteousness in this life function as a guarantee against destruction. *4 Ezra* 7:76-77 reads, "He answered me and said 'I will show you that also, but do not be associated with those who have shown scorn, nor number yourself among those who are tormented. For you have a treasure of works laid up with the Most High; but it will not be shown to you until the last times.'"

survival of the remnant.[23]

(3) *The remnant and the execution of the oppressors.* This promise to the remnant of victory over their oppressors is evident in another passage:

> The last ruler who is left alive at that time will be bound, whereas the entire host will be destroyed. And they will carry him on Mount Zion, and my Anointed One will convict him of all his wicked deeds and will assemble and set before him all the works of his hosts. And after these things he will kill him and protect the rest [i.e., remnant] of my people who will be found in the place that I have chosen (*2 Bar.* 40:2).

The Anointed One binds the last ruler while destroying his host. This passage appears in the interpretation of the apocalypse of the forest, the vine, the fountain, and the cedar (chaps. 35–40). Once again assurance is given to the oppressed community that God's protection will be upon the land and, therefore, the remnant will survive the terrors of this final apocalypse.

In summary, the remnant idea in *2 Baruch* is associated with the traditional themes found in the Old Testament—judgment, salvation, vindication, protection, covenant loyalty, and future existence. However, it is also connected to the idea of the deliverance of the land. Thus we find in *2 Baruch* a remnant concept that, like *4 Ezra*, has been territorialized.

Summary

In the non-canonical Jewish apocalyptic literature surveyed, the remnant concept has been appropriated *prima facie* from the Old Testament. Jewish apocalyptic writers used language similar to that of the Old Testament prophets. However, their concepts of the remnant differ in significant ways. In the Old Testament, the doctrine of the remnant promises that the remnant survives in order to fulfill the universalistic purpose for its election—to extend the knowledge of Israel's God into all the Gentile world (e.g., Isa 19:25; 45:20, 22; 51:5; 56:7; 66:19; Zech 8:23; 14:16). The motif of the remnant examined in the Jewish apocalyptic works is basically nationalistic (i.e., Israel, not others), sectarian (i.e., our group, not theirs), restrictive (i.e., our individual adherents, not Jews in general), and territorialized (i.e., Israel, not Rome, Egypt, etc.). Salvation was held out

---

[23]See Sayler, *Have the Promises Failed?* p. 117.

for the remnant of Israel, but rarely (and that only obliquely) for the Gentiles. The primary focus appears to be on the privilege of survival based on works of obedience in response to the covenant.

II. The Remnant in Qumran Literature

The literature of Qumran is generally dated between the second century B.C. and the first century A.D.[24] While it reflects apocalyptic perspectives, the Qumran documents also present a separatistic, exclusive, and passionately sectarian understanding of the remnant concept. As in the Old Testament, the Hebrew roots for remnant appear in Qumran documents.[25] Notable Qumran scholars have documented remnant self-con

---

[24] See Geza Vermes, *The Complete Dead Sea Scrolls in English* (New York: Penguin Books, 1998), pp. 12-14. All direct quotations are from his translations.

[25] The root š'r is translated as "remnant" or "to remain." Š'r occurs 39 times in noun forms and 15 times as verbs in Qumran literature. Examples of nominal forms of š'r may be found in CD 1:4; 2:6; 1QS 4:14; 5:13; 1QSb 1:7; 1QM 4:2; 13:8; 14:5, 8-9; etc. Verbal forms of the root š'r may be found in CD 1:4; 19:10, 13; 4QFlor 1-3ii2; 4Q368 6:2; 4Q390 1:10; and 11Q19 60:1.

The root š'r also occurs in Aramaic in the DSS a total of 37 times, although four examples appear to be reconstructions. Nominal occurrences constitute 32 uses of the root. Examples of nominal uses may be found in 4Q208 1:3; 7:2; 15:5; 17:5; 19+21:2; 20:1; 23:3; 25:4; 4Q209 5:5, 6; 6:8, and 9. Verbal forms of š'r may be seen in 4Q537 1+2+3:1; 4Q556 14:7; and 4Q561 3:5. Adjectival forms of š'r may be seen in 4Q196 13:1; 18:6. These passages reflect a strong awareness of remnant status among the covenantors. For more examples see Martin G. Abegg, *The Dead Sea Scrolls Concordance*, vol. 1, part 2 (Boston, MA: Brill, 2003), pp. 706, 929.

The Hebrew term 'aḥ°rît occurs 44 times, but with an emphasis more on the "end" or "latter" times or days, etc. Examples may be found in CD 4:4; 6:11; 1QSa 1:1; 1QpHab 2:5; 9:6; 1Q14 6:2; 4Q161 5-6:10; 4Q162 2:1, etc. Prepositional, adjectival, and adverbial forms may be seen in Abegg, ibid., vol. 1, pp. 26-28. Aramaic forms occur two times in 4Q563 and 1:4; 11Q10 38:9. Abegg, ibid., vol. 1, p. 781.

The Hebrew root ytr occurs in nominal forms 10 times where it may be translated "remainder" or "excess." Examples may be found in 1QpHab 7:7; 8:15; 9:4, 7; 4Q163 12:4; and 4Q252 4:4. Verbal forms of ytr occur 18 times and may be translated as "to survive" or "to remain." Examples may be found in CD 2:11; 3:13; 1QM 2:6, 10, 14; 4Q163 12:4; 4Q252 4:4; 4Q424 1:11, etc. There is one occurrence in Aramaic found in 4Q558 33:4. See Abegg, ibid., vol. 1, pp. 332, 849.

The Hebrew root plṭ occurs in nominal forms seven times and can be translated "survivor" or "fugitive," depending on the context. Examples of nominal forms of plṭ may be found in 1QHª 11:28; 14:25, 32; 17:29, 33, and 4Q427 14:2. Verbal forms of the root plṭ occur five times and can be translated "to escape" or "to deliver." Examples of verbal forms of plṭ may be seen in 1QSb 1:7; 1QHª 11:10; 13:18. An Aramaic form of the nominal plṭ occurs only once in 4Q206 1xxxvi18 and can be translated "deliverance." Verbal forms in Aramaic occur 11 times and can be translated "to escape." Examples include 1Q20

sciousness among the Qumran covenantors.[26] James Vanderkam expresses this consensus when he asserts: "The people who lived in and around Qumran believed firmly that they were part of that remnant raised by God to be a plant of righteousness and truth."[27] John Collins noted that the Qumran sectaries considered themselves "as an elect group within Israel . . . the true Israel."[28] Qumran viewed itself as an eschatological community.[29] Non-covenantors standing outside the Qumran *yahad* (community) were not considered members of the chosen people.[30] Thus, the Qumran texts provide an intriguing glimpse intensely sectarian readings of the Old Testament prophecies concerning salvation and remnant theology.[31] The assessment that follows presents four findings that provide a background to the vision of the remnant contained in the book of Revelation:

(1) *Qumran covenantors considered themselves to be the eschatological remnant.*[32] Succinctly, the covenantors of Qumran viewed themselves

---

11:14; 12:17; 19:20; 22:2; and 11Q10 32:2. See Abegg, ibid., vol. 2, p. 908.

The Hebrew root *mlṭ* occurs 14 times in verbal form. It can be translated "to escape" or "to rescue." Examples may be found in CD 7:14, 21; 19:10; 1QH^a 11:9; 1Q27 1:4; 4Q183 1:3, etc. No Aramaic usages occur. See Abegg, ibid., vol. 1, p. 451 for more.

[26]See, for instance, Kurt Schubert, *The Dead Sea Community: Its Origins and Teachings* (New York: Harper and Brothers, 1959), pp. 80-84; Josef Tadeusz Milik, *Ten Years of Discovery in the Wilderness* (Naperville, IL: A. R. Allenson, 1959), pp. 113-118; Jürgen Becker, *Das Heil Gottes und Sündenbegriffe in den Qumrantexten und im Neuen Testament* (Göttingen: Vandenhoeck and Ruprecht, 1964), pp. 60-64; Martin Hengel, *Judaism and Hellenism: Studies in Their Encounter in Palestine During the Early Hellenistic Period*, vol. 1 (Philadelphia, PA: Fortress Press, 1974), p. 223; Henk Jagersma, *A History of Israel from Alexander the Great to Bar Kochba,* (Philadelphia, PA: Fortress Press, 1985), p. 78; and Michael A. Knibb, *The Qumran Community* (Cambridge: Cambridge University Press, 1978), pp. 22-23.

[27]James C Vanderkam, *The Dead Sea Scrolls Today* (Grand Rapids, MI: William B. Eerdmans, 1994), p. 111.

[28]J. J. Collins, *Apocalypticism in the Dead Sea Scrolls: The Literature of the Dead Sea Scrolls* (London: Routledge, 1998), p. 91.

[29]James C. Vanderkam and Peter Flint, *The Meaning of the Dead Sea Scrolls: Their Significance for Understanding the Bible, Judaism, Jesus, and Christianity* (San Francisco, CA: Harper, 2002), pp. 362-363.

[30]Schubert, *Dead Sea Community*, p. 82.

[31]Qumran scholarship has seen the important role that Messianism plays in the beliefs of Qumran. For brief summaries on the role of Messianism in the scrolls, see Lawrence H. Schiffman, *Reclaiming the Dead Sea Scrolls: Their True Meaning for Judaism and Christianity* (New York: Doubleday, 1994), pp. 323-327; Elliot, *Survivors of Israel*, pp. 472-473; and Collins, *Apocalyptic Imagination*, pp. 157-166.

[32]Such eschatological self-understanding is disclosed in the Habakkuk *pesherim* of the Qumran community. The covenantors can speak of the last days in two senses:

as the "remnant of your people" (1QM 14:8-9). Salvation would come to them through God's mercy as the sole, true "remnant" (CD 2:11; 1QH^a 6:8; 1QM 14:9) when Israel ceased to exist (CD 3:13; 1QM 13:8). They alone practiced the "commandments" (CD 3:12) and observed the "whole Torah" (4QFlor 2:2).[33] Observance of the Torah would prepare them to survive the eschatological war. To stand apart from or to leave the sectaries was "to have no remnant or survivor" (CD 2:6-7; 19:10; 1QS 5:13).

Clearly the Qumran community reflected its own remnant self-consciousness.[34] In light of the fact that the community saw itself living in the last days, the term "remnant" is particularly appropriate for the exclusivistic self-understanding of the Qumran community. *As the self-professed remnant, the Qumran covenantors consistently affirmed that they, and they alone, enjoyed a special status before God.* They proclaimed, "We are the remnant of your people" (1QM 14:8). This self-understanding of

---

broadly and technically. For example, 1QpHab uses the phrase "end of days" in 2:5-9 when it describes apostates who are not willing to accept the message of the Teacher of Righteousness. These apostates are contemporaries of the commentator. This is the broad use of the expression. Later, the commentator seems to speak of the last days as a time in the future (9:6). For further study, see Helmer Ringgren, *The Faith of Qumran: Theology of the Dead Sea Scrolls* (Philadelphia, PA: Fortress Press, 1963), pp. 152-166; and Schulbert, *Dead Sea Community*, pp. 98-106. Against any *a priori* requirement or definition of the eschatological remnant as "those who remain after the final judgment of the wicked" (cf. James Watts, "A Critique of Remnant Theme in the New Testament" [Master's Thesis, Southern Baptist Theological Seminary, 1986], pp. 11-12), all of the Qumran community's activities, including the appropriation of the self-differentiating title of remnant, occurred with a consciousness of membership within a last-day community. Therefore, it was not necessary for the covenantors to explicitly label themselves "an eschatological remnant." Remnant identity was consciously established against a background awareness of the community's dispute with general Israelite society. This fact also contradicts Huebsch, who attempted "an exhaustive analysis of the use of remnant in Qumran sectarian literature." He used the criterion of "threat, survival, and historic-theological" relevance to determine which passages contain the remnant theme. Huebsch incorrectly concluded that the Qumran sect did not see itself as an eschatological remnant, but as a part of Israel. See Robert W. Huebsch, "The Understanding and Significance of the 'Remnant' in Qumran Literature: Including a Discussion of the Use of the Concept in the Hebrew Bible, the Apocrypha, and Pseudepigrapha" (Ph.D. dissertation, McMaster University, 1981).

[33]In this connection, John's emphatic declaration *"Here* [emphasis mine] are they that keep the commandments of God" in 14:12 may be viewed as a polemic against the competing remnant claims of Qumran.

[34]See Ellen Juhl Christiansen, "The Consciousness of Belonging to God's Covenant and What It Entails According to the Damascus Document and the Community Rule," in *Qumran Between the Old and New Testaments*, Frederick H. Cryer and Thomas L. Thompson, eds. (Sheffield: Sheffield Academic Press, 1998), pp. 69-97. Christiansen carefully outlines the significance of belonging to the *yahad* (community).

the Qumran covenantors is evident in the Damascus Rule: "But with the remnant which held fast to the commandments of God He made His Covenant with Israel for ever, revealing to them the hidden things in which all Israel had gone astray."[35]

One must agree with Vermes when he says the sectaries "not only considered themselves to be the 'remnant' of their time, but the 'remnant' of all time, the final 'remnant.'"[36] However, according to 1QS 1:16-20, other Jews could also join the community and thereby attain salvation.[37] This remnant self-consciousness resulted in the creation of social and physical distance from "mainstream" Jewish society.

(2) *Qumran represented a cultic and geographic withdrawal from Israel.* As we have seen previously, Jewish apocalyptic literature represents a "within-society" protest to Israel's perceived apostasy. However, Qumran carried that protest against Jewish secularization a step further—it demanded disassociation from the larger Jewish society. Qumran documents present remnant status and ritual purity as inseparable. Thus, the remnant concept in Qumran literature functions as an intensification of Palestinian sectarianism.[38] The Qumranites practiced a segregational remnant theology that isolated them from, and, in their judgment, insulated them against the pervasive wickedness of their times.[39]

Qumran withdrawal to the wilderness was chosen because of its connection to the prophecies of the Old Testament.[40] The covenantors saw themselves as the "sons of light" (1QS 4:22; 8:1-5) who were obligated to hate the "sons of darkness" (1QS 1:3-4, 9-10). Physical separation from them was critical. This view of their own ascetic commitment emerged from the belief that God had chosen their community and bestowed special secrets upon them (1QpHab 7:4-5). They *alone* were "the elect" (1QSa 2:7), that is, the remnant. Such confident self-assessment is evident in the War Scroll's Psalm of Return: "Among the poor in spirit [there

---

[35]Geza Vermes, *The Complete Dead Sea Scrolls*, p. 129.

[36]Ibid., pp. 68-69.

[37]Vanderkam, *Meaning of the Dead Sea Scrolls*, pp. 262-263, describes the annual ceremony of detailed rituals by which a Jewish acolyte may unite with the Qumran sect.

[38]Particularism and separatism characterize the Qumran covenantors. See Roland deVaux, *Archaeology and the Dead Sea Scrolls* (London: Oxford University Press, 1973), pp. 68-69, 81, 97-98.

[39]For examples of ritual requirements of separation and purification, see 1QS 5:13-20; 6:15-17; 3:2; 7:24; 8:23; 9:8; CD 6:17-20; 12:19-20.

[40]James C. Vanderkam, *An Introduction to Early Judaism* (Grand Rapids, MI: Eerdmans, 2001), pp. 164-165.

is power] over the hard of heart, and by the perfect of way all the nations of wickedness have come to an end: not one of their mighty men stands, but we are the remnant [of Thy people]" (1QM 14:7-8).

Remnant understanding is also evident in the Damascus Document: "For when they were unfaithful and forsook Him, He hid His face from Israel and His sanctuary and delivered them up to the sword. He left a remnant [$š^{e'}ērît$] to Israel and did not deliver it up to be destroyed" (CD 1:3-5). The Qumranites believed themselves to constitute a separated remnant that God had left to Israel (CD 1:7; 6:2-3). In fact, if Israel saw itself as God's remnant, the Qumranites considered themselves to be what we would call "the remnant" from the remnant (CD 1:4). One could conclude that the "self-identification of the Damascus communities as the remnant marks a decisive breach with the body of the Jewish people as a whole."[41] Qumran viewed itself as the exclusive bearer of covenant promises (1QpHab 2:3; CD 6:19; 8:21; 19:33-34).[42] They were the keepers of the commandments of God in anticipation of their messiahs (1QS 5:5-6; 8:5-9; 9:5; CD 3:19). Their unique form of compliance with the covenant led them to sit in judgment on fellow Israelites, as seen in the next point.

(3) *Jews outside the Qumran sect were destined for destruction.* The Damascus Document expresses the total destruction awaiting non-sect members outside of their community: "Patience and much forgiveness are with Him towards those who turn from transgression; but power, might, and great flaming wrath by the hand of all the Angels of Destruction towards those who depart from the way and abhor the Precept. They shall have no remnant or survivor" (CD 2:4-7). Having no "remnant" meant that covenant violators would be without posterity and, in turn, without continuity. The covenantors of Qumran viewed all who stood outside their community as the "sons of darkness" who forsook the covenant (CD 5:11). Those outside the covenant (i.e., apostate Israelites), would be annihilated (1QS 3:20-21; cf. 1QM 3:9-19). Logically, then, if Jews beyond their community were lost, the Gentiles would fare much worse.

(4) *Gentiles had no hope of salvation.* The covenantors manifested a decidedly negative attitude toward the Gentiles.[43] Lawrence Schiffman

---

[41]Alex Deasley, *The Shape of Qumran Theology* (Carlisle, Cumbria: Paternoster Press, 2000), p. 89.

[42]Loyalty to the covenant meant membership in God's faithful remnant. See also E. P. Sanders, *Paul and Palestinian Judaism* (Philadelphia, PA: Fortress), pp. 245-257.

[43]The war to come described in the War Scroll would be waged against the *kittîm* (see 1QM 1:2-3, 6, 9, 12). Joseph Baumgarten writes, "As one might expect, the deprecation

points out that Qumran sectarians identified themselves as separate from non-Jews in two ways: (a) they were not idol-worshipers, and (b) they were the chosen people [i.e., remnant] who would inherit the land in the End of Days.[44] But first the land would have to be purged of the incessant paganism that had never been completely eradicated in the land of Palestine.[45]

Clearly, all hope of remnant universalism disappeared from the remnant concept held by members of the Qumran community. This represents a contrast to the Old Testament's vision of the people of God's universal election. The covenantors used two terms to identify the despised and defiled Gentiles: *kittîm* and *gôyîm*. The word *kittîm* identifies the occupiers of their country.[46] This name is associated with the seacoast town of Citium on the island of Cyprus. The term became a code word within the community for the Romans (see 1QpHab 2:12; 3:4, 9; 6:4; cf. Josephus, *JW* 6.316). Covenantors were expected to shun the Gentiles. Gentiles were judged the enemies of Yahweh (1QM 12:11) and consequently would not qualify for entrance into the eschatological temple (4QFlor 1:4). They were idolaters, bereft of the presence of Yahweh (1QpHab 12:13; 13:3-4). For these reasons, the covenantors' aversion to the Gentiles became an essential feature of their faith.

Summary

The remnant concept in the Dead Sea community operated along exclusivistic, sectarian lines. The Qumranites saw themselves as the remnant of Israel. Repeatedly, they affirmed that they enjoyed special status with God because of their loyalty to the covenant. Those outside their sect were regarded as either apostates from the covenant or Gentiles. Apostates could commit to the covenant community, undertake the ascetic life of a covenantor, and thereby become a participant in the remnant community. Gentiles could not join the Qumran remnant community. Most

---

of pagans is most pronounced in the War Scroll, where expressions such as 'nations of wickedness' and 'nations of futility' are frequently found" (Joseph M. Baumgarten, "Gentiles," *EDSS*, pp. 304-305). The word *gôyîm* is used to describe the nations outside of Palestine (1QM 2:7; 4:12). They also were to be shunned (see Joseph Fitzmeyer, *Responses to 101 Questions on the Dead Sea Scrolls* [New York: Paulist Press, 1992], pp. 93-94).

[44]Lawrence Schiffman, "Israel," *EDSS*, vol. 1, p. 389.

[45]D. Flusser, "Paganism in Palestine," in *The Jewish People in the First Century*, vol. 2, S. Safrai and M. Stern, eds. (Philadelphia, PA: Fortress, 1976), p. 1065.

[46]Scholarly consensus identifies the Kittîm with the Romans. See Timothy H. Lim, "Kittim," *EDSS*, vol. 1, pp. 469-471; cf. David W. Baker, "Kittim," *ABD*, vol. 4, p. 93.

strikingly, in Qumran the "sons of light" are joined by angels to engage in combat that contributes to the defeat of the "sons of darkness" (1QM 1:10; 7:6; 19:1). In contrast, God's Combatant in the book of Revelation is the Rider on the white horse (Rev 19:11-21) who prosecutes the final battle against evil. Revelation's godly remnant are never presented as taking up physical weapons. They engage in overcoming evil by non-military means: by the "blood of the Lamb and by the word of their testimony" (Rev 12:12). In Qumran, victory over the enemies of God is *achieved*; in Revelation, victory is *received* because God prosecutes the battle against His enemies.

III. Conclusion

After the Old Testament period, specific thinking regarding the remnant continued to develop. As can be observed in the intertestamental literature sampled here, while remnant self-consciousness carried with it numerous iterations, the ideas formed present a substantially different portrait of the remnant than the picture presented in Scripture. The inclusive nature of the remnant was replaced in intertestamental literature with a very passionate sectarianism (CD 1:4; 1QM 14:8). The vision of an inclusive remnant was truncated in this literature by a narrow nationalism (*Jub.* 15:26; 24:28). In fact, distinctly anti-Gentile elements appear in the literature, while in the New Testament and particularly in Revelation, we witness the Christian faith interacting with and within Gentile environments. While the intertestamental literature surveyed contains elements of a seed theology, its idea is that the seed guarantees survival. The book of Revelation points to the "seed of the woman" and all that is related to Him as the guarantor of victory over the enemy (Rev 12:17; 2:27-29; 12:11; 14:1-3; 15:1-4). In the intertestamental period we find a remnant idea that in some cases is territorialized and connected to the land of Israel. In the Scripture the panorama is that of a "new heaven and a new earth" (Isa 65-66; Rev 21:1-5).

CHAPTER III

THE REMNANT IN THE GOSPELS

Clinton Wahlen
Associate Director
Biblical Research Institute
Silver Spring, MD

Our purpose here is to ascertain the extent to which a remnant concept is operative in Jesus' activity and/or proclamation.[1] At the outset, it is important to acknowledge that some scholars do not find the remnant theme at all in the Gospels.[2] Others insist it is "undeniably present in the Gospels."[3] One reason for diametrically opposite conclusions on this question is the lack of agreement on how remnant is to be defined. Those who argue against its presence in the Gospels tend to define it more narrowly, insisting on the presence of specific remnant terminology. Therefore, before looking at the concept of the remnant in the Gospels, it will be important to notice briefly how remnant theology appears in the post-Old Testament period, beginning with the Septuagint and continuing with later Jewish literature including the Targumim.[4] While by no means

---

[1] For a brief survey of research on Jesus and the remnant, see M. A. Elliott, "Israel," *DJG*, pp. 356-63; note also his succinct reference to "the persistent question whether Jesus intended, called or gathered a remnant, or whether this remnant was the unintended result of his divisive mission" (p. 362).

[2] Rudolf Bultmann, "Die Frage nach der Echtheit von Mt 16, 17-19," *ThBl* 20 (1941): 265-79; Joachim Jeremias, *The Parables of Jesus* (London: SCM, 1972), p. 223; Günther and Krienke, "Remnant, Leave," *NIDNTTE*, vol. 3, p. 253: "Neither the OT concept of the remnant, nor its narrower Judaistic counterpart, is to be found in the Gospels."

[3] Elliott, "Israel," p. 361; see also Ben F. Meyer, "Jesus and the Remnant of Israel," *JBL* 84 (1955): 123-30; idem, *The Aims of Jesus* (London: SCM, 1979); Hasel, "Remnant," *ISBE*, vol. 4, p. 134: "Though the noun 'remnant' is absent from the Gospels, the concept has a prominent place."

[4] The important role of the Septuagint in early Christian conceptualization is widely recognized inasmuch as it represents "the earliest commentary on the Hebrew Scriptures" and "contains the canonical Scriptures of the early Christian church" (*Greek-English Lexicon of the Septuagint*, Johan Lust, Erik Eynikel, and Katrin Hauspie, compilers [Stuttgart: Deutsche Bibelgesellschaft, 2003], p. xxi). That Jews in Palestine used the Septuagint is shown by the Qumran scrolls (ibid., p. xx). The relation of the Targumim to Judaism of the

exhaustive, this survey will highlight some elements important for our understanding of the work of John the Baptist and Jesus as regards Israel and the remnant.[5]

Background to the Remnant Concept

Jewish Concept of the Remnant

The principal Hebrew forms for "remnant" (derivatives of *š'r* and *š'ryt*) are translated in the Septuagint with various forms of *leipō* ("to leave behind"), *loipos* ("other," "the rest"), *leimma* ("remnant"), and *sōzō* ("to save," "to preserve").[6] While the first two forms occur thirty-three times in the canonical gospels, never are they used in the technical sense of a "remnant" but rather in the more general sense of "leave" or "the others."[7] Other terms, however, are used in the Septuagint in parallel with remnant terminology, including forms of *sperma* ("seed")[8] and *oligos* ("few"),[9] both of which occur in the Gospels in contexts which evoke the concept of a remnant. Notably, more specialized remnant vocabulary (various forms of *leimma*, "remnant") occurs only twice in the New Testament (Rom 9:27; 11:5) and is comparatively rare in the Septuagint.[10] Much more common are various forms of *loipos* ("the rest").[11] At the same time, it is important to keep in mind that even in the absence of

---

Second Temple period is vigorously debated but these ancient texts provide a glimpse of early Jewish Scriptural reflection which may sometimes correspond to understandings of the Hebrew Bible in the time of Jesus.

[5]All four canonical Gospels portray John the Baptist as paving the way for Jesus' work and so any consideration of Jesus must take into account this close connection.

[6]Cf. Ronald E. Clements, "*Šā'ar*," *TDOT*, vol. 14, p. 285; H. Wildberger, "*Š'r* to remain," *TLOT*, vol. 3, p. 1292; B. Kedar-Kopfstein, "*Šārîd*," *TDOT*, vol. 14, p. 216. Most important for our purposes are the use in the LXX of the following Greek terms: *kataleipō* (Deut 28:62; 3 Kgdms 19:18; Isa 7:3; 10:19, 20, 21; 11:11, 16; 28:5; Ezra 9:8, 15), *hupoleipō* (4 Kgdms 19:30; Isa 4:3; Zeph 3:12), *leimma* (4 Kgdms 19:4), *kataleimma* (Gen 45:7; 4 Kgdms 19:31; Isa 10:22; 37:31), *hupoleimma* (4 Kgdms 21:14), and *hupoloipos* (Isa 11:11; Jer 50:20).

[7]As W. Günther and H. Krienke ("Remnant," pp. 252-253) observe, there may be a significance even to this more general usage.

[8]Deut 3:3; Isa 1:9; 14:22, 30; 15:9; 37:31.

[9]Deut 4:27; Isa 16:14; 24:6; Jer 42:2 [MT 49:2]; 44:28 [MT 51:28].

[10]So also Günther and Krienke, "Remnant," p. 248; e.g., *leimma* is found only in 2 Sam 21:2 and 2 Kgs 19:4 and only the latter verse refers to Israel.

[11]The adjectives *loipos* and *kataloipos* occur more than 120 and 90 times respectively while the verbal form *kataleipō* occurs most frequently of all, nearly 300 times (ibid.).

remnant terminology a remnant theology may still be present.[12]

Further Development of the Remnant Concept

In Second Temple period Jewish literature, remnant terminology continues to be used positively in the sense of preservation and negatively in the sense of near total destruction, reflecting canonical Hebrew usage. In this section, we focus on those instances where Jewish writings significantly modify or elaborate on the underlying Hebrew text and observe how the deviations further develop the remnant concept.

1. Seed Theology. The Flood story in which only Noah and his family are spared destruction becomes a source of hope in later Jewish literature.[13] *The Wisdom of Solomon* describes it as planting a new human "seed" (*sperma*): "The hope of the world took refuge on a raft, and guided by your hand left to the world the seed of a new generation" (14:6).[14] Philo similarly likens Noah to a tree bearing three "fruits" of Israel, i.e. Abraham, Isaac, and Jacob.[15] Because his household showed itself "worthy of the divine grace" it became "a seed and a spark of a new race of mankind."[16] This moralistic emphasis continues in the Targumim, describing Noah as one who "walked *in reverence of the Lord*"[17] and "perfect *in good works*."[18]

As a counterpoint to this good "seed," the Septuagint translation occasionally introduces the idea of bad "seed" not found in the Hebrew text.[19] In recounting the defeat of Og, king of Bashan, Moses says, "We

---

[12]G. F. Hasel, "Remnant," p. 130; Similarly, in connection with Zephaniah, George W. Anderson, "The Idea of the Remnant in the Book of Zephaniah," *ASTI* 11 (1977-1978): 12; Greg King, "The Remnant in Zephaniah," *BSac* 151 (1994): 415.

[13]Already in Isa 54:9-11, the Noachic "covenant of peace" is applied to Jerusalem (and implicitly to its inhabitants) with a view to its glorious future.

[14]David Winston, *The Wisdom of Solomon: A New Translation with Introduction and Commentary* (Garden City, N.Y.: Doubleday, 1979), p. 267, notes an ANE parallel: "The Sumerian counterpart to Noah, *Ziusudra*, is similarly called the 'preserver of the seed of mankind' (*ANET*, p. 44)." See also Gerhard F. Hasel, *The Remnant: The History and Theology of the Remnant Idea from Genesis to Isaiah* (Berrien Springs, MI: Andrews University Press, 1972), pp. 135-47.

[15]*Mig* 125; cf. *Mos* 2.60.

[16]*QG* 1.96.

[17]*Tg. Onq.* Gen 6:9.

[18]*Tg. Neof.* Gen 6:9.

[19]See Kedar-Kopfstein, "*Śārîd*," p. 216; Gottfried Quell, "B. *Sperma* and Equivalents in the Old Testament," *TDNT*, vol. 7, p. 540. Further on "seed theology" in Jewish literature, see Leslie Pollard, "The Remnant in Non-Canonical Jewish Apocalyptic Works," in this volume.

struck him down until not a single survivor [śārîd] was left" (Deut 3:3).[20] The Septuagint translates the last part of the verse "until there was none of his seed [sperma] left," emphasizing the utter extermination of Israel's enemies, an idea that appears also in the *War Scroll*'s interpretation of Num 24:17-19. The messianic scepter "will smash the temples of Moab, . . . destroy all the sons of Seth . . . [and] exterminate the remnant [śārîd] of the city" (1QM 11.6-7). Interesting also is the LXX version of the Balaam oracles, in which the "dust of Jacob" becomes the "seed of Jacob" and the prophet prays, "let my seed be as their seed" (Num 23:10). Another Old Testament passage, Isa 1:9, referring to Jerusalem's survival of the Assyrian invasion, similarly translates "remnant" (śārîd) with "seed" (sperma): "Except the Lord of hosts had left us a *seed*...."[21] As these examples illustrate, the remnant concept came to include the idea of preserving a "holy seed."[22]

2. Quantifying the Remnant. In the Old Testament, the preservation of a remnant is based not on its size but on God's mercy,[23] and when the remnant is quantified in some way it is usually in terms of a small minority such as a tenth (Isa 6:13) or a third (Zech 13:8-9). The notion of a limited number of faithful people *within* Israel is first visible in the assurance to Elijah that God will leave as a remnant (š'r) seven thousand, "all the knees that have not bowed to Baal" (1 Kgs 19:18).[24] This distinction within Israel between those who are faithful to God and those who are not is further developed in such passages as Mal 3:16-18 and subsequent Jewish traditions, as well as in the New Testament in connection with the restoration of Israel[25] and, more particularly, by Jesus in terms of a penitent and purified remnant (Mark 9:11-13; cf. 4:11-12).[26]

---

[20]The NRSV is used throughout this chapter.

[21]Cf. Isa 1:4 which identifies the lawless in Israel as "bad seed" (*sperma ponēron*). See also Isa 15:9, in which "those of Moab who escape" (MT) is translated in the LXX as *to sperma Mōab* and Isa 14:22, referring to the cutting off, among other things, of Babylon's "remnant and seed" (*kataleimma kai sperma*).

[22]This is based, perhaps, on the Hebrew text of Isa 6:13 which refers to "the holy seed." Cf. 4:3 (the š'r "will be called holy") and Zeph 3:12-13: "For I will leave (š'r) in the midst of you a people humble and lowly. They shall seek refuge in the name of the LORD — the remnant (šeʾērît) of Israel; they shall do no wrong and utter no lies, nor shall a deceitful tongue be found in their mouths."

[23]Sang Hoon Park, "Š'r," *NIDOTTE*, vol. 4, p. 15.

[24]H. Wildberger, "Š'r," p. 1288.

[25]See Steven M. Bryan, *Jesus and Israel's Traditions of Judgement and Restoration* (Cambridge: Cambridge University Press, 2002), pp. 91-98.

[26]Ibid., pp. 128-29, 239, arguing convincingly that this passage clarifies Jesus' view

The Septuagint in places develops further the notion of a small remnant within Israel. In an apocalyptic view of God's judgment on the world, Isaiah sees "few people" (*anthrōpoi oligoi*) left in Israel (Isa 24:6).[27] Similarly, those entreating Jeremiah to pray for mercy mention that what is left of Israel's "remnant" has become but "a few" (*oligoi*). *Jubilees* and the Qumran literature also conceive the remnant to be small.[28]

To summarize our brief consideration of the post-Old Testament period Jewish literature, the most frequent terminology in the Septuagint for "remnant" are not forms of *leimma* ("remnant") but of *loipos* ("the rest"), demonstrating that remnant theology can be present even in the absence of the more technical remnant terminology. Furthermore, other terms such as *oligoi* ("the few") and *sperma* ("seed") are also connected with the remnant concept. Consequently, as we turn our attention to the Gospels, we will need to look more broadly as to how notions of "seed" or children, smallness, and other similar terms are utilized in order to ascertain whether and to what extent a remnant concept may be present. First, however, it will be helpful to relate the notion of remnant within the larger context of prophetic hopes of Israel's restoration and the proclamation of John the Baptist.

The Gospels and the Remnant

Closely related to the question of whether Jesus intended to gather a remnant is the nature of His mission to Israel. Some argue that the restoration of Israel better describes Jesus' mission.[29] However, the idea of restoration involves more than what is sometimes suggested. In addition, as we shall see, there is evidence not only that the remnant theme is present in the gospels but also that it plays an important role in the mission and proclamation of Jesus.[30] In order to understand the role of rem-

---

that John the Baptist called forth a remnant who prove responsive to His own kingdom proclamation. See also our discussion below.

[27]Cf. Isa 16:14 in which those left in Moab are described as "very few" (*oligostos*).

[28]*Dictionary of Judaism in the Biblical Period: 450 B.C.E. to 600 C.E.*, Jacob Neusner and William Scott Green, eds. (New York: Macmillan, 1996), p. 524. Cf. Joel Willitts, "The Remnant of Israel in 4QpIsaiah[a] (4Q161) and the Dead Sea Scrolls," *JJS* 57 (2006): 25. See Leslie Pollard, "The Remnant in Non-Canonical and Jewish Apocalyptic Works and in Qumran," in this volume.

[29]E. P. Sanders, *Jesus and Judaism* (London: SCM, 1985); James W. Watts, "The Remnant Theme: A Survey of New Testament Research, 1921-1987" *Perspectives in Religious Studies* 15 (1988): 109-29.

[30]See Bryan, *Judgement*, pp. 114-28; *pace* E. P. Sanders, *Jesus*, p. 226; Richard A.

nant ideas in the work of Jesus, it will be helpful first to look at the work of John the Baptist.

Remnant and John the Baptist

All four Gospels present John the Baptist as the forerunner of Jesus.[31] These several descriptions, taken together, present a fairly coherent picture of John's work. First John's immersing people in water was so distinctive that he became known as "the baptizer" (*ho baptistēs*).[32] Besides the obvious differentiation that this implied between those who accepted his baptism and those who did not (Matt 3:7 par.), the references to repentance in view of the coming judgment[33] and, more specifically, to a "sifting" of Israel also suggest a remnant concept may be operative. However, unlike some Jewish groups, such as that centered in Qumran, the notion of the remnant visible in John's preaching is not exclusivist but open to all who showed "fruit" demonstrating repentance (Matt 3:8).[34] Indeed,

---

Horsley, *Jesus and the Spiral of Violence: Popular Jewish Resistance in Roman Palestine* (San Francisco, CA: Harper & Row, 1987), p. 211; Martin Hengel, *The Charismatic Leader and His Followers* (Edinburgh: T. & T. Clark, 1981), pp. 59-60; Marius Reiser, *Jesus and Judgment: The Eschatological Proclamation in Its Jewish Context* (Minneapolis, MN: Fortress, 1997), p. 313.

[31] Matt 3:1-12; Mark 1:2-8; Luke 3:1-18; John 1:19-28. Darryl L. Bock, *Jesus according to Scripture: Restoring the Portrait from the Gospels* (Grand Rapids, MI.: Baker Academic, 2002), p. 78: "That the story of Jesus' ministry began with John was the common view of the church (Acts 1:21-22; 10:37)." On the varying perspectives, see John P. Meier, "John the Baptist in Matthew's Gospel," *JBL* 99 (1980): 384-86.

[32] Unlike Jewish purification rituals, which were self-administered (thus the middle form *baptisōntai* in Mark 7:4; cf. Luke 11:38), John appears to be the active agent in the immersion of others (indicated by *humas*, the direct object of the active verb in Mark 1:8a parr.), also implied by John 4:1-2 which would need to make no such clarification if the immersions were self-administered under the authority of John or Jesus; cf. Josephus, *Ant.* 18.116. See also Joan E. Taylor, *The Immerser: John the Baptist within Second Temple Judaism* (Grand Rapids, MI: Eerdmans, 1997), pp. 49-50; John P. Meier, *A Marginal Jew, Volume 2: Mentor, Message, and Miracles* (New York: Doubleday, 1994), p. 51.

[33] A common Jewish motif as evident, e.g., in Sir 5:6-7: "Do not say, 'His mercy is great, he will forgive the multitude of my sins,' for both mercy and wrath are with him, and his anger will rest on sinners. Do not delay to turn back to the Lord, and do not postpone it from day to day; for suddenly the wrath of the Lord will come upon you, and at the time of punishment you will perish"; also CD XIX.15-26 in which not only entry into the "covenant of conversion/repentance" (*bryth tshwvh*, line 16) but also separation from sin is necessary to survive the visitation of God's wrath.

[34] Meyer, "Jesus and the Remnant," pp. 128-29, who understands John's message to imply an "open remnant" in contrast to the "closed" concept of "particularist remnant groups," but see the point made by John P. Meier, "John the Baptist in Josephus: Philology and Exegesis," *JBL* 111 (1992): 231 that John's baptism was a bodily purification, conditional

in the description of John's ministry given by Josephus, it seems to be the steady increase of his following, apparently including even soldiers and tax collectors (Luke 3:12-14), that precipitated his arrest and eventual death at the hands of Herod.[35] The Gospels also characterize the Baptist's following as mainstream and influential (Mark 11:32 parr.). While the meaning of John's water baptism is disputed, the reference to a coming baptism of spirit and fire again seems to point to the expectation of an imminent separation within Israel of chaff from wheat (Matt 3:11-12 par.; cf. Amos 9:9).[36]

Jesus and the Restoration of Israel

The relation between the respective ministries of John and Jesus is complex but both seem to have criticized the Jewish tendency toward a superficial reliance on Israel's election to the exclusion of ethical purity,[37] echoing the intra-Israel concerns evident already in the later Old Testament prophetic critiques (e.g. Zech 13:7-9; Mal 3:16-18)[38] and some of the Second Temple period Jewish literature.[39] A crucial question in this connection is whether Jesus' work is best understood in terms of a restoration theology or a remnant theology. There does not yet exist any scholarly consensus to answer this question, though many tend to understand Jesus in terms of Israel's restoration.[40]

According to critical scholarship, what Jesus may have intended His work to accomplish is a complicated question.[41] Nevertheless, we can be fairly certain that one intention of Jesus was to restore or reconstitute

---

on its recipients already having been morally cleansed and practicing virtue.

[35]So Meier, "John the Baptist in Josephus," pp. 235-36 and n. 28, also observing how Josephus distinguishes John from Jewish revolutionaries like Theudas et al.

[36]Cf. Sanders, *Jesus and Judaism*, p. 92.

[37]Cf. E. P. Sanders, *Judaism: Practice and Belief, 63 BCE–66 CE* (London: SCM, 1992), p. 264, citing Matt 3:9; John 8:39. More specifically regarding Israel's election and the Jesus traditions concerning restoration, see Sanders, *Jesus and Judaism*; Bryan, *Judgement and Restoration*, pp. 86-87.

[38]As Günther and H. Krienke have observed, the remnant concept also began to be linked in such passages as Zech 8:3-13 to Yhwh's return to Zion ("Remnant," p. 250).

[39]Ibid., pp. 250-251; cf. cf. Joachim Jeremias, "Der Gedanke des 'Heiligen Restes' im Spätjudentum und in der Verkündung Jesu" *ZNW* 42 (1949): 191.

[40]E.g. E. P. Sanders (see n. 24), N. T. Wright, *Jesus and the Victory of God* (Minneapolis, MN: Fortress, 1996), et al.

[41]For an extensive bibliography on scholarship about the historical Jesus (2045 entries covering the period from 1768 to 1996), see Craig A. Evans, *Life of Jesus Research: An Annotated Bibliography* (Leiden: E.J. Brill, 1996).

Israel in some way.[42] Three principal lines of evidence support this conclusion:

1. The pervasiveness of restoration hopes. Even though Israel has suffered under God's judgment, much of the prophetic literature envisages Israel's restoration as the goal of this judgment.[43] Several features of Jesus' work serve to affirm these hopes. Less clear for us, however, is the precise form Jesus expected this restoration to take.[44]

2. Jesus' appointment of "the Twelve."[45] It has been suggested that this circle around Jesus points unambiguously to the reconstitution or "restoration" of Israel.[46] This group consisted of exactly twelve individuals, who were chosen by Jesus, and who represented at least symbolically, a "regathering of the twelve tribes" of Israel.[47] However, Jesus' promise that His followers would sit on twelve thrones judging the twelve tribes of Israel indicates a future as well as a present realization of the idea of Israel's restoration.[48]

3. The mission to Israel. The sending of the Twelve on a mission to Israel, mentioned by all three synoptic gospels (Mark 6:6-13 parr.) and the specific exclusion of Gentiles (Matt 10:5), suggests a continuing concern

---

[42]The notion of "restoration" requires further definition. At the time of Jesus, there were competing understandings of the prophetic traditions on this subject: "Restoration could be conceived of either as a return to covenant fidelity or as the re-establishment of the twelve tribes and national dominion" (Bryan, *Judgement and Restoration*, p. 107). These are not necessarily mutually exclusive, as Bryan himself points out. They also depend on how "Israel" is conceived.

[43]Graham N. Stanton, "Aspects of Early Christian-Jewish Polemic and Apologetic," *NTS* 31 (1985): 377-92; Sanders, *Jesus and Judaism*, pp. 98-106.

[44]Watts, "Remnant Themes," pp. 118-119 apparently considers remnant and restoration expectations to be mutually exclusive but this is not necessarily the case. See, e.g., Bryan, *Judgement and Restoration*, pp. 120-123 who, on the basis of Mark 9:12-13, argues that Jesus considered the restoration of Israel already accomplished in some sense through John the Baptist's preaching.

[45]Sanders, *Jesus and Judaism*, pp. 98-106; idem, *The Historical Figure of Jesus* (New York: Penguin, 1993), pp. 184-187.

[46]Sanders, *Jesus and Judaism*, p. 98.

[47]John P. Meier, "The Circle of the Twelve: Did it Exist During Jesus' Public Ministry?" *JBL* 116 (1997): 657. See also Joachim Jeremias, *New Testament Theology* (London: SCM, 1971), pp. 233-234.

[48]Meier, "The Circle of the Twelve," p. 657 n. 55, also referencing idem, *A Marginal Jew*, vol. 2, pp. 237-506. As Meier points out in his article (pp. 655-658), both forms of the saying preserve a reference to "twelve" ("twelve thrones ... twelve tribes," Matt 19:28; "twelve tribes," Luke 22:30), making clear that, in Jesus' eschatological vision of a restored Israel, the Twelve were to have positions of authority.

for the nation as a whole. Nevertheless, a failure to respond positively to the apostles' proclamation portends judgment (Mark 6:11). Furthermore, in the Matthean version of the sending discourse, the focus gradually shifts toward a more universal concern,[49] which finds further development in the great commission (Matt 28:19-20; cf. 24:14).

Even if the evidence is fairly clear that Jesus intended His work to effect Israel's restoration *in some* sense (though not as a revolutionary)[50] the question remains, is it possible to find in Jesus' proclamation and activity also the notion of a remnant theology? In order to address this issue, it is necessary to look more closely at the evidence presented in the Gospels as to what Jesus may have intended vis-à-vis Israel. First, we will look more generally at the aims and audience of Jesus' ministry before examining more specific evidence for a remnant theology in the gospels.

Jesus and the Remnant

Jesus and Israel

As with John the Baptist, Jesus' proclamation was addressed to all Israel. If to judge only from the Synoptic Gospels, it would seem that Jesus' ministry was primarily confined to Galilee. The Gospel of John, however, witnesses to a Judean ministry in an earlier stage of Jesus' work and portrays this work as having a longer time-frame than what might be inferred from the Synoptic traditions alone.[51] In addition, Luke and John show Jesus concerned also for the inclusion of Samaritans (Luke 9:52; John 4:4; cf. 8:48 but also Matt 10:5). Taken as a whole, this evidence points to a concern for all Israel, at least in a geographic sense.[52] In fact, Jesus' travels

---

[49]Further, see Clinton Wahlen, *Jesus and the Impurity of Spirits in the Synoptic Gospels* (Tübingen: Mohr, 2004), p. 136.

[50]See Matt 26:52 and Mark 14:48, cited as evidence by Markus Bockmuehl, *This Jesus: Martyr, Lord, Messiah* (Downers Grove, IL: InterVarsity, 1993), p. 118 (cf. 211 n. 36).

[51]See D. Moody Smith, "John: A Source for Jesus Research?" in *John, Jesus, and History, Volume 1: Critical Appraisals of Critical Views*, Paul N. Anderson, Felix Just, and Tom Thatcher, eds. (Atlanta, GA: SBL, 2007), p. 171.

[52]While John's Gospel as a source for historical Jesus traditions has often been questioned, more recent scholarship has increasingly found reason to consider it stemming from early recollections of Jesus independent from those preserved in the Synoptics. See e.g. John P. Meier, *A Marginal Jew: Rethinking the Historical Jesus, Volume 1: The Roots of the Problem and the Person* (New York: Doubleday, 1991), pp. 44-45; F. J. Moloney, "The Fourth Gospel and the Jesus of History," *NTS* 46 (2000): 42-58; James D. G. Dunn, *Jesus Remembered* (Grand Rapids, MI: Eerdmans, 2003), pp. 165-167; Paul N. Anderson, *The Fourth Gospel and the Quest for Jesus* (New York: T. & T. Clark, 2006); and now, the studies stemming from the SBL group by the same name, *John, Jesus, and History* (see n. 51 above

to areas near Tyre and Sidon and across the Sea of Galilee to the Decapolis may suggest an expansive notion of Israel's borders, also possibly the reconstitution of Israel to include Gentiles.[53]

In addition, as with the Baptist, Jesus spoke openly to large and diverse groups of people which included the ranks of the privileged, women as followers, and outcasts.[54] On the one hand, Jesus' gospel proclamation was a generalized call to repentance (Mark 1:15; cf. Matt 3:8 par.).[55] But, like the response to John's call,[56] the four gospels witness to the rejection also of Jesus' proclamation by the majority in Israel.[57] This poses a problem if we understand Jesus' kingdom proclamation as eschatological: Why did it not eventuate in a restored national Israel?[58]

As we mentioned in connection with the promise of sitting on twelve thrones,[59] there is evidence that Jesus' proclamation anticipated more than simply a revival of the nation based on kingdom ethics—there would be an eschatological judgment and sifting, using language similar to what we find on the lips of John the Baptist.[60] The similarity between the mes-

---

for the complete bibliographic information).

[53] Wahlen, *Jesus and the Impurity of Spirits*, pp. 130-131 and n. 119; Dunn, *Jesus Remembered*, pp. 322-323.

[54] Some of Jesus' disciples seem to have had privileged access to the ruling priests (i.e. Judas Iscariot; the beloved disciple, on which see Oscar Cullmann, *Der johanneische Kreis* [Tübingen: Mohr, 1975], pp. 67-88 who considers him the primary witness behind the Fourth Gospel; Richard Bauckham, *Jesus and the Eyewitnesses: The Gospels as Eyewitness Testimony* [Grand Rapids, MI: Eerdmans, 2006], pp. 384-411, who identifies this disciple as early but also outside the circle of the Twelve; Craig S. Keener, *The Gospel of John: A Commentary* [Peabody, MA: Hendrickson, 2003], pp. 82-115 defending at length the traditional view that this disciple is John the son of Zebedee). Other well-placed followers include the owner of the upper room (Mark 14:12-16); Joseph of Arimathea (Mark 15:43; John 19:38); women able to provide financial support, including Joanna, the wife of Herod's steward (Luke 8:2-3; 24:10; on which see Dunn, *Jesus Remembered*, pp. 322, 534-537); and, as Dunn (p. 540) puts it, "sympathetic Pharisees" (Luke 7:36; 11:37; 14:1). A toll collector even appears among the Twelve in Matthew's list (10:3; cf. 9:9; Mark 2:14) as does a zealot named Simon (Matt 10:4; cf. Mark 3:18/Luke 6:15).

[55] Jeremias, *New Testament Theology*, pp. 152-56; Dunn, *Jesus Remembered*, p. 499; *pace* Sanders, *Historical Figure of Jesus*, p. 233, who states that Jesus "was not a repentance-minded reformer."

[56] Matt 21:42; Luke 7:32-35. See Dunn, *Jesus Remembered*, pp. 722-723, 797.

[57] Meier, *A Marginal Jew*, vol. 1, p. 177.

[58] One solution, of course, is that of Albert Schweitzer: Jesus failed to bring in the eschaton, on which see the chapter entitled "Did Jesus Fail?" in Bockmuehl, *This Jesus*, pp. 77-102.

[59] See n. 43 above.

[60] This eschatological judgment includes but goes beyond the notion of "eschatological

sages of John and Jesus with respect to judgment comes most clearly to the fore in the litany of sayings that follow the Beelzebul controversy (Matt 12:30-45 par.), beginning with the affirmation that "whoever is not with me is against me, and whoever does not gather with me scatters" (12:30; cf. 3:12). It continues with warnings about blasphemy against the Holy Spirit (12:31-32; cf. 3:11), a tree and its fruit (12:33-37; cf. 3:8, 10), the sign of Jonah (12:38-42) and the return of the unclean spirit (12:43-45). As is evident from the references cited, most of these sayings have their parallel already in the proclamation of judgment by John the Baptist.[61] As the gospel narratives present it, this sifting already begins in a very real sense with the gathering of those who choose to follow Jesus, his spiritual "family" (Mark 3:31-35), and the exclusive disclosures to the Twelve in recognition that many were not accepting His gospel of the kingdom (4:11-12).[62]

The implications of the exclusiveness and ultimacy of Jesus' proclamation, centered not around the temple but Himself, constituted the most likely cause of opposition.[63] Jesus' triumphal entry and taking charge in the temple brought the religious leadership face to face with this question of authority. We see the extrapolation of their rejection of Him in the judgment parables (e.g. Matt 22:11-14; 25:1-13)[64] but the prospect of many not willing to accept His proclamation is suggested already in the Sermon on the Mount (7:21-27; cf. Luke 6:46-49; 13:25-27) and in the

---

reversal" described by Dunn, *Jesus Remembered*, pp. 412-417; nor is it simply self-referential of Jesus' own demise or to be relegated to the final judgment at the end of the age (as Dunn also argues, pp. 808, 420-25).

[61]Further, see Wahlen, *Jesus and the Impurity of Spirits*, p. 128. Some but not all of these parallels might be explicable on the basis of the Matthean tendency toward paralleling Jesus with John the Baptist (see Meier, "John the Baptist in Matthew," pp. 383-405), but not all (as Meier himself recognizes, ibid., p. 398 n. 50).

[62]From the Markan narrative, it appears that opposition leads directly to Jesus teaching in parables (3:23; 4:2). We cannot here enter in to the discussion of the role of Isaianic expectations of rejection (Isa 53:1; cf. John 12:38) but, in view of Jesus' characterization of His ministry in thoroughly Isaianic terms (e.g. Luke 7:22-23 par.), it would be surprising if He did not find it meaningful as opposition to His proclamation intensified (so e.g. Bockmuehl, *Martyr, Lord, Messiah*," pp. 90-91 but cf. Dunn, *Jesus Remembered*, pp. 809-818). As Horst Dietrich Preuss (*Old Testament Theology*, vol. 1 [Louisville, KY: Knox, 1995], p. 56) reminds us, Isaiah of Jerusalem responded to widespread unbelief of his prophetic message by gathering faithful disciples around him (Isa 8:16, 18).

[63]See Sanders, *Historical Figure of Jesus*, pp. 236-237.

[64]In the context of the temple episode, the parables contain an implicit judgment on Israel's leadership (esp. Mark 12:1-12); further, see Clinton Wahlen, "The Temple in Mark and Contested Authority," *BibInt* 15 (2007): 248-267.

sifting of the wheat from the tares, echoing John's warning of imminent judgment (Matt 13:24-30, 47-50; cf. 3:11-12).

Jesus and Remnant Theology

In view of the similarity of the proclamations about judgment by John the Baptist and Jesus, it would be natural to anticipate that a similar theology of the remnant may be operative also in their proclamations.[65] The idea of Israel's restoration is not incompatible with a remnant theology. In fact, the Old Testament concept of the "faithful remnant" is not completely separable from the notion of "Israel" itself, since the former involves the separating out of a recognizable group of faithful Israelites that are preserved while the rest are excluded from Israel through divine judgment.[66] Similarly, Jesus' announcement of kingdom terms, centered on one's relation to Him and His teaching, implicitly excludes all who would reject Him and thereby effects, to a certain extent at least, not the restoration of all Israel but a division within it.

Images of the Remnant

An important question at this juncture of our study is whether or not division was a conscious result of Jesus' activity and proclamation.[67] That Jesus not only anticipated but even intended His ministry to be divisive is suggested by Luke 12:51: "Do you think that I have come to bring peace to the earth? No, I tell you, but rather division!" (cf. Matt 10:34). Turning to a consideration of possible remnant images and terminology in the

---

[65]So Meyer, "Jesus and the Remnant," p. 127 and, most recently, Bryan who distinguishes between Jesus and John on the basis of Hasel's distinction between a faithful remnant and the eschatological remnant, with John calling out the former and those responding to Jesus' message of the kingdom comprising the latter (*Judgement and Restoration*, pp. 117, 239). Watts' critique ("Remnant Themes," esp. p. 112) falters on his failure to consider the notion of a faithful remnant alongside his discussion of the historical and eschatological remnants.

[66]For the distinction between historical, faithful, and eschatological remnants and a more detailed consideration of the concept of the remnant in the OT, see Hasel, "Remnant," pp. 130-134 and Tarsee Li, "The Remnant in the Old Testament," in this volume. As Meyer ("Jesus and the Remnant," p. 127) points out, "in biblical and extrabiblical literature, everywhere, always, and without exception, the remnant is defined by judgment." While Meyer also considers the converse true (i.e. that mention of judgment presupposes the existence of a remnant), this is not necessarily so but should be signaled by the presence of relevant terminology.

[67]The contention here that Jesus intended the restoration of all Israel implies that the consequent division within Israel was neither a necessary nor ideal result (cf. n. 1 above).

Gospels, we shall see indications that this is indeed the case.[68]

In the first part of this study, dealing with relevant Jewish background material to the remnant concept, we found that Septuagint terminology centers more around various forms of *loipos* ("other," "the rest"), indications of smallness, and "seed" theology in addition to the expected *leimma*-terminology ("remnant"). This is significant because, as we have also observed, the Septuagint witnesses to developing Jewish reflections on the Hebrew Bible of a kind not unlike those which are visible in the indisputably indigenous Judaism of the Qumran literature and the Aramaic Targums. We now know that the older scholarly distinction between Hellenistic and Palestinian Judaism is untenable.[69] It should not be surprising therefore to find similar ideas about the remnant in a variety of Jewish writings whether they originated in Palestine or in the Diaspora, whether in Hebrew, Aramaic or Greek.[70]

1. The term *loipos* ("other," "the rest") is found in the Gospels thirteen times, usually in a negative sense.[71] At least one notable exception is found in Luke.[72] In the parable of the Pharisee and the Tax Collector, the self-righteous Pharisee distinguishes himself from the "rest of mankind," specifically listing "thieves, rogues, adulterers" but also "this tax collector" (18:11; cf. v. 9). At first glance, this would seem to fit the other negative examples but for the surprise ending, which identifies the tax collector rather than the Pharisee as being the one who went away from the temple "justified." This might not seem especially significant except that the parable is closely connected with the preceding verses in which Jesus affirms that God will grant "justice" to His "elect" (*eklektōn*). By way of conclusion to some judgment passages *eklektoi* ("chosen ones") ap-

---

[68]Meyer, "Jesus and the Remnant," pp. 129-130 and Hasel, "Remnant," p. 134, briefly highlight much of this remnant terminology.

[69]Martin Hengel, *Judaism and Hellenism: Studies in their Encounter in Palestine during the Early Hellenistic Period* (London: SCM, 1981).

[70]Cf. n. 4 above. Although Jesus (with arguable exceptions) worked among Aramaic-speaking Jews, the pervasiveness of Greek influence on Jewish ideas even within Israel proper permits a comparison of the terminology in the LXX with the Gospels.

[71]Sometimes the negative reference is to people (Matt 22:6; 25:11; 27:49; [16:13]; Luke 8:10; 24:9, cf. 11; similar to the usage in Paul [Günther and Krienke, "Remnant," p. 252]); other times it refers negatively to things (Mark 4:19; Luke 12:26). Twice *loipos* is used adverbially in the accusative singular (Matt 26:45; Mark 14:41).

[72]Luke 24:10 may be another one, referring to "other" women (*loipai*) who reported to the eleven disciples and all "the rest" (*loipoi*, v. 9) that they found the tomb empty and that two glorious beings said that Jesus had risen from the dead and would meet them in Galilee. But v. 11 indicates that those who heard this story considered it an "idle tale."

pears as a referent to a remnant-like group.[73]

2. Seed imagery is used in the parable of the Wheat and Tares (Matt 13:24-30) to represent two contrasting groups. The interpretation of the imagery identifies "the good seed" (*to...kalon sperma*) as "the sons of the kingdom" and "the tares" (*ta zizania*) as "the sons of the evil one." The same phrase also can be used negatively: "the sons of the kingdom" will be cast into outer darkness (Matt 8:12; cf. 12:27). This is similar to the good seed/bad seed contrast mentioned earlier in our survey of Jewish literature. Similar imagery using "sons" is also quite frequent: peacemakers will be called "sons of God" (Matt 5:9); those who love their enemies will be called "sons of the Most High" (Luke 6:35 par.). But Jesus can also refer to the "sons of those who murdered the prophets" (Matt 23:31; cf. Luke 11:47) and "the sons of this age" in contrast to the "sons of light" (Luke 16:8; similarly 20:34, 36). Jesus also mentions the "sons of light" in John 12:36.[74] While similar language used in the Qumran literature points to an exclusive notion of the remnant, Jesus, like John the Baptist (Luke 3:8 par.), broadens the concept to include others from outside of Israel (Matt 8:10; Luke 13:29).

3. Building and Planting. Jesus speaks of building His *ekklēsia* or "congregation" (Matt 16:18; cf. 18:17)[75] and the uprooting of "every plant that my heavenly Father has not planted" (15:13). Similar language is found in a remnant context of Jeremiah (24:6-7), the larger context of which also contrasts "good figs" with "bad figs," referring to two groups of people in Judah.[76]

4. Shepherd imagery. In a variety of traditions, Jesus describes Himself (or God) as a shepherd (Matt 26:31; John 10:16; cf. Jer 23:4; 50:19) and the disciples as the sheep (Matt 26:31; Luke 12:32). He also speaks of gathering the "lost sheep" of Israel (Matt 10:6; 15:24), evoking a remnant image familiar from such Old Testament remnant passages as Jer 23:2-3[77]

---

[73] "For many are called, but few are chosen" (Matt 22:14; cf. 19:30; 20:16); God sends His angels to "gather his elect" (24:31).

[74] Cf. the reference to the "sons of light" and "sons of darkness" in the writings of Qumran (e.g. 1QS I.9-10).

[75] On the Jewish background for *ekklēsia* stemming from the Hebrew usage of *qahal*, see K. E. Stendahl, "Kirche im Urchristentum" in *Religion in Geschichte und Gegenwart*, vol. 3, K. Galling, ed. (Tübingen: Mohr, 1959), cols. 1297-1304.

[76] Kenneth Mulzac, "The Remnant and the New Covenant in the Book of Jeremiah," *AUSS* 34 (1996): 242, linking these verses with the mention of remnant in 23:4 as representing the divine initiative in a new work of preserving/saving.

[77] See Kenneth D. Mulzac, "'The Remnant of My Sheep': A Study of Jeremiah 23:1-8 in its Biblical and Theological Contexts," *JATS* 13/1 (2002): 138-141.

The Remnant in the Gospels

and Zeph 3:19-20.[78] Further, Jesus' mention of "other sheep" which are "not of this fold" (John 10:16) points to an expansive notion of the remnant, drawing on prior prophetic hopes for the inclusion of Gentiles in the future kingdom (e.g., Isa 49:6; 56:6-8).

5. Quantifying terminology. In a way similar to what we found in Jewish literature of the Second Temple period, Jesus refers to His followers with a variety of terms that suggest a small group. He refers to the "few" (*oligoi*) who find the way to life (Matt 7:14; cf. Luke 13:23) and affirms that, though "many" are called "few" (*oligoi*) are chosen/elect (Matt 22:14). To the "poor" (*ptōchoi*), Jesus proclaims good news (Matt 11:5; Luke 4:18; 7:22) and these also are blessed (Luke 6:20 par.). Finally, Jesus also employs the term "little ones" (*mikroi*) for those who believe in Him (Matt 10:42; Mark 9:42; Luke 17:2) and refers to His disciples as "the little flock" (*to micron poimnion*, Luke 12:32).

While few if any of these terms of reference by themselves would be sufficient to consider that Jesus conceived of His followers as a "remnant," the multiplicity of expressions taken together are significant. Furthermore, Jesus' use of terms which parallel remnant terminology in Second Temple period Jewish literature suggests that a remnant theology is present. There are also indications that His concept of the remnant was inclusive.

Conclusion

This study of the Gospels has examined to what extent the concept of a remnant can be traced to Jesus. A comparison of remnant terminology used in Jewish literature with the Gospels shows that a similar usage can be found in the sayings of Jesus. Furthermore, we have observed that the proclamations of John the Baptist and Jesus share some common features relevant for this study. In particular, both were addressed to Israel as a whole and yet also precipitated further division within Israel based on individual responses to their messages. We also noticed a similarity in their respective proclamations of judgment, including use of the same imagery: gathering and scattering, trees and fruit, sifting of wheat from chaff, etc. Both John and Jesus employed this imagery in the context of opposition to their proclamations. These considerations suggest that a theology of the remnant was operative in both cases. Intriguingly, their proclamations also lend an element of inclusiveness to the concept of a faithful remnant.

---

[78]Cf. King, "Remnant," p. 415 on the remnant "concept" in these verses.

The primary difference between them is that, whereas the horizon of John the Baptist's proclamation was future, Jesus connected judgment to His proclamation of the kingdom as a *present* as well as a future reality and that Israel's *present* response to Him would be a decisive factor in the judgment. At the same time, the proclamation of Jesus was also connected with the prophetic hope of Israel's restoration. Remnant theology and restoration hopes are paradoxically combined in the activities and sayings of Jesus. On the one hand, the sending of the apostles on a mission to Israel suggests restoration, though even this hinges on the people's response. On the other hand, the calling and mission of the Twelve seem to represent the beginnings of a remnant from Israel grounded in one's response to Jesus. The election of a remnant would seem to imply a negative judgment on Israel. Nevertheless, hope remains for Israel because, while the nation largely turned away from Jesus and His kingdom proclamation, Jesus' gathering work continues to be realized through the Twelve, whose proclamation eventuates in the emergence of an Israel of faith.

CHAPTER IV

THE REMNANT IN PAULINE THOUGHT

Leslie N. Pollard
Vice President
Loma Linda University
Loma Linda, CA

This chapter will explore the presence and use of the remnant motif in the eschatological preaching and teaching of Paul. We will carefully examine the *explicit* reference to the remnant motif found in Rom 9–11, analyzing key usages of remnant language in these chapters. This analysis will reveal that the trajectory toward a borderless (versus territorialized) remnant evidenced in the Gospels matures in Paul. He uses *loipos* and its derivatives outside the contexts of judgment and salvation, i.e., non-technically. But it is in Rom 9–11 that we find the most theologically developed use of remnant terminology in the New Testament. In the climax[1] of his epistle, Paul uses the noun *leimma* to argue that the promises of election are perpetuated in a "remnant" of Israel (11:5).

I. Paul Asserts a Remnant

Romans 9:1-5 introduces the key question: "Does Israel's unbelief mean the Word of God has failed?" Paul's unequivocal answer is "No!" But Paul's "No!" is in a sense conditional. For him, "Israel" denotes a particular covenantal relationship between God and the chosen nation (cf. Eph 2:12). Paul's "No!" means that the privileges associated with the historic election of Israel, including eschatological salvation, have been extended to believing "Israelites." To state it concisely: Paul distinguishes his remnant from biological and empirical Israel ("Israel *kata sarka*/according to the flesh").

In support for his view, Paul appropriates and applies remnant passages from the Old Testament leading to his culminating conclusion in Romans 11:5.[2] Paul seems to divide Israel into "the *historical* people of God"

---

[1] For an excellent treatment of Paul's handling of the issue of Israel's stumbling, see Krister Stendahl, *Paul Among Jews and Gentiles* (Philadelphia: Fortress Press, 1976), pp. 78-96.

[2] G. Schrenk, "*Leimma*," *TDNT*, vol. 4, p. 210: "This [Rom 11:5ff] is the climax and

and "the 'people of promise'; and this involves a theological distinction that enables Paul to differentiate two groups of people in the present."[3] He relocated unbelieving Jews over and against believing Jews and believing Gentiles. Lester Meyer asserts tersely that, for Paul, only "those Jews who accept his gospel constitute the remnant."[4]

Questions on Remnant

In his treatment of the remnant idea in Rom 9–11, Paul uses a combination of citations from the Old Testament to substantiate his conclusions concerning the relationship between "Israel *kata sarka*" ("according to the flesh") and "Israel *kata pneuma*" ("according to the Spirit") (Hos 1:10; 2:23; Isa 1:9; 1 Kgs 19:10, 18). Through the use of diatribe, he answers three questions:[5] (1) What does the history of Israel mean? (2) How valid is the covenantal promise? and (3) Since the majority of Israel chose not to believe, can God be faithful while including the Gentiles in the covenant?[6] In Rom 1–8 Paul provides the foundation for asserting salvation by faith in Christ alone. Paul's purpose in Rom 9–11 is to demonstrate that God did not totally cast off His people but preserved His covenant through a faithful remnant (i.e., *hypoleimma* in 9:27). In Paul's purview, this faithful remnant of the Israelites constituted the nation of the saved. Romans 9–11 is critical to the New Testament presentation of the remnant because it represents the core of Pauline thinking on the relationship between Israel as the historical remnant and the redefined reality of Christ's faithful/soteriological remnant according to the election of grace.

In fact, *Paul uses Old Testament remnant passages to expand the breadth and scope of God's faithful remnant.* A closer look at the way Paul uses the remnant passages of the Old Testament demonstrates the scope of his remnant theology. Romans 9:6-13 constitutes the first set of passages that frames an internal differentiation within Israel. The table

---

conclusion of the exposition thus far . . ."

[3]J. W. Aageson, "Typology, Correspondence, and the Application of Scripture in Romans 9-11," *JSNT* 31 (1987): 54-55.

[4]Lester V. Meyer, "Remnant," *ABD*, vol. 5, p. 671.

[5]Ernst Käsemann, *Commentary on Romans* (Grand Rapids, MI: Eerdmans, 1980), p. 261, shows that three similar questions are the core of Paul's discussion of God, Israel, and the Gentiles. Käsemann sees the dilemma: "If the promise to the Jews has lost its validity, the gospel can no longer give final assurance and everything will depend on personal faith which no longer has any previously given basis."

[6]In light of Israel's unbelief, W. S. Campbell, "Israel," *DPL*, p. 442, states, "The true Israel [therefore] is 'of Israel' but not coextensive with historical Israel."

below presents the Pauline contrast between biological Israel and the Israel of faith.

Table
Biological Israel and the Israel of Faith Contrasted

Biological Israel	Israel of Faith: "A remnant according to grace"
ou hoi (not the ones) *ek* ("from") Israel, i.e., biological Israel (9:6b)	"[but] *houtoi* those of Israel" i.e., according to the promise (9:6b)
[not] Abraham's *sperma* (seed) (seed = descendants in 9:7a)	[but] Abraham's *tekna* (children in 9:7a) *En Isaak* is *sperma* (seed) (9:7b)
not *the tekna tēs sarkos* 9:8a (children of the flesh)	[but the] *tekna tou Theou* (children of God) (9:8b) = *tekna tes epangelias* (children of the promise) (9:8c) = [Abraham's] *sperma* (seed) (9:8c)
not *ek ergōn* (9:12a) (of works)	But *ek tou kalountas* (by Him who calls) (9:12b)
[not] Esau (9:13c)	[but] Jacob (9:13b)

Paul's understanding[7] of Israel in 9:6-13 is crucial to his[8] argument for the existence of a faithful remnant. Israel's collective failure precipitated a division of the faithful (i.e., *ek Israel* versus "of Israel"[9:6]). *Ek Israel* is most probably ablative, denoting separation.[9] Paul asserts that the previous covenantal boundaries of historic Israel were primarily expressed in the limitations indicated by *sarkos* (flesh), *ergon* (work), *thelontas* (the one willing), and *trechontas* (the one running). However, in Paul's reconstruction of Israel, the children of God are those who, through grace, moved beyond any reliance on a corporate historical election as a means of salvation (Rom 9:8, 11; cf. 9:32; 11:6). *Sperma* ("seed") in Rom 9:6-9 primarily denotes the biological descendants of Abraham through Isaac, the son of the promise. At the same time, Paul's gospel asserts that God, in fulfillment of the Old Testament promises, expanded the covenantal

---

[7]Bruce W. Longnecker, "Different Answers to Different Issues: Israel, the Gentiles, and Salvation History in Romans 9-11," *JSNT* 36 (1989): 96, calls this Paul's "redefinition" of Israel. The contrast is between unbelieving Jews and Jewish Christians. Here Paul denies the causative and salvific centrality of the law.

[8]James D. G. Dunn, *Romans 9–16* (Dallas, TX: Word, 1988), pp. 547.

[9]Cf., C.E.B. Cranfield, *Romans*, vol. 2 (Edinburgh: T. and T. Clark, 1979), pp. 470-471; John Piper, *The Justification of God: An Exegetical and Theological Study of Romans 9:1-23* (Grand Rapids, MI: Baker, 1983), p. 21.

remnant of the faithful Jews by also calling the Gentiles (Rom 3:29-30; 9:24; 10:10-13; Gal 3:28-29).[10] This expanded community is possible because of the existence of the faithful remnant of Israel.

Paul cites Gen 21:12 to validate his point. The passage is excerpted verbatim from the LXX to assert that in Isaac alone is the "seed" named.[11] Isaac represents the child of the covenant promise.[12] Syntactically, the preposition *en* as used in this verse is restrictive, "only in Isaac." Isaac stands as a symbol of those birthed through the "promise" within the Israel of faith.

The second text appropriated by Paul is Mal 1:2-3 in Rom 9:13. The words *agapaō* and *miseō* ("love" and "hate") form an antithesis frequently found in Jewish writings (Deut 21:15; 22:13; 24:3; Judg 14:16; Prov 13:24; 15:32; Mal 1:2-3) and is not to be taken as literal hate. "Jacob I loved" (i.e., chose) and "Esau I hated" (i.e., did not choose) shows "that election depends on divine rather than human action."[13] This passage demonstrates God's freedom and sovereignty in the election of Israel. Just as Jacob was preferred prior to his birth and irrespective of his subsequent conduct, so Israel had been similarly chosen. Thus God's freedom to continue His covenant by His own prerogative independent of Israel's effort (i.e., law-keeping) and/or consent simply underscores His sovereign mercy.

Paul's Theological Reasoning

In Paul's theological reasoning we encounter "divine reversal."[14] The Old Testament records numerous examples of the reverse ordering of sons.[15] Paul asserts that it is the call and merciful initiative of God (9:16b)

---

[10]See Stendahl, *Jews and Gentiles,* pp. 78-96.

[11]Dunn, *Romans,* p. 547, comments that "God had told Abraham that his promise of seed and land applied only to the line of descent through Isaac, that so far as his covenant with Abraham was concerned, only Isaac and his offspring would be recognized as Abraham's seed."

[12]The wording in Romans 9:7 is the exact rendition of the LXX *en Isaak klēthēsetai soi sperma.* God's naming or "calling" creates this salvific reality. See Rom 4:17; 8:28; 29; 9:12, 24-26.

[13]Aageson, "Typology," p. 56.

[14]See also Jerome H. Neyrey, *Paul in Other Words: A Cultural Reading of His Letters* (Louisville, KY: Westminster/John Knox, 1990), pp. 60-63. He writes, "As much as he defends God's fidelity to his promises . . . Paul also argues for God's freedom to be gracious to a new people, the Gentiles."

[15]See Ronald E. Clements, *Abraham and David: Genesis XV and Its Meaning for Israelite Tradition* (Naperville, IL: Alec R. Allenson, 1967), pp. 47-60. Clements notes the preference for Abel over Cain, Isaac over Ishmael, Joseph over his brothers, David over his

that sustains and defines the covenant, not Israel's merit, entitlement, or preconceptions. For Paul, God is free to choose and reject at His pleasure. From this perspective, Paul's remnant conception is consistent with the Old Testament prophets. It has been correctly stated that "the prophets saw Israel as a whole as rebellious and disobedient . . . Still there remained within the faithless nation a remnant of believers who were the object of God's care. Here in the believing remnant was the true people of God."[16] Further, Paul utilizes Hos 2:1, in 9:25-26, to argue his point. The Gentiles, who were "not a people," God will call[17] (*kaleso*) "my people." Douglas Stuart is correct in saying that "Israel's population will be immeasurably expanded, partly by the inclusion of people not originally Israelite."[18] Thus, the Pauline remnant is primarily an expansive and inclusive concept.

Paul further propounds his understanding of the remnant more insistently in Rom 9:27.[19] In the MT, Isa 10:22 uses the words *šeʾar . . . yašûb* ("a remnant will return/repent"[20]), where the LXX translates *yašûb* as *sōthēsetai* ("will be saved"). Paul's use of the Greek term *krazein*[21] ("cries out"), in connection with LXX Isaiah, has a prophetic edge to it.[22] Further, v. 28 promises *logon . . . poiēsei* ("to execute sentence") on the earth. In this pericope, Paul connects the faithful remnant to the judgment/salvation schema to which the notion of the remnant is inextricably paired in the Old Testament. Paul apparently saw that Isaiah's words applied to his situation. He used this quotation from Isaiah to indicate that in his day, this prophecy concerning Israel was already fulfilled in the experi-

---

brothers, and Solomon over his royal brothers.

[16]George E. Ladd, *Theology of the NT* (Grand Rapids, MI: Eerdmans, 1974), p. 108.

[17]See Käsemann, *Romans*, p. 274; Aageson, "Typology," pp. 56-57; Christopher D. Stanley, *Paul and the Language of Scripture: Citation Technique in the Pauline Epistles and Contemporary Literature* (Cambridge: Cambridge University Press, 1992), p. 110.

[18]Douglas Stuart, *Hosea-Jonah* (Waco, TX: Word Books, 1987), p. 37.

[19]After elaborating on God's freedom to show mercy (Rom 9:19-26) in a way that allows Him to save the Gentiles, Paul invokes a word from the remnant lexicon of the LXX (MT *šeʾar*, LXX *kataleimma, hypoleimma*) in 9:27. He quotes Isa 10:22-23 "And Isaiah cries out concerning Israel, though the number of the sons of Israel [be] as the sand of the sea '*to kataleimma auton sōthēsetai*' (the remnant will be saved)."

[20]*Yašûb* can designate a physical return or a change of mind by repentance. See Jacob Milgrom, "Repentance in the Old Testament," *IDBSup*, pp. 736-738. However, this might be a wordplay on the name of Isaiah's son in Isa 7:3. See John D. W. Watts, *Isaiah 1-33* (Waco, TX: Word, 1985), pp. 90-91.

[21]Dunn, *Romans*, p. 572, notes that "*krazei* is not merely stylistic, but probably indicates a degree of intensity or urgency."

[22]Cranfield, *Romans*, vol. 2, p. 501.

ence of Israel. His use of remnant language, therefore, presupposes that there has been a judgment, a division in Israel precipitated by the Christ event.[23] Aageson writes perceptively, "The discussion which began as an attempt to demonstrate that both Jews and Gentiles have been called concludes with a distinction between Israel as the whole people of God and the remnant."[24]

But Paul's remnant theology is two-sided. Israel under judgment is emphasized in 9:27-28. In 9:29 Paul uses a contrasting example through which assurance is highlighted. Paul uses Isa 1:9: "If the Lord of hosts had not left us [*egkatelipen*] a few survivors [LXX *sperma*, "seed"], we would have been like Sodom, and become like Gomorrah"(NRSV).[25] "Seed" in 9:29 is synonymous with "remnant" in 9:27.[26] Later in 11:4, Paul will use the perfect tense (*katelipon*) to demonstrate God's preservation of the remnant in Elijah's day.[27] His remnant theology asserts that Israel has not been completely decimated.[28] She is not like Sodom and Gomorrah. It was common to compare Israel to Sodom and Gomorrah (Matt 10:15; Luke 10:12; Matt 11:23-24; Luke 17:28-29). Unlike Sodom, God has preserved a "seed" for Israel. Barrett points out that "the term *sperma* refers to Israelites who are truly the children of Abraham, the genuine children of God."[29] Paul connects assurance to his remnant understanding—hope remains for Israel. This prepares the way for his readers to reconsider Israel in the next round of his argument.

---

[23]Schrenk, "*Leimma*," p. 213: "The new turn in Paul is that the remnant is now related only to the Christ who has appeared. The remnant has its existence only in Him. It consists, not only of those who are faithful to Yahweh, but rather to those who believe in God's righteousness in Christ."

[24]Aageson, "Typology," p. 57.

[25]Joseph A. Fitzmeyer, *Romans: A New Translation with Introduction and Commentary* (New York: Doubleday, 1993), p. 574, notes that Israel deserved the same fate as Sodom and Gomorrah, but God left a "remnant," and thus it was spared.

[26]See also Charles K. Barrett, *A Commentary on the Epistle to the Romans* (London: Black, 1991), p. 178; Dunn, *Romans*, p. 574; Cranfield, *Romans*, vol. 2, p. 503.

[27]In Rev 12:17, we note that "seed" and "remnant" theologies coalesce in the eschatological warfare of the Apocalypse.

[28]Thomas R. Schreiner, *Romans* (Grand Rapids, MI: Baker, 1998), p. 529: "As we saw in the exposition of Rom 9:6-9, the term *sperma* refers to Israelites who are truly the children of Abraham, the genuine children of God. It is merely another way of describing the remnant of verse 27." See also John Paul Heil, "From Remnant to Seed of Hope for Israel," *CBQ* 64 (2002): 718-720.

[29]Barrett, *Romans*, p. 178. Also Dunn, *Romans*, p. 574. In Gal 3:29 we find Paul's argument for Gentile believers' classification as "Abraham's seed according to the promise."

II. Paul's Final Argument

In Paul's final summation, before proceeding to a series of admonitions in Rom 12–16, he addresses the issue of God's faithfulness. In Rom 11:1-6, Paul employs LXX remnant terminology (*leimma*) to make his point. This passage functions as a summary of the preceding argument and as a transition to the final phase of the argument. In vv. 8-10, Paul uses passages from the three sections of the Old Testament—Law (cf. Deut 29:4), Prophets (cf. Isa 29:10), and Writings (cf. Ps 69:22-23). He raises and answers the essential question, "Has God rejected His people?" His first proof is *pro hominem*: "I myself am an Israelite . . ."[30] Paul, as a messianic Jew, appeals to his own ancestry to prove that God has not rejected Israel.[31]

In his next assertion, Paul appropriates an episode from the Old Testament—Elijah's plea against Israel. The Elijah story in Rom 11:4 simply illustrates two things. First, Paul held that a part of Israel was apostate, and second, that God had chosen a remnant.[32] In Qumran, the conception of the remnant is based on obedience to the law. In contrast, Paul asserts that an authentic remnant has been preserved by "grace." Paul's correlation of Israel (and by implication his own ministry[33]) with Elijah elucidates his conception that believers in Christ are akin to the faithful in Elijah's day. Analogous to Elijah's day, when God did not cast off His people, He has not done so *en tō nūn kairō* ("at the present time;" 11:5). Horne is thus correct when he writes that "the salvation of a small remnant from the total mass is ample proof that God's true people have not been, are not now, nor will be cast off."[34]

---

[30]Cranfield, *Romans*, vol. 2, p. 543, writes that Paul is arguing as follows: "God would hardly have chosen a Jew to be His special apostle to the Gentiles, had He cast off His people, the Jews." See also Hendriksen, *Exposition of Paul's Epistle to the Romans* (Grand Rapids, MI: Baker, 1980), p. 361; Käsemann, *Romans,* p. 299.

[31]See James D. G. Dunn, *Theology of the Apostle Paul* (Grand Rapids, MI: Eerdmans, 1998), pp. 520-521.

[32]Käseman, *Romans,* p. 301.

[33]See Johannes Munck, *Christ and Israel an Interpretation of Romans 9-11,* (Philadelphia, PA: Frotress, 1967), p. 13, where he shows that the analogy to Elijah strikingly parallels the ministry of the apostle Paul as he interacted with Israel and the Gentiles. He says, "And just as Elijah returned from his stay among the Gentiles in order to settle matters between Baal and Yahweh . . . so Paul is now on his way from the Gentiles so that stubborn Israel may be shown the obedience of faith as it is to be found among the Gentile believers."

[34]Charles Horne, "The Meaning of the Phrase 'And Thus All Israel Will Be Saved'

Theologically, the existence of a remnant is temporary.[35] The remnant will be consummated into one eschatological community. It "will become the totality. It is thus a productive number, not an unchangeable minority."[36] The salvation of believing Jews and Gentiles prepares the way for complete vindication of the covenant promises of the Old Testament. Thus, the apostle ends with the summary in Rom 11:26: "All Israel will be saved." The remnant [i.e., Israel] will stand as the ultimate witness to the covenant faithfulness of God.[37]

III. Conclusion

In the writings of Paul, the open remnant doctrine is made explicit as Paul wrestles with the question of the relationship between God's faithfulness and Israel's rejection of the Messiah. In Paul, we find the explicit doctrine of a faithful remnant consisting of believing Jews joined by believing Gentiles. To them were granted the covenantal titles of national Israel, and thus they were placed squarely in the stream of God's soteriological activity. In Romans, Paul freely used explicit remnant language since his target audience in Romans lay outside of Palestine. Further, such language clearly assured Paul's Jewish audience in Rome that Israel's promised salvation was possible, but through Christ. This Paul did using remnant language in Rom 9–11.

(Romans 11:26)," *JETS* 21 (1978): 330.

[35] Paul Achtemeier, *Romans* (Atlanta, GA: John Knox, 1985), p. 180, comments, "What was the purpose of the hardening of Israel? Were they hardened so that God could have an excuse to condemn them? Did they, as Paul frames it, 'stumble in order to fall' (v. 11)? The answer to that question is clear, and it is final: No! Were that the case, God's final purpose would not be grace, and his election would serve purposes other than redemption. Rather, Israel's stumbling was the occasion for redemption to be opened to gentiles."

[36] Schrenk, "*Leimma*," p. 212.

[37] D. G. Johnson, "The Structure and Meaning of Romans 11," *CBQ* 46 (1984): 99, insightfully says that "the remnant did not serve as a witness to the faithfulness of certain individuals (and thus by implication the rejection of others), but as a witness to the faithfulness of God and his elective purposes for Israel."

CHAPTER V

THE REMNANT IN THE BOOK OF REVELATION

Richard P. Lehmann
Former President
Salève Adventist University
France

The study of the topic of the remnant in the book of Revelation should not be limited to its explicit reference in 12:17. The topic is in fact a common one in the Old Testament,[1] widespread in intertestamental literature,[2] and present elsewhere in the New Testament.[3] This study examines more specifically the presence and nuances of the concept of the remnant in the book of Revelation. This will allow us to ascertain the richness of the remnant motif and how it relates to the church of Christ as a whole. Since Revelation is permeated with Old Testament imagery and terminology, we shall uncover notions and recollections that are particularly present in the Old Testament. Since the literary style of the book of Revelation is apocalyptic in nature, it echoes the common stream of popular views found in the related literature of that time, a fact we should also keep in mind in our exposition of the topic.

To achieve our purpose, we will first examine the *concept* of the remnant scattered throughout the book of Revelation. Then we will look into the rich and meaningful contribution of Rev 12 to our understanding of the concept. Our study will not be limited to the occurrences of remnant terminology (Greek *loipos* or *oligos*)[4] but will also look into and discuss passages in which the concept is present. Concerning remnant terminology, it is to some extent correct to say that because of its diversity of usage,

---

[1]See Li, "The Remnant in the Old Testament," in this volume; and F. Dreyfus, "Reste d'Israël," *DBS*, vol. 10, cols. 414-437.

[2]See Leslie Pollard, "The Remnant in Non-Canonical Jewish Apocalyptic Works and in Qumran," in this volume; and Richard Lehmann, "L'Eglise du reste," in *L'Eglise de Jésus-Christ: sa mission et son ministère dans le monde* (Dammarie-lès-Lys: Vie et Santé, 1995), p. 83.

[3]See chapters three and four in this volume.

[4]Two other Greek words are used by Paul: *leimma*, in Rom 11:5, and *hypoleimma* in Rom 9:27.

it is not as precise and technical as we would like it to be. Looking at the concept of the remnant in the book of Revelation is important because of the omnipresence and centrality of the theme for the book. Revelation 12:17 is not only at the epicentre of the book;[5] more importantly, it is one of the central themes of the book.

I. Concepts Related to the Remnant

As a general introduction to the discussion of the remnant in Revelation, let us review the three main applications of the concept found in the Old Testament and other Jewish literature.[6] The literature allows us to talk about *a surviving or historical remnant*. This remnant could designate an entity representing in part or as a whole those through whom God is pursuing His plan of redemption. Without their survival of catastrophes such as the Flood, religious challenges as encountered by the prophet Elijah, moral dilemmas as faced by Amos, military impasses such as the deportation mentioned by Jeremiah, or mixtures of all of the above, the promise of Gen 3:15 could not come to pass. This group of survivors is found in a special way throughout the Old Testament.[7]

There is also *an elite or faithful remnant*. This notion is found in Paul and among the people of Qumran.[8] This expression

> designates, within the sociological makeup of God's people, the religious elite. In the eyes of God they are the only genuinely vibrant segment, the only one that truly represents the whole and are able to carry forward the religious future of Israel. . . . They are different from the surviving remnant, the lone survivors; the elite remnant coexists with the other members of the people who appear spiritually but not physically dead, such as is the surviving remnant.[9]

---

[5]With Ekkehardt Mueller, "The End Time Remnant in Revelation," *JATS* 11 (2000): 189.

[6]See Li, "The Remnant in the Old Testament," in this volume; and Dreyfus, "Reste," cols. 414-437.

[7]See Hasel, *Remnant*, p. 386.

[8]Dreyfus calls it the elite remnant. He focuses on the remnant vocabulary ("Reste," col. 433).

[9]Ibid., col. 432. To strengthen the concept, we would like to refer to the use of the term "generation," common in the Old Testament. It not only designates a people of a particular period, but typifies a trans-generational group—usually in a pejorative way. For instance, Ps 78:8 refers to the "stubborn and rebellious generation," implying multiple generations. Likewise in Prov 30:11-14, the wicked "generation" spans centuries. Rabbinic literature speaks of the generation of infidels that spans all times. It includes that of Cain,

The concept of *an eschatological remnant* is very common in the book of Revelation. It brings together aspects of the two preceding views and is in fact an expression of the historical and faithful group that faces and endures anguishing challenges. This is the "remnant" considered in Rev 12, a remnant fully involved in spiritual conflicts and willing to testify in the midst of a sweeping religious disaster. We will explore in detail this particular view of the end-time remnant in Revelation.

II. The Remnant Concept in the Book of Revelation

Remnant Terminology

The substantive *loipos*, found in Rev 12:17, is used eight times in Revelation.[10] It is in all instances employed in the plural and could be trans-

---

that of the antediluvians, that of the departed ones in the desert. Hence, the righteous Noah is not considered to belong to the generation of the flood (*Gen. Rab.* XXX 1/62a). He is a survivor. Elsewhere, Moses, Joshua, and Caleb are rescued from the wicked wilderness generation. For numerous references, see Evald Lövestam, "The η γενεα αυτη (*hē gēnea autē*): Eschatology in Mk 13, 30 parr.," in *L'Apocalypse johannique et l'Apocalyptique dans le Nouveau Testament*, J. Lambrecht, ed. (Leuven: Leuven University Press, 1980), pp. 403-413.

By contrast, the faithful generation establishes itself on obedience (*Jub.* 20:3). A "generation of light" will be seated on a throne of light (*1 Enoch* 108:11). That same book breaks down history in seven weeks. The seventh week brings a perverse generation out of which "the righteous will be brought forth as witnesses of truth" (*1 Enoch* 93: 4-10). Thus, we find in that literature, both concepts of "generations" co-mingled throughout the ages: The adulterated and wicked generation, and the faithful "remnant."

The Essenes of Qumran constituted a community preoccupied by eschatological concerns. They were convinced that they were the true remnant, holding the critical truth that God had ordained for "the end time." They considered themselves a privileged "remnant," intended by God to proclaim the "truth" (*War Rule* XIII. 8-9). This "remnant" claimed to be distinctive through purity and holiness in the midst of a perverse generation (*Hymns* VI. 8- 9). They were dedicated to the study of prophecy, the proclamation of the coming Messiah, the end of this wicked world, and the establishment of a new system of worship.

They were recognizable because of their fidelity to God's commandments and for being particularly careful in the observance of the high Sabbaths and other ordinances of truths expected to bring longevity and happiness. The lost and forgotten truths of Israel were somehow revealed to them in order to live by them and testify about them (*CD* 12-16). While other believers were considered infidel and cursed for belonging to an impure and sullied religion, they considered themselves the glorious representatives of Divine grace (*CD* XIII, 2-9). The eschatological setting they embraced led them to prescribe a total separation from the "irreligious"—even from their material and financial life (*1QS* IX. 8- 9). It would be surprising if John the Baptist had ignored this trend and related views with some roots in the Old Testament.

[10] Rev 2:24; 3:2; 8:13; 9:20; 11:13; 12:17; 19:21; 20:5.

lated as a plural or a singular.[11] The verbal form *leipō*, which means "to leave," "to miss," does not occur in Revelation. The most common usage of the noun refers to "the others," but it could be used to convey the idea of a remnant.[12] The word may be linked to objects (the trumpets, 8:13) or persons. It may designate a lost group (19:21; 20:5), conceivably one that is rescued (9:20; 11:13), a portion of the church (2:24; 3:2), or the entire church (12:17). In our case, Rev 12:17 "is of special importance, since the remnant is not confined to a local setting (3:2; 2:24) but rather is the universal remnant, namely the remnant of the overall church."[13] Only the context makes it possible to distinguish an eschatological remnant from the church of which it is a part.

Another term, *oligos*, is used four times. In two instances, the reference is to time (12:12; 17:10), and in one instance, to accusations (2:14). Revelation 3:4 is the only place where it is used to designate a small group within the church of Sardis, whose promise of white robes compares closely with the promises given to the martyrs (6:11) and the countless multitude of the redeemed (7:9, 13). In Rev 3:4, the term *oliga* (a plural form of *oligos*) is used and means "some," "a few." Since the term by itself carries no necessary theological significance, it is important for us to pay particular attention to the context and to focus on the study of the *notion* or the *theme* of the remnant.

John and the Remnant

Exiled to the island of Patmos because of the *Word of God* and the *testimony of Jesus*, John is depicted from the outset as sharing the tribulation and the patience of Jesus (1:9). He is implicitly identified as a survivor of the tribulations endured by the church. The following table indicates that the terms he uses to describe his experience are part of the remnant language used in various parts of Revelation.

Rev 1:9	Rev 12:17	Rev 19:10	Rev 20:4
I John, who also am your brother, and companion in	And the dragon was wroth with the woman, and	And I fell at his feet to worship him. And he said	And I saw thrones, and they sat upon them, and

---

[11]Cf. M. Carrez, *Lexique grec du Nouveau Testament* (Neuchatel, Paris: Delachaux et Niestlé, 1966), p. 107.

[12]If we want to keep the plural, we could translate it in some texts as "the survivors" or "the rescued" (3:2; 9:20; 11:13).

[13]Mueller, "Remnant," p. 189.

Rev 1:9	Rev 12:17	Rev 19:10	Rev 20:4
tribulation, and in the kingdom and patience of Jesus Christ, was on the isle that is called Patmos, *for the word of God*, and for the *testimony of Jesus Christ* (KJV).	went to make war with the remnant of her seed, which keep the *commandments of God*, and have the *testimony of Jesus Christ* (KJV).	unto me, See thou do it not: I am thy fellow servant, and of thy brethren that have the testimony of Jesus: *worship God*: for the *testimony of Jesus* is the spirit of prophecy (KJV).	judgment was given unto them: and I saw the souls of them that were beheaded for the *witness of Jesus,* and for the *word of God*, and which had not worshipped the beast . . . (KJV).

The four texts refer to severe trials, and they all imply faithfulness to God, to His commandments, and to His Word. They all refer to the testimony of Jesus. It is debatable whether in Rev 20:4 the reference is to two distinct groups—those who are beheaded and those who refuse to worship the beast—or whether they are both the same group of people. Regardless, they are all believers and faithful in the face of death and persecution. They have remained faithful to God, His Word, and His commandments—all of which are basically describing a fundamental commitment to God.

Notice that both 1:9 and 19:10 refer specifically to John's personal experience. Notice also that 12:17 refers to the remnant attacked by the dragon and that 20:4 portrays those who have rejected the worship of the beast, his image, and its mark. Both passages express resistance to the evil, coercive power through faithfulness to the Word of God and the testimony of Jesus. John is thus, in his day, emblematic of a remnant able to stand firm against the Roman dragon and who shares the tribulations, loyalty, and patience of the saints in Jesus (1:9; 14:12).

Overcomers as Remnant

The messages to the seven churches have traditionally been understood in Adventist circles as encompassing the history of the church as a whole.[14] Each message addresses the Christian church as a whole during

---

[14]See Roy A. Anderson, *Unfolding the Revelation* (Mountain View, CA: Pacific Press, 1981), pp. 6-8; C. Mervyn Maxwell, *God Cares*, vol. 2 (Boise, ID: Pacific Press, 1985), pp. 120-132, 142-144; William Shea, "The Covenant Form of the Letters to the Seven Churches," *AUSS* 21/1 (1983): 71-84; Richard Lehmann, *Apocalypse de Jean*, vol. 1 (Collonges sous Salève: Faculté adventiste de Théologie, 2002), pp. 66-67; Clinton Wahlen, "Heaven's View of the Church in Revelation 2 and 3," *JAAS* 9.2 (2006): 145-156. Today some are expressing reservations about this approach. Hans K. LaRondelle, *How to Understand the End-Time Prophecies of the Bible* (Sarasota, FL: First Impression, 1997), p. 90, sees them

a given period of history. One could also say that each Christian church throughout history may have been impacted by the messages. In each letter Jesus calls for conversion out of which a remnant may be formed.

In each of the messages to the seven churches, a promise is made to the overcomer. Although Jesus issues a direct statement ("I know thy works"), He uses an indirect form of expression when speaking to the overcomer ("to him that overcomes I will give . . ."). In a sense, the promise is not offered to the church as a whole but to him/her (singular) who, within the church, is victorious by living according to the warning given to the church. The call is clearly given on a personal and individual basis. The message to Laodicea involves Christianity as a whole, just as was the case with the messages to other churches. In Rev 12:11, the elect are partakers of the afflictions of Christ, but in 3:21 they are viewed as participants in the victory of Christ. There is also a remnant raised from within the church represented by Laodicea.

The structure of the book is divided into promises (Rev 2–3) and fulfillments (Rev 21–22),[15] portraying the redeemed as being composed exclusively of overcomers. Indeed, the final reward is reserved for the overcomer (21:7). In the New Jerusalem the elect are the overcomers. Therefore, it could be suggested that the term "overcomer" refers to a remnant made up of those who have overcome the trials of their day. An overcomer is by definition a remnant, considering that not everyone is victorious and that only the conquerors will benefit from the promises. It is very important to observe that the remnant is not made up of faithful ones who simply escaped the apostasy of the world. They are also those located within the Christian church who embraced the words of Christ in the midst of Christian apostasy.

The overcomers mentioned in the hymn of Rev 12:11 are directly related to the "remnant" mentioned in the same chapter. The Christological hymn, recorded in Rev 12:10-12, clarifies that the victory of the remnant was made possible through Christ's victory. The remnant resisted the assaults of the beast. Such is also the case of the overcomers who will stand on the sea of glass (15:2).

---

only as "prototypes of the future church development in the entire world" and "seven ecclesiastical conditions that exist in His expanding church till the end." Jon K. Paulien, "The Hermeneutics of Biblical Apocalyptic," in *Understanding Scripture: An Adventist Approach*, George W. Reid, ed. (Silver Spring, MD: Biblical Research Institute, 2005), p. 253, cautiously says, "While many commentators have seen a historical sequence in the letters, it may not be the primary purpose of the text."

[15]Cf. LaRondelle, *Prophecies*, p. 100.

Thus we find that there are overcomers in all historical periods covered by the seven churches—each with its own challenges. They all had critical choices to make: either to obey Christ and His commandments or to follow the general trend. The closing chapters of history also produce its overcomers, namely those who will stand on the sea of glass and who have been victorious "over the beast and his image and over the number of his name" (15:2). The remnant in each era acquire its own distinguishing marks. The remnant in the closing moments of history is characterized by faithfulness to the Word of God (Rev 12–14) and closeness to Jesus (Laodicea). Their lives must be fully imbued with Christ's character. Overcoming is not theirs merely by virtue of His example; it is theirs experientially—by His presence in every fiber of their being.[16]

The messages to the seven churches reveal that Christ focuses His attention upon all of His church, faithful or not. It is implied that in the church are both faithful and unfaithful persons (cf. Matt 13:24-30). However, salvation is not obtained corporately because it is not the result of belonging to a given community. It is a personal choice, an individual response to the call of Christ and His offer of salvation. This suggests that the remnant spring forth from within the Christian Church. This remnant is made up of victors or conquerors. We are suggesting that Revelation affirms both the existence of a faithful remnant able to subsist throughout history and an eschatological remnant within the last church.

The 144,000 and the Remnant

The sequence of the seven seals concludes with a dramatic question: "For the great day of his wrath is come; and who shall be able to stand?" (6:17). In other words, considering the wrath of the Lamb as the only possibility for deliverance, will there be a remnant still standing? Revelation 7 functions as a parenthesis and provides an answer to that specific question through the reference to the 144,000 or the great multitude. The 144,000 and the great multitude designate the same entity.[17] While the 144,000 are depicted in the framework of an audition, the multitude appears in a vision (v. 9). This schematic construction parallels that of

---

[16]Kenneth A. Strand, "Overcomer: A Study in the Macrodynamic of the Theme Development in the Book of Revelation," *AUSS* 28 (1990): 252.

[17]See Richard Lehmann, *Apocalypse de Jean*, vol. II (Collonges-sous-Salève: Faculté adventiste de théologie, 2002), pp. 127-158. Also, Ranko Stefanovic, *Revelation of Jesus Christ: Commentary on the Book of Revelation* (Berrien Springs, MI: Andrews University Press, 2002), p. 266; and LaRondelle, *Prophecies*, p. 149.

Rev 1:12-13, where John hears a voice telling him to write what he sees, and then he sees Christ. The vision clarifies the audible content. In Rev 5, Christ is announced as a lion (v. 5) before He is seen as a lamb (v. 6). In Rev 9:16-17, John hears the number of horsemen and then sees the horses. The same sequence of hearing before seeing is also present in Rev 6:2, 5, 8. We also find a reverse sequence: In Rev 21, John sees the New Jerusalem (v. 2), followed by an audible explanation (v. 3). Regardless of the sequence, the same entity is present in each case.

Let us carry this thought further. The 144,000 described in Rev 14:1-5 reveal the same characteristics as the multitude: They are standing before the throne (14:3; 7:9) and are depicted as redeemed (14:3; cf., 7:10). While the redeemed multitude have washed their robes in the blood of the Lamb (7:14), the 144,000 were not defiled with women, that is, the harlot Babylon and her daughters (14:4; 17:5).

The symbolic number 144,000 can be viewed as the "innumerable" size of the multitude (7:9). There appears to be here an echo of the promise made to Abraham that his posterity would be innumerable, represented by the 12 tribes, all nations, languages, and peoples (7:9).[18] There seems to be a relationship between the Lamb who leads the multitude to the fountains of waters (7:17) and the 144,000 who follow the Lamb wherever He goes (14:4).

The question of the elders—"who are those who have been clothed with white robes (*oi peribeblēmenoi tas stolas tas leukas*)?" (7:13)—is obviously referring back to the multitude clothed with white robes (*peribeblēmenous stolas leukas*) (7:9). But now it is added that it passed through a mysterious, unspecified great tribulation (*tēs thlipseōs tēs megalēs*) and yet benefitted from the eschatological promises.[19] They are

---

[18]Twelve is the number of the tribes of ancient Israel and of the new Israel based on the 12 apostles. This theme is again present in Rev 21:12-14 with 12 gates with the names of the 12 patriarchs, and the 12 foundations with the names of the 12 apostles, thus emphasizing the direct connection between Israel and the messianic community. See also A. Vanhoye, "L'utilisation du livre d'Ezechiel dans l'Apocalypse," *Bib* 43 (1962): 436-476.

[19]Compare:

Rev 7:15-17 (KJV)	Rev 21:3-4 (KJV)
7:15 Therefore are they before the throne of God, and serve him day and night in his temple: and he that sitteth on the throne shall dwell among them.	21:3 And I heard a great voice out of heaven saying, Behold the tabernacle of God is with men, and he will dwell with them, and they shall be his

The Remnant in the Book of Revelation

sealed on their forehead with the name of the Lamb and of the Father. Their white robe implies their priestly function.[20] The connection between the 144,000 (composed of 12 tribes) and the multitude underlines the continuity between the promises made to Israel and the salvation of the Gentiles (cf. Gal 3:26-29).[21]

Not all human beings are sealed with the seal of God, only those who have been redeemed from the earth. Since they are referred to as "first fruits," it follows that the 144,000 are indeed a remnant.[22] They are characterized by the following experiences: (1) they have not defiled themselves with women (14:4)—in other words, they have not prostituted themselves with Babylon, the mother of harlots (17:1-6); (2) they follow the Lamb (14:4), not the beast or the false prophet;[23] and (3) they did not participate in the lies (14:5) of the false prophet (prophet of lies) (13:11-17; 16:13; 20:10). In other words, they possess all the characteristics of the remnant described in Rev 12–14.

They chose God's side in the midst of references to the wrath of the Lamb (6:17), of God (14:10), and that of the dragon and his followers (12:12, 17). They are the remnant confronted by the combined powers

Rev 7:15-17 (KJV)	Rev 21:3-4 (KJV)
7:16 They shall hunger no more, neither thirst any more; neither shall the sun light on them, nor any heat. 7:17 For the Lamb which is in the midst of the throne shall feed them, and shall lead them unto living fountains of waters: and God shall wipe all tears from their eyes.	people, and God himself shall be with them *and be* their God. 21:4 And God shall wipe away all tears from their eyes; and there shall be no more death, neither sorrow, nor crying, neither shall there be any more pain: for the former things are passed away.

---

[20]Cf. Beatrice S. Neal, "Sealed Saints and the Tribulation," in *Symposium on Revelation—Book I*, Frank B. Holbrook, ed. (Silver Spring, MD: Biblical Research Institute, 1992), p. 264.

[21]See Hans K. LaRondelle, *The Israel of God in Prophecy: Principles of Prophetic Interpretation* (Berrien Springs, MI: Andrews University Press, 1983), pp. 98-114.

[22]Also Hans K. LaRondelle, "The Remnant and the Three Angels' Messages," in *Handbook of Adventist Theology*, R. Dederen, ed. (Hagerstown, MD: Review and Herald, 2000), p. 870.

[23]Following Christ is a theme that runs through the whole New Testament. It is explicit in Matt 16:24-25 and illustrated by the Christological hymn in Phil 2:6-11. It is the model that all believers are invited to follow.

of darkness. The reference to the remnant composed of 144,000 goes beyond the Elijah-type conflict and places them at the level of the moral and spiritual component of the remnant in the prophets of the Old Testament. Those who bear the name of God and of the Lamb are expected to witness for Him by manifesting through word and action the loving kindness of Christ to humanity. Confronted with the beasts whose mainstay is violence, the remnant witnesses to the "gentleness of Christ" (2 Cor 10:1; Phil 4:5).

Two Witnesses and the Remnant

The cycle of the seven trumpets also provides the stage for the presence of a remnant. The vision of the two witnesses occupies the same structural position as the 144,000 in the cycle of the seals—it is placed as a parenthesis between the sixth and the seventh trumpets (Rev 10–11). When studying the concept of the remnant in Revelation, we cannot ignore the importance of this parenthesis. It provides for us three important pieces of information. First, there is a prophetic time period identical to that of chapter 12, namely the 1260 days (11:3). Second, they are attacked by the beast that rises out of the abyss (11:7). Third, the two witnesses give "testimony" (11:7).

The sixth seal ends with an ominous question: "Who shall be able to stand?" (6:17, KJV). The answer given is, the 144,000. At the close of the sixth trumpet, no specific question is asked. We are told that after the tribulations of the sixth trumpet, the survivors (*hoi loipoi*) do not repent of their wicked deeds; they continue to worship idols (9:20). There is apparently no hope any longer for humanity because its remnant have not repented. The content of chapters 10 and 11 provide a reassuring response to such a catastrophic scenario. The tenth chapter announces good news: When the seventh trumpet shall be heard, the mystery of God will find its fulfillment (10:7). Meanwhile, John is called to prophesy to many peoples and nations (10:11). There is still hope; the prophecy must still be heard. Chapter 11 shows how this prophetic work will be fulfilled by two witnesses clothed in sackcloth.

The mission of the two witnesses is related to the notion of the remnant in various ways. First, their ministry is comparable to that of Elijah. The account of Elijah is suggestive of the remnant (1 Kgs 19:14). Jezebel destroyed the core of God's worship as represented by both the priestly and prophetic ministries of the Lord. The situation seems to have been hopeless and divested of the possibility of redemption. Elijah concluded that he alone was the remnant.

Second, the ministry of the two witnesses can also be compared to that of Moses, who turned the water of the Nile into blood and brought upon the land many calamities (11:6). The Exodus led by Moses could be understood within the framework of a remnant[24] that escapes a disaster. Without God's intervention, the plan of salvation would have ended in Egypt, through Pharaoh's methodical genocide of the Jews.

Third, in Rev 11:4, the two witnesses are compared to a pair of olive trees, familiar symbols in Jewish tradition of two anointed individuals recognized as Joshua and Zerubbabel.[25] The experience of Joshua, described in Zech 3, is clearly related to that of Rev 12. In both passages Satan is the accuser, and the statement regarding the brand plucked from the fire is akin to the remnant (Zech 3:2).[26] The reference to Joshua and Zerubbabel implies two witnesses representing both the priestly and prophetic agencies. This should not be surprising because God's purpose was to raise up a priestly people (cf. Exod 19:6; Rev 1:6; 5:10).

A question arises: If both witnesses make up a remnant, what might their relationship be to the woman of Rev 12? This question is all the more relevant because they are both in some way associated with the 1260-day prophecy (11:3; 12:6). Both of the witnesses are attacked. One is attacked by the dragon, and the other by the beast who poses as a double of the dragon. Notice also that in chapter 12, Christ is the posterity of the woman and that the two witnesses share the experience of Christ. Their death is identified with His, and, like Him, they rise again and ascend to heaven "in a cloud"—another Christological feature (11:8, 12).

Kenneth Strand has shown that the two witnesses are the Old and New Testaments,[27] the written Word of God; Christ being the incarnated Word. He goes on to suggest that they could also represent the persecuted people of God who bore testimony to both Testaments.[28] We can assume that the woman in the wilderness and the witnesses clothed in sackcloth have something in common. Revelation 12 offers little information about the woman; however, the marks of the two witnesses suggest that the woman-church is recognized by her faithfulness to the Holy Scriptures and the testimony of the prophets. She constitutes the faithful remnant that knows the Scriptures—the two witnesses—and testifies

---

[24]See Isa 11:11, 16.

[25]Cf., Pierre Prigent, *L'Apocalypse de Saint Jean* (Genève: Labor & Fides, 2000), p. 271.

[26]Cf. 2 Sam 14:7; Amos 4:11.

[27]Cf. Ellen G. White, *The Great Controversy* (Mountain View, CA: Pacific Press, 1911), p. 267.

[28]Kenneth Strand, "The Two Witnesses of Revelation 11:3-12," *AUSS* 19 (1981): 135; idem, "The Two Olive Trees of Zechariah 4 and Revelation 11," *AUSS* 20 (1982): 257-261.

from the wilderness. The remnant of the seed of the woman is also in line and descended from it. They remain steadfast to the commandments of God and the faith of Jesus. Just as Rev 11:13 suggests that a remnant will glorify God (v. 13; *hoi loipoi*), at the end of Rev 12 it is indicated that there is a surviving remnant of the seed of the woman.

The remnant testifies to the validity of the content of the little book (10:10-11)—"that there should be time no longer. But in the days of the voice of the seventh angel, when he shall begin to sound, the mystery of God should be finished, as he hath declared to his servants the prophets" (10:6b, 7, KJV). Therefore, it bears witness to the Word of God as it is contained in the Scriptures. Following the hidden, holy remnant in the wilderness, there is an eschatological remnant. The possible connection between the two witnesses and the woman, implicit in Rev 11, helps to clarify the nature and identity of the woman, while chapter 12 clarifies the nature of the eschatological remnant. Together they demonstrate that the eschatological remnant is not the product of a spontaneous generation. The "seed of the woman" is heir to a prophetic testimony contained in both the Old and New Testaments, which has been carried forward through the centuries by God's faithful remnant.

Finally, if the concept of the two witnesses required by the law undergirds the book of Revelation[29] as it also seems to permeate the New Testament,[30] and if the two witnesses imply the activity of the people of God as those who are truthful to Scripture, then the common reference to both "the word of God" and the "testimony" (6:9), "the commandments of God and the "testimony of Jesus" (Rev 14:12), and "the testimony of Jesus and the spirit of prophecy" (19:10) must be interconnected. Again, the remnant is in the line of the faithful people of God who bear testimony to what God has revealed (His commandments) and what Jesus has revealed through those who are called "prophets."[31]

Servants and the Remnant

From the first verse of the book of Revelation, we are told that the book is addressed to the servants of God (1:1), a notion repeated at the end of the book (22:6). It informs them of things to come soon as revealed in the book as a whole. The servants of God receive His seal (7:3),

---

[29]Cf. Strand, "Two Witnesses," p. 132.

[30]Cf. Gerhard Pfandl, "The Remnant Church and the Spirit of Prophecy," in *Symposium on Revelation—Book II*, Frank B. Holbrook, ed. (Silver Spring, MD: Biblical Research Institute, 1992), p. 311. See also Matt 18:16; John 5:31-36, 37, 39.

[31]Cf. 1 Pet 1:10; 1 Cor 12:28; Eph 2:20; 3:5; 1 Thess 2:15.

are linked to the 144,000, and join them in a chorus of praise (19:5; 14:3). Babylon may have spilled their blood (19:2), but God will reward their faithfulness (11:8). The usage of the term "servants" brings out the notion that their conflict and their victory are identical to those of both the surviving, historical remnant and the eschatological remnant. Given that the central issue of the conflict is a matter of worshiping either God or the beast, the worshipers are by definition servants of whomever they choose to worship.

If the theme of the remnant is central to the book of Revelation, it is because the book is addressed to the church. As such, it addresses the remnant of all ages, those who have constituted the true people of God, the church as the body of Christ. He is the suffering Servant par excellence (Isa 53).

The Book of Life and the Remnant

If the only ones who will enter the city of God are those whose names are written in the Lamb's book of life (21:27), then the victorious remnant must obviously be among them. The book of life is featured at the last judgment (20:12) and is mentioned in the context of the conflict instigated by Babylon and the beast that supports her (17:8). This serves to distinguish between those who worship the beast and the saints (13:8). Some may detect an element of predestination in the fact that the names have been written in the book "from the foundation of the world" (17:8, KJV). However paradoxical it may seem, this detail is theologically meaningful. In fact, whatever titles may be given to the remnant, they are called to be courageous, to perseverance, to faithfulness, and to obedience to the Lord to the point of almost sounding legalistic. The truth is that the final judgment is based on the works of each individual. This is mentioned twice in Revelation (20:12-13). The book of life is also mentioned twice in the context of the final judgment (20:12, 15). The reference to the names written in the book of life "from the foundation of the world" serves to remind us that all is of grace, even our works.

Faithfulness to the commandments of God may be decisive, but none can pride him/herself in having kept them because victory was granted to each one by God's grace. Although the bride wears pure white linen representing the righteous works of the saints, this also is God's gift to her (19:8). No one forces her to accept the gift; she accepts the robe with gratitude.[32] According to Rev 7:14, the members of

---

[32]See Richard Lehmann, "The Two Suppers," in *Symposium on Revelation—Book II*, pp. 207, 223.

the great multitude "have washed their robes and made them white in the blood of the Lamb." It is their choice but the result depends on the blood of the Lamb. In this case the message of John corresponds to that of Paul, though presented in a slightly different way: "He chose us in him before the creation of the world to be holy and blameless in his sight" (Eph 1:4). "Chosen to be holy" is the call particularly given to the remnant.

Kingdom of Priests and the Remnant

The holiness of the remnant brings us back to God's great plan intended to bring together those who exclusively belong to Him: "You shall be to me a kingdom of priests and a holy nation. These are the words which you shall speak to the children of Israel" (Exod 19:6, NKJV). Revelation develops the theme of true worship and identifies the redeemed ones as priests. In what appears to be a Christological hymn or a confession of faith, Christ is praised because through His blood, He constituted the saved ones "priests unto God" (1:5-6). In another hymn, the Lamb is praised because He *"redeemed us"* and *"made us unto our God kings and priests"* (5:9-10, KJV). In the end, those who have resisted the beast and his image for the sake of the testimony of Jesus and the Word of God are declared blessed. To them it is promised that "they shall be *priests of God and of Christ* and shall *reign* with him" (20:6, KJV, emphasis mine).

As already indicated, the 144,000 represent the totality of the end-time people of God. Following the theme of Exod 19, the people of God are all priests (the so-called priesthood of all believers). Here is how the first epistle of Peter presents it: "But you are a chosen race, a royal priesthood, a holy nation, God's own people, that you may declare the wonderful deeds of him who called you out of darkness into his marvelous light" (1 Pet 2:9, RSV).

The adoration and worship due to God is the theme of Revelation. It stands in contrast to the will of the beast and its image. This brings us to Exod 19, where we find the origin of these priestly people. The priests are guardians of the law. It is their duty to teach it to the people.[33] The priests are also mediators between humans and God. They link the two through sacrifices. The law given to His people is not intended to make legislators out of them; rather, it is to appoint advocates whose duty is to intercede on behalf of transgressors. Thus, the remnant are to function as media-

---

[33]Deut 31:9; 33:8-10.

tors, not through their own sacrifice but through the blood of the Lamb that was slain.[34]

This is a vital concept. When we focus exclusively on the remnant's capacity to keep the commandments of God, we tend to forget that their role and mission is primarily to plead for the guilty and intercede for sinners. They are a testimony to the mission of Jesus who came "not to call the righteous, but sinners" (Matt 9:13, RSV). The three monsters cut themselves off from the grace of God and incur His wrath because of their persecuting activity. They organize a worship of pride and violence. Dressed as priests of old in white robes, the new priests are the remnant whose robes have been made white by the blood of the Lamb. Thus, they declare forever that God is love and that salvation is God's work of grace.

The call to holiness is not only individual but also collective. When God calls His people to holiness, it is always in the plural.[35] Holiness is a community concern, for "no one can live in the image of God and remain alone."[36] Holiness is not just a separation from evil; it is a commitment to God and to fellow humans while striving for fitness to meet God[37] and to serve others.

Conclusion

These diverse approaches to the study of the remnant provide us with a broad appreciation for its uniqueness. Revelation presents a remnant that survives through history. Without this remnant, sustained by the grace of God, the promised redemption would fail. Christ, the posterity of the woman, according to the promise of Gen 3:15, takes on a larger significance when we consider that His church becomes His body. This body takes on the form of a remnant beneficiary of His grace (cf. Rom 11:5). It is a unique and multifaceted remnant whose features include John, the overcomers, the 144,000, the kingdom of priests, and the servants whose names are written in the Lamb's book of life. This remnant is identified with both a surviving or historical remnant and a holy remnant, depending on the circumstances. However, in the closing days of history, there will be an eschatological remnant whose nature takes over the na-

---

[34] LaRondelle, "Remnant," p. 859.

[35] "I am the LORD your God; sanctifies yourselves therefore, and be holy, for I am holy" (Lev 11:44; 20:7; NRSV). See also 1 Pet 1:16.

[36] Paul Beauchamp, *D'une montagne à l'autre: la loi de Dieu* (Paris: Seuil, 1999), p. 84.

[37] André Bouart, "Sacré," *DEB*, p. 1146.

ture of its predecessors but who lives through particularly challenging circumstances.

Studying the remnant in Revelation has made it possible for us to recognize its richness and its complexity. The remnant is made up of overcomers who have stood firm in the face of persecutions from the dragon and his followers. It is a remnant whose suffering is somewhat comparable to that of Christ. It is a faithful remnant, wholly made up of those who keep the commandments of God as Jesus kept the commandments of His Father.[38] The entire book of Revelation revolves around the difference between the worship of the only true God and other forms of worship that betray the Decalogue.

The Old Testament tells of priests and prophets opposing one another, but the remnant of Revelation resemble Jesus Christ—it holds both functions. This remnant announces the good news of salvation and intercedes while fulfilling the prophetic role as keeper of the Word of God and the book of Revelation (22:9-10). It is a remnant grounded in prophetic tradition awaiting the One who is coming. Finally, it is an eschatological remnant that emerges to bear witness through the last judgment, calling God's people to come out of Babylon (18:4-5).

III. The Remnant in Revelation 12

The Remnant and the Commandments of God

The reference to the commandments of God in Revelation is not of secondary importance. Not only do we find it mentioned twice (12:17 and 14:12), each time using the same basic terminology (commandments of God and the testimony/faith of Jesus), but it is also present in the confrontational context involving the dragon, the beast, and the false prophet in their opposition to the Decalogue. It is also found in the call to obedience proclaimed by the three angels. The dragon is introduced at the very beginning as a murderer (sixth commandment). His intention is to destroy the posterity of the woman in the form of the child (12:5) or the remnant (12:17). He is identified as the devil, Satan (12:9), the one whom Jesus called a murderer from the very beginning (John 8:44). The beast from the sea appears on the scene of the conflict, blaspheming (13:1, 5-6). Its language disregards the third commandment. The dragon and the beast of the sea demand worship in defiance of the first commandment ordaining exclusive worship to God, the Redeemer (13:4). The

---

[38] A theme dear to John (John 15:10; 1 John 2:3-4; 3:22, 24; 5:2-3; 2 John 1:6).

land beast promotes idolatry and murder (second and sixth commandments; 13:15).

By contrast, the call of the three angels is directed to true worship, implying obedience to the law.[39] The reference to the creator God ("worship Him who has made the heavens and the earth"), the Redeeming God ("the everlasting Gospel"), and the judging God ("the hour of His judgment has come") allude to the first table of the Law proclaiming God as Creator (Exod 20:11), Savior (20:2), and Judge (20:5-6). Unquestionably there are several parallels between Rev 14 and the fourth commandment.[40] In fact, the background of Rev 14 is woven into a covenant that requires faithfulness and obedience.[41] All the necessary structures of a covenant are present: a preamble (14:6-7), an historical prologue (14:6), requirements (14:7, 12) and witnesses (14:10, 13). It is also clear that there is a parallel between Revelation 12:17—"those who obey God's commandments and hold to the testimony of Jesus" (NIV)—and the reference in Rev 14:12 (KJV) to those who "keep the commandments of God, and the faith of Jesus."

The verb "keep" (*tēreō*) is important. In the Johannine literature, it refers specifically to the keeping of the traditional catechetic content, traced back to the teachings of Jesus, and is considered to be normative for believers[42] (John 14:21-24; 15:20). The observation of God's commandments or those of Jesus are considered as a sign of Christian vitality. Thus, in Revelation, keeping the commandments of God is a matter of remaining faithful to the prophetic message and tradition as given and transmitted by the prophets since the beginning to the end. The remnant stand out because of their grasp of Scripture expressed in their obedience to God's commandments; it is the authentic posterity of the woman.

The faith of Jesus is the same faith He relied on during the temptations in the wilderness, based on "*It is written*" (Matt 4:4, 7). Without this kind of faith in the Word of God, it is impossible to render Him a pleasing worship (Heb 11:6). Briefly stated, the fondness of the remnant for the faith of Jesus and the commandments of God identifies the group as the prophetic witness to the authenticity and validity of the

---

[39]Roberto Badenas, "Vraie et fausse adoration dans les messages des trois anges: Apoc. 14:6-13," in *Etudes sur l'Apocalypse: signification des messages des trois anges aujourd'hui* (Collonges sous Salève: Institut adventiste du Salève, 1988), pp. 152-153.

[40]See Mathilde Frey, "Sabbath Theology in the book of Revelation," and Johannes Kovar, "The Remnant and God's Commandments," in this volume.

[41]Badenas, "Vraie et fausse," p. 156.

[42]Cf. E. H. Riesenfeld, "*Tēreō*," *TDNT*, vol. 7, p. 144.

Word of God. The remnant is prophetic in that, in a world inclined toward the worship of the beast and its image, the group witnesses with Jesus on behalf of the true worship of the creator God, to whom it gives allegiance.

It is unquestionable that the conflict between the three beasts and the posterity of the woman is directly related to true worship and obedience to the commandments of God. The remnant is a holy remnant, recognizable because of the group's faithfulness to the long prophetic tradition held by Scripture.

The Testimony of Jesus and the Remnant

The second characteristic of the remnant is that they have the testimony of Jesus. The first question is whether the remnant testifies about Jesus or whether Jesus gives His testimony to the remnant. In other words, is the genitive subjective or objective? Both have been defended.[43] Adventists have traditionally taken the genitive as a subjective genitive, as used in other cases in the book of Revelation.[44] This means that the testimony is that rendered by Jesus.

In Rev 19:10, "the testimony of Jesus" is identified with the spirit of prophecy. The statement is set within a rather surprising incident in which John attempts to worship an angel; this would be contrary to all other teachings of his book. All exegetes have pondered the meaning of this dual incidence (22:8-9). This has suggested to some that John might have been reacting to a tendency among some in the church to worship angels, denouncing it.[45] Clearly the two passages denounce the worship of a person other than God.

Moreover, the two episodes testify about Jesus, whose words are contained in the book of Revelation:

19:10: *Thy brethren that have the testimony of Jesus.*

22:9: *Thy brethren the prophets, and of them which keep the sayings of this book* [KJV].

This is not surprising because the book is introduced from the start as a "revelation of Jesus Christ" (1:1). Jesus is both the author and the object of the revelation. To be a true prophet who has the testimony of Jesus implies faithfulness to the message of Revelation. Anyone who makes that claim but proclaims anything other than the message contained in Rev-

---

[43]For a discussion of the issues see Pfandl, "Remnant Church," pp. 295-333, *idem*, "Identifying Marks of the Remnant in the Book of Revelation," in this volume.

[44]Ibid., p. 321.

[45]Cf. E. Corsini, *L'Apocalypse maintenant* (Paris: Le Seuil, 1984), p. 123.

elation would have to be a false prophet, one not sanctioned by the spirit of prophecy (Rev 22:18-19).

The other congruence confirms this point:

19:10: *For the testimony of Jesus is the spirit of prophecy.*

22:10: *Seal not the sayings of the prophecy of this book: for the time is at hand* [KJV].

According to these parallel statements, Jesus renders His testimony through His prophets and particularly through the book of Revelation. Blessed is he that keeps the words therein (1:3; 22:7). To carry this point further, it is essential to analyze the nature and function of the false prophet whose character is prevalent in the second half of the book. It would have been surprising that John would discuss the spirit of prophecy that energizes the true prophets without also dealing with the false prophet.

Let us take a brief look at the telling signs of the false prophet.[46] The beast out of the earth has the appearance of a lamb. Its ecological system is thus religious in nature. It accomplishes many great wonders[47] to feed a universal frenzy of devotion to the sea beast. It counterfeits the miracles of Jesus to draw the attention of the crowds away from Him (cf. John 2:12, 24). The beast increases its works[48] and attempts to seduce people through overwhelming activism. Its actions involve a discourse inspired by demonic spirits and energized by violence (16:13-14). The discourse is inspired by the ancient king of Babylon, whose intent was to impose idol worship by coercion (Dan 3; cf. Rev 13:15). The false prophet also imposes the mark of the first beast (13:16). It is the counterpart of the two witnesses who speak as prophets of God (11:3). Although the two witnesses are able to produce miracles, none of them is considered to be a "sign." They have power (*exousia*) and the potential to use it but do not make use of it.[49] On the contrary, they are clad in sackcloth and do the works that will lead them to share in the fate of Christ (11:9, 11). Their cadavers are seen in the street of the *great city*, a formula used exclusively to identify Babylon.[50]

---

[46]For more details, see Richard Lehmann, "Le faux prophète et l'image de la bête," in *Etudes sur l'Apocalypse*, pp. 168-186.

[47]The word *sēmeion* is employed seven times in Revelation; three times in the singular referring to a sign under the control of God (12:1, 3; 15:1), and four times in the plural to qualify the action of the false prophet (13:13-14; 16:14; 19:20).

[48]Of the 30 usages of the verb *poieō* ("to do" "to make") in Revelation, 11 are about the false prophet and eight of them are in Rev 13:12-16.

[49]In v. 5, an active present tense (*thelei*) is balanced by the use of a subjunctive aorist with a conditional meaning (*thelēsē*).

[50]Rev 16:19; 17:18; 18:10, 16, 18-19, 21.

The false prophet takes on a priestly function founded on the sacrilegious worship of an image. His actions are contrary to the teachings of all the prophets of old, whose objective was to turn Israel away from idol worship.[51] Far from returning to "the law and to the testimony," he promotes working with spirits and mediums (cf. Isa 8:19; Rev 16:13).

It appears that the spirit of prophecy, which energizes the remnant of the seed of the woman, is connected to the revelation of the true God as given in His Word, and is not only a manifestation of the spirit of prophecy in their midst. The remnant receives its vigor from the teachings of Jesus in the Old Testament and in His own ministry, and through the testimony of the apostles, which includes the Revelation of John. This total reliance on Scripture allows the remnant to use it to identify the manifestation of the prophetic gift in their midst. Consequently, the Adventist Church has recognized that the ministry of Ellen G. White is a manifestation of the gift of prophecy. The remnant is thus anchored in prophetic tradition, witnesses to it, and experiences it.

In this line, the three messages proclaimed by the angels in Rev 14 are fully in harmony with the convictions of the remnant. The first message is related to the Word of God as indicated by the reference to the commandments of God.[52] The second message condemns Babylon for persecuting the remnant. And the third one is related to the beast, which is the instrument of the dragon against the remnant. The remnant fully proclaim these messages as they express their convictions and experience.[53]

The Woman and the Remnant

In Revelation the remnant people are directly related to the woman in chapter 12. The woman has been interpreted in different ways (e.g., Mary the mother of Jesus or the worship of Artemis[54]). We will take for granted that the woman represents the people of God[55] without distinguishing between the Old and New Testaments. In Rev 12:6, she is escaping to the wilderness. This seems to point to the Exodus of Israel to the desert and also to the escape of the prophet Elijah when threatened by the wrath of Jezebel (1 Kgs 17:1-7). This last possibility can be supported

---

[51]1 Kgs 18:18-21.

[52]Cf. Badenas, "Vraie et fausse," pp. 156-158.

[53]See LaRondelle, "Remnant," pp. 872-880.

[54]H. D. Saffrey, "Relire l'Apocalypse à Patmos," *RB* 92 (1975): 385-417. For an analysis of the different views, see Prigent, *L'Apocalypse*, pp. 283-289.

[55]With Stefanovic, *Revelation*, p. 378, and many others.

by the fact that there are other places in Revelation that seem to allude to the ministry of Elijah (11:5-6; 13:13). The experience of Elijah should not be separated from the notion of a remnant[56] that survive in the midst of apostasy and persecution, particularly when the basic issue is one of worship (1 Kgs 19:14, 18). As already indicated, that theme is particularly important in Revelation.

The second passage describing the woman's escape to the wilderness uses images derived from the vocabulary of the exodus (Rev 12:14-16). The two wings of an eagle refer to Exod 19:4 and Deut 32:11. The wilderness is the location where the gift of manna was received (Exod 16). The reference to the river (or flood) swallowed by the earth (Rev 12:15) may go back to the song of Moses and Miriam (Exod 15:12) explicitly mentioned in Rev 15:3. It is also useful to remember that the dragon is a symbol of Egypt (Isa 51:9-10; Ezek 29:3; 32:2) and Babylon (Jer 51:34). The woman, like the remnant, is able to escape the threat of total destruction through religious motivations.[57]

The description of the woman in Revelation uses vocabulary associated with the remnant. The woman is persecuted by the dragon, as the remnant of her posterity will be. She is the heir of the original promise but also the object of aggression by the ancient serpent (cf. Gen 3:15; Rev 12:9). The eschatological remnant is not the only one that suffers persecution. The church, symbolized by the woman, had the same experience. There is continuity between the woman and the remnant. Therefore, it could be suggested that, from the historical point of view, the persecuted church appears to be identified as an historical and faithful remnant in hiding during the 1260 days.

One could be led to think that there are only two central characters in this story: the dragon and the woman. However, Rev 13 reveals that the dragon makes use of two beasts to war against the saints (13:7) and to kill them (13:15). In Rev 17 we find the mystery of another woman, also a mother, but this time drunk with the blood of the saints (17:6). She is supported by a beast that, like the dragon, has seven heads and ten horns (17:7; 12:3).[58] This woman, like the dragon, also has made war against the saints. If a woman is the symbol of the church, it is obvious that the

---

[56]Paul himself made the link in Rom 11:2-5.

[57]Exod 7:16, 26; 8:4, 16, 21-24, etc.

[58]It is noteworthy that the heads and horns of the beast in chapter 17 are given in the same order as those of the dragon (12:3), but not of the beast (13:1). This suggests that the beast is a clone of the dragon, doing the same work as in chapter 12 but through the woman called Babylon.

reality of the "church" exists on two different levels. The woman/church persecuted during the 1260 days represents the remnant persecuted by another entity that is also a "woman/church," but this one is to be identified as Babylon.

The reference to the woman helps us to clarify the theological notion of "remnant" as a church. We can speak about a remnant that is identified with the ongoing church. It is heir to the promises of God and the object of the dragon's wrath throughout history. This is where it takes on a diachronic dimension. But this remnant is not alone in the world as if it were the church all by itself. There also exists another component of the church, a somber woman called Babylon. Therefore, the remnant represents both a "sequential" concept (found throughout history) and a "central" concept (particularly located at the end of history). But in contrast to the exclusivism found in the Qumran discourse that condemns those not of their own,[59] Revelation is consistently inclusive. It is true that it divides humanity into only two groups, namely the redeemed and the lost, but the underlying message is that it is still possible for the unredeemed to make a choice. The remnant proclaims the final call to "My [God's] people" to come out of Babylon (18:4). Far from being the church on its own, the remnant is its dazzling face, its main attraction, and the symbol of its distinctiveness. It is God's extended hand of rescue toward His children who are experiencing the seduction of the three beasts.

A Christological Hymn and the Remnant

It is not possible to fully explain the nature of the remnant in Rev 12 without taking into consideration the hymn placed between the two references to the woman fleeing to the wilderness to escape the dragon (vv. 6, 14). Verses 7-9 portray a major war taking place in heaven. Michael and His angels are the victors and, as a result, the defeated dragon is cast out of heaven. This description of the war has a dual function. It reaffirms the faith of the remnant as they face the threats of the dragon against them. They will be facing a defeated dragon. From a structural point of view,[60] Rev 12 portrays the dragon as ineffective. It is agitated, it wants to devour the child, it fights against Michael and His angels, it pursues the woman, and it vomits a flood against her. Confronting it all along is this unshakeable Being who challenges its actions and faces it with an

---

[59]See Pollard, "The Remnant in Non-Canonical and Jewish Apocalyptic Works and in Qumran," in this volume.

[60]See J. Calloud, "Apocalypse 12–13: Essai d'analyse semiotique," *FoiVie* 75 (1976/4): 26-78.

iron fist. God removes the child, prepares for the woman a safe place in the wilderness, provides her with wings like a great eagle, and causes the earth to swallow the flood. God alone is efficient. Michael embodies Him in the struggle. The remnant has nothing to fear in the face of the dragon's wrath.

The second function of the war narrative is to remind the remnant that salvation does not come by merit, but that it is based on and determined by the victory of Christ. The dragon uses its mouth to devour, vomit, and accuse. It carries its purpose more on a spiritual level than a physical one. Faced by Satan's accusations, the proclamation of the Christological hymn in vv. 10-12 resounds with joy. The sounds of rejoicing break out in heaven with the announcement that the dragon has been cast out. The reason for his expulsion is given: "He accused [the brethren] before God day and night" (v. 10). The setting is judicial. Satan is now powerless against the plan of salvation. Since the accuser is eliminated, all obstacles to divine forgiveness are removed. There is rejoicing in heaven, not so much because the dragon has been cast out, but because the dragon can no longer carry out his destructive work in heaven. As with similar hymns in Rev 4–5, the inhabitants of heaven are involved in the salvation of the saints. After singing praises to God the Creator and Christ the Savior, they can now sing songs of praise because the plan of salvation has been fulfilled (Rev 12).

Revelation 12:11 provides the prerequisites for victory: The death of Christ on the cross and the commitment of believers to the Savior. The text deals more with martyrdom than with baptism. The death of the believer is presented as being intimately connected with that of Christ and His victory over death. However, the hymn makes it clear that victory is not gained through the martyrdom of believers. Martyrdom is not held as an instrument of salvation. Only the blood of the Lamb can save. Martyrdom is merely an act of communion through a common destiny.

Considering the reality of its own *kenosis*, the remnant faintly participates in that of the crucified Christ. It is a living testimony. Subjected to the attacks of Satan, as was Christ, they testify by faith to the victory of Christ now accomplished on the cross. Woes may strike the earth, but heaven breaks out in a song of victory. There is hope, as Christ has vanquished the enemy and is exalted again to heaven. Thus, the notion of the remnant goes beyond the mere legalistic observation of God's commandments. It implies a living testimony of faithfulness in spite of obvious weaknesses. Moreover, it testifies that although on the cross God may have appeared to have been at His weakest point, He was in fact at the height of His power. The mention of God's commandments, primarily in chapters 13 and 14 where the focus is on the first four commandments, is a challenge to having faith in God alone as efforts are being made to bring about a new form of worship. The context is truly a reflection of Elijah's experience.

The book of Revelation is set a midst power struggle involving two conflicting kingdoms and the question of worship: The kingdom of God and His Christ, challenged by the kingdom of the dragon and the beasts. Only a remnant emerges victorious from the struggle. Revelation assigns names to the remnant, each one intended to be specifically descriptive. The woes of earth are overcome by faith in what has been accomplished in heaven and on the cross. The eschatological victory of the remnant is already a current reality.[61]

IV. The Adventist Church and the Remnant

An Affirmation

The Seventh-day Adventist Church has always claimed to be the "remnant church," although the exact phrase is not found in the church's official statement of fundamental doctrines. The subject, however, is discussed in the preparation of baptismal candidates.[62] Since its beginning, the Seventh-day Adventist Church has perceived itself to be the remnant characterized by the following attributes:

1. It is ethical—faithful to the commandments of God.
2. It is prophetic—has the spirit of prophecy.
3. It is ecclesiastical—a distinctive remnant; the church of God.
4. It is missiological—called to proclaim God's last message to the world.
5. It is eschatological—the end-time remnant.

These positions have been held as a whole since the inception of our church. Although areas of emphasis may have shifted, none of these positions has been discarded. Today the church favors a more theologically defined position. Bible prophecy is the foundation upon which it identifies itself with the remnant.[63] The position is not derived from a sociologi-

---

[61] See the study by William Shea, "The Parallel Literary Structure of Revelation 12 and 20," *AUSS* 23 (1985): 37-54.

[62] Belief no. 12, formulated in 1980, limits itself to mentioning the existence of a remnant. The word "Church" is reserved for the universal church. However, the *Church Manual*, in the section dealing with the baptismal vow, affirms "that the Seventh-day Adventist Church is the remnant church of Bible prophecy" (*AdvChManual*, p. 34).

[63] Ibid.

cal outlook; it is built on a biblical exegesis sustained by faith, not by sight (cf. 2 Cor 5:7).

The question of the legitimacy of the Seventh-day Adventist Church remains. This is particularly so in the context of the "Perth Declaration" of 1991, in which it is claimed that the Seventh-day Adventist Church is a "prophetic movement . . . the remnant called of God to bear a unique message to earth's last generations, to announce the imminent return of Christ in power and glory."[64] The answer to the question of legitimacy will be considered first on the grounds of hermeneutics. Numerous studies have been devoted to the character of apocalyptic literature.[65] However, many consider the book of Revelation to be a highly spiritual work of edification and encouragement, refusing to recognize as apocalyptic the book that has given its name to this form of literature. This literary genre is different from prophetic works in general in that it does not look at history from the perspective of human experience, but from that of God.[66] "In answer to the prophet's cry, 'How long, O Lord, how long?' the apocalyptists gave the year, the day and the hour!"[67] The implication is that prophecy was no longer understood as a simple promise about the future, but as the announcement of events that needed to be fulfilled. Apocalyptic interpretation came to be seen as calculations and predictions.[68]

In the book of Revelation, this remnant identifies itself through a number of distinctive features that single it out. One of its strongest attributes is its ability to survive by the grace of God revealed through the blood of the sacrificed Lamb It is in and through Him that a people arise whose calling is to follow the Lamb wherever He goes. It is therefore thanks to the grace of God that there is a remnant. In other words, the remnant is not known for its intrinsic qualities, but because of its faithful devotion to the divine plan.

---

[64]"The Perth Declaration," *AdvR*, Nov 7, 1991, p. 7.

[65]Cf. Hans K. LaRondelle, "Interpretation of Prophetic and Apocalyptic Prophecy," in *Symposium on Biblical Hermeneutics*, Gordon H. Hyde, ed. (Washington, DC: Review and Herald, 1974), pp. 225-249; Kenneth A. Strand, *Interpreting the Book of Revelation: Hermeneutical Guidelines, with Brief Introduction to the Literary Analysis* (Naples, FL: Ann Arbor Publishers, 1979), pp. 11-16; Richard Lehmann, "Relationships Between Daniel and Revelation," in *Symposium on Revelation—Book I*, pp. 131-144; and LaRondelle, *Prophecies*, pp. 6-12.

[66]See Strand, *Revelation*, pp. 18-22.

[67]D. S. Russell, *Method and Message of Jewish Apocalyptic* (Philadelphia, PA: Westminster, 1964), p. 183.

[68]See P. Fruchon, "Sur l'interprétation des apocalypses," in *Apocalypses et théologies de l'espérance. Congrès de Toulouse 1975*, L. Mouloubou, ed. (Paris: Seuil, 1977), p. 435.

The Remnant and the Visible Church

To avoid a parochial conclusion, some have tended to apply the term "remnant" to all sincere Christians, not only those in the Adventist church.[69] In doing this, we are in danger of reducing the authentic remnant to an invisible entity comprised of those who are "perfect" or "saints," chosen from within the Adventist church and other churches. In this setting, the authentic remnant church would be an invisible group. It is true that in the letters to the seven Churches, the overcomer is always referred to in the singular. However, in the rest of the book, the concept is that of God's new group of people. The backdrop for the 144,000 is the constitution of the Israel of faith. The connection with Exod 19 follows the same line of thought. The existence of a visible reality is always implied. As we have suggested, the vocabulary chosen in the account of the two witnesses connects them to the notion of the church as a group of people.[70]

Our study has shown that in biblical theology and particularly in Revelation, the remnant is of essential value. Every period of history has had its remnant, and the time of the end is no exception. If we consider the literary specificity of Revelation and acknowledge that our days are eschatological in nature, we should have no doubt that a remnant exists today. This remnant can only be a remnant *church*. As we have seen, the remnant is not only recognizable because of its opposition to Babylon but also because of its direct connection to the woman of Rev 12. The symbol of the woman is used to designate the people of God as a whole. If the prophets of the Old Testament insist that only a remnant will be saved, it is clear in their view that it is Israel who will survive through this remnant. There is no instance in the New Testament of an author individually addressing a mystical group that is distinct from the concrete community of which they are members. John conveys that same sense of community.

The Bible mentions an historical remnant formed by a family or a people that survives an ecological, military, religious, moral or spiritual catastrophe. This suggests that God's plan has realized itself through a remnant as a community. This community is characterized by its faithfulness to God. It is the faithful generation who, at any time, has put its faith in the grace of God. History has also an end, and this end is both present

---

[69] Cf. *Seventh-day Adventists Answer Questions on Doctrine: An Explanation of Certain Major Aspects of Seventh-day Adventist Belief* (Washington, DC: Review and Herald, 1957), pp. 186-196.

[70] Cf. E. G. White, *The Great Controversy* (Mountain View, CA: Pacific Press, 1911), p. 268.

and future. Today there is an eschatological remnant, but this remnant is not the fullness of the final, glorious, and innumerable remnant of God (144,000, the great multitude). In the book of Revelation, the remnant is a communal, ecclesiastical, and social reality, made up of those who have been called, constituting an assembly (*ekklēsia*) of God's faithful worshipers. Nothing allows us to escape the notion that the remnant is a visible, identifiable,[71] ecclesiastical entity. Of course, it is also both a sociological and spiritual reality.[72]

The Remnant and the Totality of the Church

From our discussion it clearly follows that the Seventh-day Adventist Church as the remnant of prophecy does not by itself constitute the whole church. The mystery of the church is such that at a particular time in history, a specific body of believers may be fully the church without being the church in its entirety. It could be recognized as the expression of the church of God without being the totality of the church of God.[73] The remnant carries within it the complete identity of the church, but as a point of reference without excluding others. Just as every cell of the body contains the complete identity of the whole, the *ecclesia* of the remnant is really the church, without being the whole body. In other words, the visible body of the remnant church can claim to be the church of God without excluding a larger Christian body of believers. God considers many other faithful and sincere believers outside the Adventist church to be part of His people.[74]

The church remains the church of God in spite of its errors or the sins of its members. It is not cursed; it is called by Christ to make radical changes. The love of Christ for His church remains constant whether or not the church is faithful. The theme of the remnant is a warning that reinforces the validity of the prophetic calls, for only a remnant will be saved. However, this does not reduce the Lord's love for the church that

---

[71] In LaRondelle's outline of the history of the remnant, he speaks of "remnant groups," then mentions "Churches," opting more often for the word "movement" ("Remnant," pp. 880-882).

[72] Ibid. See also Clifford Goldstein, *The Remnant* (Boise, ID: Pacific Press, 1994), pp. 78-79.

[73] Compare 1 Cor 1:2 ("To the church of God in Corinth, to those sanctified in Christ Jesus and called to be holy, together with all those everywhere who call on the name of our Lord Jesus Christ—their Lord and ours"), with 1 Cor 14:36 ("Did the word of God originate with you? Or are you the only people it has reached?").

[74] For further discussion, see Rodríguez, "Concluding Essay" in this volume.

is constantly called upon to reform and to return to its originator. Thus, the claim of the Seventh-day Adventist Church to be the remnant church of Bible prophecy is a statement of fact that remains a challenge. The remnant church remains always under the test of the Word of God. The call to come out of Babylon is always relevant and permanent. It not only addresses those who are in Babylon, but also those who are tempted to go back to Babylon, as Israel was tempted to return to Egypt. Pride and arrogance are particularly peculiar to Babylon, but they are never far from those who claim to be faithful to God.

V. Conclusion

A people cannot be the Remnant Church without having the humility to accept this as a gift of grace from God. The identity of the remnant should be considered on a theological basis. Its implications are as follows:

1. To the extent that the book of Revelation discusses and proclaims the end of history and the existence of a faithful remnant that is faithful to the commandments of God and the faith of Jesus, which is prompted by the spirit of prophecy and which witnesses to and works on behalf of others, the Seventh-day Adventist Church can be identified with that remnant. The church should then respond to its divine calling as it is revealed in Scripture.

2. To the extent that the Adventist church embodies the various expectations of an eschatological remnant, it can affirm by faith that it is the remnant identified with the three angels' messages of Rev 14. This acknowledgement is not exclusive; rather, it is open to anyone who responds to God's call to become a part of the end-time remnant.

3. The biblical remnant should not be limited to a specific ecclesiastical structure because the structure's primary role is to promote, in an organized way, the mission of the remnant.

The tension between the human reality and the ideal view of the remnant present in the book of Revelation is resolved only by the overabundance of God's grace (cf. Rom 5:20). The claim of the Seventh-day Adventist Church to be the remnant church described in Bible prophecy is more of a challenge than a report, more a call than an assessment, more a test of faith than the sum total of its deeds. It is not possible to be the remnant church without humbly receiving it by the grace of God while agreeing in fullness of heart to participate in the divine project described in the Bible and particularly in the Revelation of John.

CHAPTER VI

THE REMNANT AND GOD'S COMMANDMENTS: REVELATION 12:17[1]

Johannes Kovar
Lecturer in Greek and New Testament
Seminar Schloss Bogenhofen
Austria

Revelation 12:17 mentions together "the commandments of God "and" the spirit of prophecy." The phrase "the spirit of prophecy" is already addressed in this volume;[2] therefore, we will concentrate on the study of the other phrase, "the commandments of God." In what follows we will attempt to clarify the meaning of the term "commandments" (*entolas*) as well as the Greek verb *tēreō*—"to keep, observe, watch over." In so doing, we should bear in mind the context provided by the book of Revelation itself and the extent to which the Old Testament has influenced John's choice of that terminology.

I. Clarification of terms

Keeping the Commandments

The noun *entolē* can be translated in different ways ("command, order, commandment, law").[3] In the New Testament it designates instructions or commandments given by the people, Jesus, or God, and could

---

[1] This chapter is a revised and abridged version of an article first published in German in *"For You Have Strengthened Me": Biblical and Theological Studies in Honor of Gerhard Pfandl in Celebration of His Sixty-Fifth Birthday*, Martin Pröbstle, ed. (St. Peter am Hart, Austria: Seminar Schloss Bogenhofen, 2007), pp. 241-263. I thank Rachel Brupbacher for providing an English translation and Stella Bradley for proofreading.

[2] See Gerhard Pfandl, "Identifying Marks of the End-Time Remnant"; also idem, "The Remnant Church and the Spirit of Prophecy," in *Symposium on Revelation: Exegetical and General Studies—Book II*, Frank B. Holbrook, ed. (Silver Spring, MD: Biblical Research Institute, 1992), pp. 295-334.

[3] See Fredeick W. Danker and Walter Bauer, *A Greek-English Lexicon of the New Testament and Other Early Christian Literature* (Chicago, IL: University of Chicago Press, 2000), p. 340.

designate a single commandment or refer to God's law as a whole. The commandments of God can be connected to different verbs without showing any significant disparity of meaning. In the following table we will provide examples from the writings of John, where the noun *entolē* is used in conjunction with different verbs:[4]

Tēreō	To keep, preserve	1 John 3:22	Hoti tas entolas autou tēroumen	because we obey his commandments (NIV) because we keep his commandments (ASV, KJV, RSV)
Echō	have	John 14:21	Ho echōn tas entolas mou kai tērōn autas	He who has my commandments and keeps them (RSV)
Lambanō	receive, take	2 John 4	Kathōs entolēn elabomen para tou patros	as we have received a commandment from the Father (KJV)
Poieō	do, observe	1 John 5:2	Hotan ton theon agapōmen kai tas entolas autou poiōmen	when we love God and do his commandments (ASV) and keep his commandments (KJV)
Peripateō	walk	2 John 6	Hina peripatōmen kata tas entolas autou	This is the commandment, even as ye heard from the beginning, that ye should walk in it (ASV)
Phulassō	keep, watch, guard	Deut 8:6, LXX (often; cf. John 12:47)	Kai phulaxē tas entolas kuriou tou theou sou	Therefore thou shalt keep the commandments of the LORD thy God (KJV)

In the Septuagint the verb *phulassō* (in the active or middle voice) is frequently mentioned in the context of law, and commandments. This is also the case in extrabiblical literature. The verb actually means "to guard, protect, preserve," and when connected to a commandment or law it specifically means "to protect from violation = keep, observe, follow."[5] The same is true of *tēreō*, which means "to keep, keep un-

---

[4]The noun *entolē* is used in the writings of John more times than in any other New Testament writer; see H. H. Esser, "*Entolē*," NIDNTT, vol. 1, p. 334.

[5]See Danker and Bauer, *Gree-English Lexicon*, p. 1068.

der guard, protect, guard." In conjunction with a commandment/law, it means "to keep, observe, obey, hold fast."[6] In fact, *phulassō* and *tēreō* are synonyms. While the LXX gives preference to *phulassō*, the New Testament uses *tēreō* more often, particularly in the book of John.[7] The two verbs, *phulassō* and *tēreō*, are thus equally common.[8] They are used in parallelism,[9] in phrases carrying the same meanings (e.g., *phulassein tas entolas* ["to keep the commandments"] and *tērein tas entolas* ["keep the commandments"]), as well as in the interesting example of the rich young man whom Jesus required to keep (*tēreō*) the commandments (Matt 19:17), which he claimed to already be keeping (*phulassō*; 19:20).

"God's Commandments"

It is not always clear what the Bible means by "God's commandments." Sometimes it seems to be the entire Torah, and sometimes it refers specifically to the Ten Commandments or a single commandment. Arguably, since the love commandment plays a crucial role in the Synoptic Gospels (e.g., Mark 12:28-31), in Paul's writings (e.g., Rom 13:9), and in the writings of John (e.g., John 13:34; 1 John 4:21), Rev 12:17 must be referring to that commandment.[10] But, since in Revelation the love commandment is not emphasized at all, we should be careful and not read it into the text. Besides, texts such as Matt 15:3-4 (= Mark 7:9-10); 19:17-20; Rom 13:9 clearly reveal that the Ten Commandments are of utmost importance for the same writers and that they use the expression "God's commandments" to refer to them; and James calls them the "law" (Jas 2:10-12). The nouns "commandments" and "law" are both used in referring to the Decalogue.[11]

---

[6] See ibid., p. 1002.

[7] Harald Riesenfeld, "*Tēreō*," TDNT, vol. 8, p. 144.

[8] Ernst Lohmeyer, *Die Offenbarung des Johannes* (Tübingen: Mohr, 1953), p. 9. He thinks that *tēreō* particularly refers to those who observe the commandments. But this does not seem accurate to me. It is interesting that R. H. Charles, *A Critical and Exegetical Commentary on the Revelation of St. John*, vol. 1 (Edinburgh: T. & T. Clark, 1920), p. 369, does not take into consideration that the two verbs are synonymous.

[9] Prov 2:11; 4:23; 13:3; 16:17; 19:16; Dan 9:4; John 17:12; see also H.-G. Schütz, "*tēreō*," NIDNTT, vol. 2, pp. 132-133; and *idem*, "*phulassō*," NIDNTT, vol. 2, pp. 134-135.

[10] See, e.g., Louis A. Vos, *The Synoptic Traditions in the Apocalypse* (Kampen: Kok, 1965), p. 203. He argues that "God's Word" as mentioned in Revelation is the gospel tradition, and that in 12:17, it refers to the love commandment.

[11] See Exod 24:12: "and I will give you the tablets of stone, with the law and the commandment, which I have written for their instruction" (NRSV).

Hence it is reasonable to expect that John would have had in mind at least the Ten Commandments in the book of Revelation when using the phrase "keep the commandments of God." On the basis of literary analysis, it has been suggested that Rev 12:17 describes the final stage of the conflict between the woman and the dragon,[12] in which God's law will play a significant role.

II. The Commandments in Rev 12:17

In Revelation the term *entolē* is found in only two passages,[13] the content of which are somewhat similar. Revelation 12:17: "And the dragon was wroth with the woman, and went to make war with the remnant of her seed, which keep the commandments of God [*tōn tērountōn tas entolas tou theou*] and have the testimony of Jesus" (KJV). Revelation 14:12: "Here is the patience of the saints: here are they that keep the commandments of God [*hoi tērountes tas entolas tou theou*], and the faith of Jesus" (KJV). Both texts list some characteristics of God's people. The 'keeping God's commandments' is mentioned in both passages, suggesting that this idea is particularly meaningful to John. In both instances the terms *entolē* and *tēreō* are tied together and are more closely defined by the genitive "of God," a subjective genitive, meaning that the commandments are from God.

Scholars disagree concerning the meaning of the phrase "God's commandments" in Rev 12:17. Many do not deal with this issue at all, leaving the question open,[14] while others interpret it in a general sense (similar to 1 Cor 7:19).[15] We also find commentators who find in it a reference to

---

[12]William H. Shea, "The Parallel Literary Structure of Revelation 12 and 20" *AUSS* 23 (1985): 37-54, especially pp. 45 and 49. See also David E. Aune, *Revelation 6–16* (Nashville, TN: Thomas Nelson, 1998), pp. 709, 712; Simon J. Kistemaker, *New Testament Commentary: Exposition of the Book of Revelation* (Grand Rapids, MI: Baker, 2002), p. 370; Grant R. Osborne, *Revelation* (Grand Rapids, MI: Baker, 2002), pp. 452, 486. G. K. Beale, *The Book of Revelation: A Commentary on the Greek Text* (Grand Rapids, MI: Eerdmans, 1999), pp. 678-680, appears to be uncertain.

[13]A third place would be Rev 22:14, but because of some textual problems it is excluded from the discussion.

[14]Charles, *Revelation*, vol. 1, pp. 331-332; Leon Morris, *The Book of Revelation: An Introduction and Commentary* (Leicester, IL: InterVarsity, 1996), p. 160; Ben Witherington III, *Revelation* (Cambridge: Cambridge University Press, 2003), pp. 171-172.

[15]Robert H. Mounce, *The Book of Revelation* (Grand Rapids, MI: Eerdmans, 1998), p. 242.

all of the commandments in God's Word, especially the ethical demands[16] or the entire revelation of both Old and New Testaments.[17] Those who favor a reference to specific commandments argue for the love commandment[18] or for the second part of the Ten Commandments and the love commandment.[19] Adventists have always regarded "God's commandments" as the Ten Commandments. There are a number of arguments that support this position.

Context and structure

The text of Rev 12:17 is embedded in the context of chapters 12–14. This section of Revelation is introduced by the initial vision found in Rev 11:15-19 and concludes with another heavenly vision in Rev 15:1-8, both related to the heavenly temple.[20] The first one references the ark of the covenant located inside the most holy place (Rev 11:19). The second one is about the "temple of the tabernacle [tent] of the testimony in heaven" (Rev 15:5). The phrase "tent of the testimony" was used in the Old Testament to designate the sanctuary as the place where the Ten Commandments were located. In other words, the term "testimony" referred to the Decalogue as the covenant law.[21] Commentators have recognized that in Rev 15:5, "the testimony" designates the law of God, the Ten Commandments.[22] The reference to the Decalogue could hardly be clearer. A reader in the first century would undoubtedly associate the ark of the covenant with the Ten Commandments, since in the Old Testament the two are

---

[16]So Osborne, *Revelation*, pp. 486, 543.

[17]Beale, *Revelation*, p. 766; Kistemaker, *Revelation*, p. 370.

[18]Vos, *Apocalypse*, p. 203.

[19]Aune, *Revelation 6–16*, pp. 709-712.

[20]The question, to what extent this section looks in two directions (backward and forward), is discussed by Anthony MacPherson, "The Mark of the Beast as a 'Sign Commandment' and 'Anti-Sabbath' in the Worship Crisis of Revelation 12–14" *AUSS* 43 (2005): 272-273. Concerning 11:19 Adventist interpreters agree that it announces the section of chapters 12-22; see, e.g., Ekkehardt Mueller, "Recapitulation in Revelation 4–11" *JATS* 9 (1998): 275.

[21]See H. Simian-Yofre, "ʿwd," *TDOT*, vol. 10, pp. 512-513.

[22]Stephen S. Smalley, *The Revelation of John: A Commentary on the Greek Text of the Apocalypse* (Downers Grove, IL: InterVarsity, 2005), pp. 389-390, comments that "the tent of the testimony" was so designated "because it contained the ark, or tablets, of the covenant; that is, the Ten Commandments which Moses received from God." He then concludes, "The 'testimony' to which reference is made in [Rev 15] verse 5, may include not only the Law of God but also the 'witness to (or by) Jesus,' since he fulfils in himself the covenantal requirements of the Father." A similar reasoning is found in Beale, *Revelation*, p. 809.

closely connected.²³ One could confidently argue that Rev 11:9 and 15:5 form a kind of *inclusio* around chapters 12–14, with the intent of turning the reader's attention to what was inside the inner compartment of the temple, more specifically, to the ark of the covenant, inside which were the Ten Commandments. These commandments will become a central theme in the final and crucial struggle in Revelation.²⁴

A look at the key elements in the structure of Rev 9:19–15:5 suggests that the commandments are of particular significance in that section. The following diagram should clarify this:²⁵

A	Sanctuary Scene–Ark of the Covenant (Ten Commandments)	Rev 11:19
B	Call to Keep the Commandments of God	Rev 12:17
C	Call to Worship the Creature	Rev 13:14-17
C'	Call to Worship the True Creator	Rev 14:6-7
B'	Call to Keep the Commandments of God	Rev 14:12
A'	Sanctuary Scene–Tabernacle (Ten Commandments)	Rev 15:5

Since much of what is found in the introductory vision of Rev 11:15-19 is taken up again in chapters 12–22, it is not surprising that the issue of the commandments, implicit in 11:19, later becomes even more prominent and explicit (12:17; 14:12). Due to the reference to the ark of the covenant in the introductory vision, we can conclude that in 12:17 and 14:12 John was referring to the Decalogue.

In certain respects, Rev 12:17 serves as a heading for what will follow in detail in subsequent chapters.²⁶ Chapter 13 describes the struggle, while chapter 14 discusses the nature and message of the remnant people. The theme of worship is undoubtedly a central concern in this whole section. The emphasis on worship²⁷ becomes particularly significant in

---

²³Exod 25:16. This text is especially significant because the Ark of the Covenant is mentioned here for the first time in the Old Testament and its function is to serve as the repository of the Ten Commandments; see also Exod 25:21; 30:6; Deut 10:1-5; 1 Kgs 8:9; 2 Chr 5:10; Heb 9:4.

²⁴MacPherson, "Sign Commandment," p. 275. Ekkehardt Mueller, *Microstructural Analysis of Revelation 4–11* (Berrien Springs, MI: Andrews University Press, 1996), pp. 575-578, finds a microstructural relationship between the genitive "God's" from 11:19 ("God's Temple") and 12:17 ("God's commandments"). I would prefer to emphasize the content, which suggests a connection between the ark of the covenant and the commandments.

²⁵William H. Shea, "The Controversy over the Commandments in the Central Chiasm of Revelation" *JATS* 11 (2000): 229. See also Rodríguez, "Concluding Essay," in this volume.

²⁶Jon Paulien, "Revisiting the Sabbath in the Book of Revelation" *JATS* 9 (1998): 182.

²⁷Rev 13:4, 8, 12, 15; 14:9, 11. The listing is according to Paulien, ibid., p. 182. The

the striking appeal of one of the angels to worship God the Creator (Rev 14:7), which alludes to Exodus 20:11.[28]

The Ten Commandments in Revelation

There are allusions to and use of the language of the Ten Commandments before and after Rev 12:17.[29] We will list some of those passages.

Rev 5:3

	Rev 5:3 (RSV)	Exod 20:4 = Deut 5:8 (LXX) (KJV)
Sabbath allusion	And no one **in heaven** or **on earth** or **under the earth** was able to open the scroll or to look into it	You shall not make for yourself a graven image, or any likeness of anything that is **in heaven** above, or that is **in earth beneath**, or that is in the water **under the earth**.

The Nestle-Aland Greek Text (26th and 27th editions, but not the older editions[30]) mentions these parallels in the margins. They are also acknowledged by some commentators.[31]

Rev 9:20-21

	Rev 9:20-21 (RSV)	Exod 20 (LXX) (KJV)
worshiping idols	nor give up **worshiping** demons and **idols**	Thou shalt not make to thyself an **idol** (v. 4) Thou shalt not **bow down** to them, nor serve them (v. 5)
killing	nor did they repent of their **murders**	Thou shalt not **kill** (v. 13 [LXX 15])

---

frequent mention of the verb "to worship" shows that this is a main topic in the section.

[28] For details see Paulien, "Sabbath," pp. 183-185.

[29] Skip MacCarty, *In Granite or Ingrained? What the Old and New Covenants Reveal About the Gospel, the Law, and the Sabbath* (Berrien Springs, MI: Andrews University, 2007), pp. 199-200, suggests the following allusions to the Ten Commandments: Rev 1:10; 2:14, 20; 3:8; 9:20-21; 11:18-19; 12:17; 14:7, 12; 15:5; 21:8. I will add some other references.

[30] At the same time Nestle-Aland[26, 27] refer to the similar text of Rev 5:13, which, however, is printed without reference to the Old Testament and which is not mentioned in the appendix.

[31] Charles, *Revelation*, vol. 1, p. 139; he cites Exod 20:4, 11; Osborne, *Revelation*, p. 261, refers to the same texts.

	Rev 9:20-21 (RSV)	Exod 20 (LXX) (KJV)
committing adultery	their **immorality**	Thou shalt not **commit adultery** (v. 14 [LXX 13])
stealing	their immorality or their **thefts**	Thou shalt not **steal** (v. 15 [LXX 14])

There are many commentators who regard the Decalogue as the Old Testament model for Rev 9:20-21.[32]

Rev 10:6

Content	Rev 10:6 (NEB)	Exod 20:11 (LXX) (RSV)
Sabbath and Creation	and swore by the one who lives forever and ever, who **created heaven** and **earth** and **sea** and **all that is in them**	for in six days the LORD **made heaven** and **earth**, the **sea**, and **all that is in them**, and rested the seventh day

Scholars have also found here a connection to the Ten Commandments.[33]

Rev 13–14

Content	Rev 13–14	Exod 20 (LXX)
making of an image[34]	that they should **make** an **image** to the beast (13:14) (KJV) He was given power to give breath to the **image** of the first beast, so that it could speak and cause all who refused to worship the **image** to be killed (13:15) (NIV) If any one worships the beast and its **image** (14:9) (NIV) who worship the beast and his **image** (14:11) (NIV)	You shall not **make** for yourself a carved **image** (v. 4) (NKJV)

---

[32] See, e.g., Nestle-Aland,[27] where Exod 20:13-15 is given as a parallel to Rev 9:20-21 in the margin. See also Aune, *Revelation 6–16*, p. 544; Charles, *Revelation*, vol. 1, p. 255; Lohmeyer, *Offenbarung*, p. 83; Mounce, *Revelation*, p. 198; Heinz Giesen, *Die Offenbarung des Johannes* (Regensburg: Pustet, 1997), p. 226; Heinrich Kraft, *Die Offenbarung des Johannes* (Tübingen: Mohr, 1974), p. 144; Ulrich B. Müller, *Die Offenbarung des Johannes* (Gütersloh: Mohn, 1984), p. 198. Osborne, *Revelation*, p. 387, finds a reference to commandments 2, 6, 7, and 8.

[33] See the margins in Nestle-Aland,[27] as well as the older editions (starting with Nestle[1] 1898), all of which make reference to Exod 20:11. The same is found in Mounce, *Revelation*, p. 206; Charles, *Revelation*, vol. 1, p. 263; Aune, *Revelation 6–16*, p. 565.

[34] J. Massyngberde Ford, *Revelation: Introduction, Translation and Commentary* (Gar-

Content	Rev. 13–14	Exod 20 (LXX)
worshiping idols[35]	And they **worshiped** the dragon which gave power unto the beast: and they **worshiped** the beast (13:4) (KJV) and all who dwell on earth will **worship** it (13:8) (RSV) and makes the earth and its inhabitants **worship** the first beast (13:12) (RSV) speak and cause all who refused to **worship** the image to be killed (13:15) (NIV) if anyone **worships** the beast and its image (14:9) (NIV) who **worship** the beast and his image (14:11) (NIV)	You shall not bow down to them or **worship** them (v. 5) (NIV)
misuse of God's name[36]	upon his heads the **name** of **blasphemy** (13:1) (KJV) to utter proud words and **blasphemies** (13:5) (NIV) he opened his mouth in **blasphemy** against God, to **blaspheme** his name (13:6) (KJV)	Thou shalt not take the **name** of the Lord thy God **in vain** (v. 7) (KJV)
no work	so that no one can buy or sell unless he has the mark (13:17) (RSV)	but the seventh day is a Sabbath to the LORD your God. On it you shall not do any work (v. 10) (NIV)
long listing of people	Also it causes all, both small and great, both rich and poor, both free and slave, to be marked on the right hand or the forehead (13:16) (RSV)	neither you, nor your son or daughter, nor your manservant or maidservant, nor your animals, nor the stranger within your gates (v. 10) (NIV)

---

den City, NY: Doubleday, 1975), p. 224, comments, "The actual making of an image for the monster is a direct infringement of Exod 20:3-4." Similarly Alan F. Johnson, "Revelation" in *The Expositor's Bible Commentary*, Frank E. Gaebelein, ed. (Grand Rapids, MI: Zondervan, 1981), vol. 12, p. 531.

[35]Osborne, *Revelation*, p. 497, cites Exod 20:3 as a parallel.
[36]Ibid., p. 500.

Content	Rev 13–14	Exod 20 (LXX)
killing	he who **kills** with the sword must be **killed** with the sword (13:10) (NKJV) and cause as many as would not worship the image of the beast to be **killed** (13:15) (NKVJ)	You shall not **kill** (v. 13 [LXX 15]) (RSV)
committing adultery	These are the ones who were not **defiled with women**, for they are **virgins** (14:4) (NKJV) drink of the wine of the wrath of her **fornication** (14:8) (NKJV)	You shall not **commit adultery** (v. 14 [LXX 13]) (RSV)
lying	and in their mouth no **lie** was found (14:5) (NRSV)	You shall not bear **false witness** against your neighbor (v. 16) (RSV)

Scholars have identified parallels for the first half of the Decalogue[37] but, as we can see, the references should not be limited to the first four commandments. John's interest is in the Decalogue itself.

Rev 14:7

	Rev 14:7 (NRSV)	Exod 20:11 (LXX)) (NIV)
Creator	and worship Him who **made heaven** and **earth**, the **sea** and springs of water	For in six days the Lord **made** the **heaven** and the **earth**, and the **sea** and all that is in them

This text too has been considered to contain a reference to the Ten Commandments, specifically to the Sabbath.[38] These very clear references or allusions to the Ten Commandments significantly increase the likelihood that they are also being referenced in Rev 12:17. While almost all of the

---

[37]Paulien, "Sabbath," pp. 184-185; MacPherson, "Sign Commandment," pp. 276-278.

[38]Paulien, "Sabbath," pp. 179-186; Ranko Stefanovic, *Revelation of Jesus Christ: Commentary on the Book of Revelation* (Berrien Springs, MI: Andrews University Press, 2002), p. 416. Exodus 20:11 is mentioned in the *The Greek New Testament*, K. Aland, Matthew Black, C. M. Martini, B. M. Metzger, and A. Wikgren, eds. (Germany: United Bible Societies,¹1966 to ⁴1993). But this reference is already found earlier in the margins and as a reference to the Old Testament in the text (in bold print) of the editions of Eberhard and Erwin Nestle, *Novum Testamentum Graece* (¹1898 to ²⁵1963). The current edition of the German Bible Society's *Novum Testamentum Graece et Latine* (³1994) mentions Exod

commandments of the Decalogue are mentioned in Revelation, the language of the Sabbath commandment particularly stands out.

The Book of Daniel and the Law

When we look through the references to Dan 7 in the Nestle-Aland Greek Text (27th edition), it is not difficult to see that this Old Testament chapter plays an outstanding role in Revelation. I would like to list all the parallels from passages listed in Nestle-Aland and, at the same time, supplement them:

Daniel	Revelation	
7:2	7:1	four winds
7:3	11:7; 13:1	beast comes up
7:4-6	13:2	description of the beasts
7:7	12:3; 13:1	ten horns
7:8	13:5, 7	mouth speaking great things
7:9	1:14; 20:4, 11	white hair, thrones
7:10	5:11; 20:12	thousands, ten thousands, books opened
7:11	13:5; 19:20	blasphemy, punishment by fire
7:13	1:7, 13; 14:14	clouds, son of man
7:14	11:15	everlasting dominion
7:18	22:5	everlasting dominion
7:20	13:5; 17:12	mouth speaking great things, ten horns
7:21	11:7; 13:7	war against the saints, they are defeated
7:22	20:4	Judgment
7:24	12:3; 13:1; 17:12	ten horns
7:25	12:14; 13:6, 7	3½ times, blasphemy, war against the saints
7:27	11:15; 20:4; 22:5	everlasting kingdom
my proposed additions:		
7:8, 21	12:17	makes war against the saints
7:25	12:17	changing of the law/preserving it

20:11 next to the Latin text, which, however, is not present in the Greek section. All the editions of Augustinus Merk, *Novum Testamentum Graece et Latine* (Rome: Pontificio Istituto Biblico,[11]1992), include a reference to Exod 20:11. The reference to the Sabbath commandment in Rev 12:17 is first missing from Nestle-Aland,[26] although it has remained in Rev 10:6 up to the current edition.

In the case of Dan 7:25, we find what I would call a thematic parallel with Rev 12.[39] This is particularly the case in Rev 12:17.[40] There are actually some common elements: war, the faithful, the law,[41] and efforts to change it (Dan) or to keep it (Rev). We can compare this shift, from the changing of the law in Daniel to its protection in Revelation, to other similar changes:

Daniel		Revelation	
7:3, 7, 19	different beasts	13:4	who is like the beast
7:4	lion with eagle's wings	12:14	woman with eagle's wings
7:18, 22, 27	saints receive power and kingdom	13:5, 7	beast receives authority
7:21, 25	horn defeats and wears out the saints	12:6, 14-17	woman protected
7:25	horn changes law	12:17	the remnant keeps the commandments
8:10	horn grows up to heaven	12:9, 13	dragon cast down to earth

From this evidence we get the impression that what the beast/horn in Dan 7 succeeded in doing is, at the end, denied to the dragon. Now the saints escape and are preserved. It is true that some elements in the description found in Daniel are also said of the believers in Revelation. But concerning the "changing" of the law, a noticeable shift occurs by affirming the "keeping" of the commandments.

---

[39]Ian Paul, "The Use of the Old Testament in Revelation 12" in *The Old Testament in the New Testament*, Steve Moyise, ed. (Sheffield: Sheffield Academic Press, 2000), pp. 256-274. He concludes: "All four types of allusions (verbal allusion to words, verbal allusion to themes, thematic allusion to words, thematic allusion to themes) occur in this chapter" (p. 269)

[40]Stephen Pattemore, *The People of God in the Apocalypse: Discourse, Structure and Exegeses* (Cambridge: Cambridge University Press, 2004), p. 120: He sees a connection between Dan 7:21, 25 and Rev 12:7, 17; 13:7, as well as between Dan 7:25 and Rev 13:5, 7.

[41]Commentators interpret the "law" in Dan 7:25 nearly always in the context of Antiochus IV and refer to texts like 1 Macc 1:45 and 2 Macc 6:6, which are also concerned with the Sabbath; e.g., John J. Collins, *Daniel* (Minneapolis, MN: Fortress, 1993), p. 322.

The Role of the Law in Eschatology

We find in the New Testament several hints indicating that, close to the end of world history, there will be a rebellion against God's law.[42] The terms "lawlessness" and "lawless" (*anomia, anomos*) are employed by Jesus (Matt 7:23; 13:41; 24:12) and Paul (2 Thess 2:3, 7-8) in the context of the end-time. The term "*anomia* refers primarily simply to the fact of *lawlessness*. The *anomos*, then, is *one for whom there is no such thing as a—or the—law*."[43] Such a person behaves "contrary to the law."[44] According to Jesus, there was to be an increase of *anomia*—lawlessness or the breaking of the law—in the world shortly before His coming (Matt 24:12). The Antichrist is described by Paul as a person who has no regard for the law of God (2 Thess 2:3, 8). Unquestionably, in the description of the first beast in Rev 13, John is going back to the apocalyptic visions of Daniel,[45] where one of the prominent signs of the so-called Antichrist is the rejection of the law (Dan 7:25). According to Revelation, God's eschatological people are loyal to the commandments at a time when God's enemies are characterized by rebellion against the divine law (Rev 12:17 and 14:12). It is practically impossible to deny that the law in that context is God's law particularly as embodied in the Decalogue. The divine law will play a central role in the final conflict between God and the forces of evil.

V. Summary

This investigation has examined the use and meaning of the phrase "keep the commandments of God" in the book of Revelation and concluded that there are good reasons to believe that it refers primarily to the Ten Commandments. This is supported by the immediate context, with its reference to the most holy place of the heavenly temple and specifically to the ark of the covenant inside which were placed the tablets of stone of the Ten Commandments. Additionally, the Ten Commandments are a central issue of concern in the book of Revelation. The book is interested not only in the first tablet—with its emphasis on worshipping God—but also in the rest of the commandments as an indispensable ethical and religious guide for God's end-time people. Practically all of them

---

[42] This is indicated by MacPherson, "Sign Commandment," p. 269.

[43] M. Limbeck, "*Anomia* lawlessness, breaking the law," *EDNT*, vol. 1, p. 106.

[44] BDAG, p. 85.

[45] See e.g., G. K. Beale, *The Use of Daniel in Jewish Apocalyptic Literature and in the Revelation of St. John* (Lanham, MD: University of America Press, 1984), p. 247.

are mentioned in one way or another in Revelation. The role of the law of God in the cosmic conflict is mentioned by Daniel. Evil powers altered the divine law. The New Testament also witnesses to the fact that the law will become an issue of contention at the end of time. It is in that context that Revelation makes clear that, at the end, there is a group of people, God's remnant people, who keep the commandments of God.

CHAPTER VII

SABBATH THEOLOGY IN THE BOOK OF REVELATION[1]

Mathilde Frey
Assistant Professor
Adventist International Institute of Advanced Studies
Philippines

The word "Sabbath" does not occur in the book of Revelation, but its theology seems to permeate it. This study investigates the presence of that theology in the book and suggests that the theme of the Sabbath may have served the author as an underlying theological concept with regard to the sevenfold division of the book, its chiastic structure, and its prominent use of the number seven. We will examine the presence of language and allusions to the Sabbath and the linguistic indicators for the concept of the Sabbath.

The background for John's theology of the Sabbath is provided by the Old Testament, but I will also suggest that two other sources from the intertestamental period may have served as a background for the Sabbath concept in the book of Revelation. These would be Philo's Sabbath theology[2] and the *Songs of the Sabbath Sacrifice* of the Qumran community.[3] Philo developed his theology of the Sabbath based upon the holistic concept of the number seven, the universal significance of the Sabbath as the birthday of the world, and the meaning of resting, equality, and freedom included in the theme of the Sabbath.[4] The liturgical scrolls of

---

[1]This is a revised and abridged version of my paper, "The Theological Concept of the Sabbath in the Book of Revelation," in *"For You Have Strengthened Me": Biblical and Theological Studies in Honor of Gerhard Pfandl in Celebration of His Sixty-Fifth Birthday*, Martin Probstle, ed. (St. Peter am Hart, Austria: Seminar Schloss Bogenhofen, 2007), pp. 223-239.

[2]Sakae Kubo, "The Sabbath in the Intertestamental Period," in *The Sabbath in Scripture and History*, K. A. Strand, ed. (Washington, D.C.: Review and Herald, 1982), p. 57.

[3]Carol A. Newsom, "Songs of the Sabbath Sacrifice (4Q400-407, 11Q17, MASIK)," in *Dictionary of New Testament Background*, C. A. Evans and S. E. Porter, eds. (Downers Grove, IL: InterVarsity, 2000), p. 1139.

[4]*Moses* 1. 37; 2. 39; *The Special Laws* 2. 15, 16; *Allegorical Interpretation* 1. 2-6; *On*

the *Songs of the Sabbath Sacrifice*, dated to the first century B.C., show certain similarities to the book of Revelation. Carol A. Newsom concludes that the frequent use of the number seven derived from the Sabbath, as the dateline of both documents, and from the chiastic structure of Revelation, in which balancing sections of sevens may be found.[5]

I. Structural Indicators for the Concept of the Sabbath

The number seven plays a central role in the book of Revelation, not only because it is explicitly mentioned many times but also because it provides a structural frame for the organization of the material found in the book. We will examine these elements.

Sevenfold Division of the Book of Revelation

The ongoing debate among biblical scholars regarding the literary structure of the book of Revelation leads Adela Yarbo Collins to state that "there are almost as many [structural] outlines of the book as there are interpreters."[6] This variety of opinions, however, has been considered by others to be "a direct testimony to the literary genius of the author."[7] Therefore, it is legitimate to ask about the structural model used by the biblical writer to convey the message of the book.[8] Among the many attempts toward detecting the literary structure of the book of Revelation, the major contributions seem to argue for an outline based on a sevenfold division of the book.[9] Jon Paulien demonstrates that the sevenfold

---

the *Creation* 30, 31, 33-42; *On the Cherubim* 26; *The Special Laws* 2. 15, 16, 48. See Kubo, "Sabbath," p. 67.

[5]Newsom, "Songs of the Sabbath Sacrifice," p. 1139. See also William H. Shea, "Sabbath Hymns for the Heavenly Sanctuary (Qumran)," in *Sabbath in Scripture*, p. 406.

[6]Adela Y. Collins, *The Combat Myth in the Book of Revelation* (Missoula, MT: Scholars, 1976), p. 8.

[7]Gilbert Desrosiers, *An Introduction to Revelation: A Pathway to Interpretation* (New York: Continuum, 2000), p. 57.

[8]See Phyllis Trible, *Rhetorical Criticism: Context, Method, and the Book of Jonah* (Minneapolis, MN: Fortress, 1994), pp. 101-106; Felise Tavo, "The Structure of the Apocalypse: Reexamining a Perennial Problem," *NovT* 47 (2005): 47-68.

[9]Collins, *Combat Myth*, pp. 13-55; Elisabeth Schüssler Fiorenza, *The Book of Revelation: Justice and Judgment* (Philadelphia, PA: Fortress, 1985), pp. 159-180; Kenneth A. Strand, *Interpreting the Book of Revelation* (Worthington, MI: Ann Arbor, 1976), pp. 43-49; Jon Paulien, *The Deep Things of God* (Hagerstown, MD: Review and Herald, 2004), p. 126; Jacques B. Doukhan, *Secrets of Revelation: The Apocalypse through Hebrew Eyes* (Hagerstown, MD: Review and Herald, 2002), pp. 13-14.

division consists of seven introductory scenes followed by seven cycles and that it seems to be built upon the sanctuary and its services in the Hebrew Bible.[10] Specifically, he suggests:

Prologue (1:1-8)
1. Introductory Scene (1:9-20)
    The Seven Churches (2:1–3:22)
2. Introductory Scene (4:1–5:14)
    The Seven Seals (6:1–8:1)
3. Introductory Scene (8:2-6)
    The Seven Trumpets (8:7–11:18)
4. Introductory Scene (11:19)
    The Fight of the Nations (12:1–14:20)
5. Introductory Scene (15:1-8)
    The Wrath of God (16:1–18:24)
6. Introductory Scene (19:1-10)
    The Final Judgment (19:11–20:15)
7. Introductory Scene (21:1-8)
    The New Jerusalem (21:9-22:5)
Epilogue (22:6-21)

It has also been suggested that a sevenfold division seems to be close to the author's intended structure with "repetitive and intensifying character," leading to the climactic final vision of the New Jerusalem.[11] This heptadic structure seems to be modeled after the heptadic pattern of the six days of the creation week leading to the climax of the seventh day (Gen 1:1–2:3) and after the heptadic pattern of the six speeches of the Lord for the building of the sanctuary (Exod 25–31), culminating with the seventh speech on the Sabbath commandment (Exod 31:12-17).

The book of Exodus introduces the building of the sanctuary by seven speeches of the Lord, with the Sabbath commandment as the seventh speech and the climax of the sequence (Exod 25:1; 30:11, 17, 22, 34; 31:1, 12). As pointed out by Peter J. Kearney[12] and further developed by Moshe Weinfeld,[13] the last speech links the whole sequence to the creation ac-

---

[10]Paulien, *Deep Things*, p. 126; Doukhan, *Secrets of Revelation*, pp. 13-14.

[11]Tavo, "Structure," pp. 47-68.

[12]Peter J. Kearney, "Creation and Liturgy: The P Redaction of Ex 25-40," *ZAW* 89 (1977): 375-386.

[13]Moshe Weinfeld, "Sabbath, Temple and the Enthronement of the Lord: The Problem

count (Gen 1:1–2:3). Its final words relate directly to the seven days of creation.[14] Jacob Milgrom recognizes the Sabbath in Exod 31:12-17 as the climax of creation, the divine temple in time, which God builds by Himself,[15] just as Abraham Heschel describes it in a poetic way as "a sanctuary in time."[16]

Duane Garrett recognizes the heptadic structure of Gen 1 as a literary form that is more precisely a 6 + 1 structure of the creation week.[17] Interestingly, Garrett then observes: "As a literary form, this structure reappears in only one other place. Remarkably, this place is the book of Revelation in the New Testament."[18] He points out further that Gen 1 and the book of Revelation are both visionary and alike in intent, because both give the divine view of the outer limits of world history, the beginning and the end, with a view toward its culmination. The culmination of the beginning of world history is the realization of the creation Sabbath (Gen 2:1-3), and the culmination of the end of world history is the realization of the New Jerusalem (Rev 21:9–22:5).

The climactic character of the vision of the New Jerusalem is rarely recognized in modern interpretation.[19] However, the one-word message of the seventh bowl, "it is finished" (Rev 16:17), suggests the total eradication of all who stand in God's way. The same one-word message is reiterated from the throne in Rev 21:6, thus forming an *inclusio* that delineates the events happening in between.[20] Also, the reappearance of

---

of the *Sitz im Leben* of Genesis 1:1–2:3," in *Mélanges bibliques et orientaux en l'honneur de M. Henri Cazelles*, A. Caquot and M. Delcor, eds. (Neukirchen-Vluyn: Neukirchener Verlagsgesellschaft, 1981), pp. 501-512.

[14]"In six days the Lord made heaven and earth, and on the seventh day he rested, and was refreshed" (Exod 31:17, NRSV; cf. Gen 2:2).

[15]Jacob Milgrom, *Leviticus 23–27: A New Translation with Introduction* (New York: Doubleday, 2001), p. 2285. Cf. Gerald J. Janzen, *Exodus* (Louisville, KY: Westminster John Knox, 1997), p. 224. The Sabbath as the climax of Exod 25-31 signifies that the sanctuary is depicted as a microcosm of the whole creation. Just as the six days of creation reach their climax in the seventh day, the new world, architecturally represented by the sanctuary, has its climax in the Sabbath.

[16]Abraham J. Heschel, *The Sabbath: Its Meaning for Modern Man* (New York: Wolff, 1951), p. 29.

[17]Duane A. Garrett, *Rethinking Genesis* (Grand Rapids, MI: Baker, 1991), p. 192.

[18]Ibid.

[19]Tavo, "Structure," pp. 54-55; Jan Lambrecht, "A Structuration of Revelation 4, 1-22, 5," in *L'Apocalypse johannique et l' Apocalyptique dans le Nouveau Testament*, J. Lambrecht, ed. (Leuven: University Press, 1980), pp. 77-104.

[20]Tavo, "Structure," p. 59.

one of the bowl angels in Rev 21:9 implies that what the angel showed the apostle John in Rev 17:1 has now run its course in history, and Rev 21:9 marks a new starting point. This is confirmed by the antithetical parallelism between Babylon depicted as a harlot (Rev 17:1-6) and the New Jerusalem portrayed as a bride (Rev 21:9-11). Thus, the final vision of the New Jerusalem cannot be seen as part of the seven bowls, as J. Lambrecht argues,[21] but as the expected destiny of a world that is finally cleansed of all evil. A first-century hearer of the book of Revelation, who is aware of the climactic character of the Sabbath in the creation account (Gen 1:1–2:3) and of the seventh speech concerning the Sabbath in the instructions given for the construction of the wilderness sanctuary (Exod 25–31), would probably detect in the final vision of the book of Revelation concerning the New Jerusalem the climax of the whole book.

Chiastic Structure of the Book of Revelation

Elisabeth Schüssler Fiorenza suggests a concentric structure of the book of Revelation with an A-B-A pattern.[22] David Barr, who views the book of Revelation as a story to be heard, not a text to be studied, shows that a concentric structure is inherent to the book in order to be understood by a first-century audience.[23] Following K. A. Strand's chiastic structure of the book of Revelation,[24] Paulien suggests that the center of the chiasm be Rev 12–14 and observes that "this section, with its messages from three angels, is what the whole structure works toward and away from. It is the key to understanding the whole book. And the center of the center is the three angels' messages (Rev 14:6-12)."[25] This very passage, calling on people to fear God and to worship the Creator, contains, as we shall argue in a moment, a direct allusion to the Sabbath commandment of the book of Exodus (Exod 20:8-11; 31:12-17).

Thus, both the sevenfold division and the chiastic structure of the book of Revelation suggest that the theological concept of the Sabbath

---

[21]Lambrecht, "Structuration," p. 103.

[22]Schüssler Fiorenza, Book of Revelation, p. 175.

[23]David L. Barr, Tales of the End: A Narrative Commentary on the Book of Revelation (Santa Rosa, CA: Polebridge, 1998), p. 149. Barr identifies a letter frame, a vision report frame, a letter scroll, a worship scroll, and a war scroll. The worship scroll (4:1-11:18) forms the heart and center of the work.

[24]Kenneth A. Strand, "Foundational Principles of Interpretation," in Symposium on Revelation—Book I (Silver Spring, MD: Biblical Research Institute, 1992), pp. 35-49.

[25]Paulien, Deep Things, 122; see also Jon Paulien, "Seals and Trumpets: Some Current Discussions," in Symposium on Revelation—Book I, pp. 183-198.

seems to be an underlying element in its structure and a central thematic principle. As the principle for the center of the book, it points to the Ten Commandments and particularly to the Sabbath commandment. The sevenfold division of the book of Revelation seems to draw on the structure of the creation account and on the outline of the seven speeches of the Lord that culminates in the Sabbath commandment of Exod 31:12-17, which in turn points to the actual realization of the building of the sanctuary in Exod 40, a chapter that clearly employs Creation-Sabbath language.[26]

The Number Seven

It has been observed that, from the most remote times, the number seven has had symbolic value.[27] The Sumerians, Babylonians, Canaanites, and Israelites regarded the number seven as the symbol of totality and perfection.[28] During the intertestamental period, number symbolism, especially of the number seven, was very popular.[29] As we already indicated, Carol Newsom has attested to the similarities between the *Songs of the Sabbath Sacrifice* and the book of Revelation based on the use of the number seven. She explains that its prominence is derived from the number of the Sabbath day.[30] In the New Testament, the number seven occurs a total of 88 times, 55 of which are found in the book of Revelation. There are seven lampstands, seven stars, seven seals, seven spirits, seven angels, seven plagues, seven horns, seven mountains, etc. John molded the book of Revelation around the number seven.

Even more intriguing is the sevenfold occurrence of the designation *Christ*,[31] the 14 occurrences of *Jesus*, the 28 occurrences of the word *Lamb*

---

[26]Note the parallels: "*God saw all that He had made, and behold, it was very good. And there was evening and there was morning, the sixth day. Thus the heavens and the earth were completed, and all their hosts. By the seventh day God completed His work which He had done*, and He rested on the seventh day from all His work, which He had done. Then *God blessed the seventh day* and sanctified it, because in it He rested from all His work which God had created and made" (Gen 1:31–2:3, NASB). "And Moses examined all the work and behold, they had done it; just as the LORD had commanded, this they had done. So *Moses blessed them*" (Exod 39:43, NASB). "*Thus Moses finished the work*" (Exod 40:33, NASB).

[27]Doukhan, *Secrets of Revelation*, p. 27.

[28]See, Otto, "*Šebaʿ*," *TDOT*, vol. 14, pp. 344-360.

[29]Doukhan, *Secrets of Revelation*, p. 27.

[30]Newsom, "Songs of the Sabbath Sacrifice," p. 1139; Shea, "Sabbath Hymns," p. 406.

[31]Revelation 1:1, 2, 5; 11:15; 12:10; 20:4, 6. See Richard Bauckham, *The Climax of Prophecy: Studies on the Book of Revelation* (Edinburgh: Clark, 1993), pp. 30-31, for this

referring to Christ, the sevenfold use of the declaration *I am coming*,[32] the seven occurrences of significant divine titles,[33] and the seven beatitudes scattered throughout the book of Revelation.[34]

Richard Bauckham shows that John has deliberately used certain words and phrases either four times, seven times, 14 times, or 28 times to convey theological truth.[35] Gregory Beale supports this observation, saying that "these patterns involve the Apocalypse's most crucial theological and anthropological terms."[36] Within the context of Scripture, this frequent use of the number seven as the number of completeness and fullness justifies the suggestion that, through it, the writer of Revelation may be alluding to the seventh-day Sabbath.

II. Linguistic Indicators for the Concept of the Sabbath

"The Lord's Day" in Revelation 1:10

John makes three basic statements before he describes his first vision. First, defines the specific place where he received the heavenly visions ("[I] was on the island called Patmos," Rev 1:9); then the cause for his stay on the island of Patmos ("because of the word of God and the testimony of Jesus," Rev 1:9); and also the specific time when he heard the loud voice behind him ("I was in the Spirit on the Lord's day," Rev 1:10, NASB). Patmos kept him as a prisoner, but in the Spirit he was free on "the Lord's day" to hear the voice and to see the Lord. The Greek phrase *tē kuriakē hēmera* ("the Lord's day") is unique in the biblical text and, consequently, different interpretations have been given to it, among which are the following:

1. *Sunday*. The vast majority of commentaries interpret the phrase "the Lord's day" as a reference to Sunday, the day of worship on which Christians allegedly gathered to read the book of Revelation.[37] There is

---

and for the further examples which follow.

[32]Revelation 2:5, 16; 3:11; 16:15; 22:7, 12, 20.

[33]Titles: "I am the Alpha and the Omega" (1:8); "I am the first and the last" (1:17); "I am the Alpha and the Omega, the beginning and the end" (21:6); "I am the Alpha and the Omega, the first and the last, the beginning and the end" (22:13).

[34]Revelation 1:3; 14:13; 16:15; 19:9; 20:6; 22:7, 14.

[35]Bauckham, *Climax of Prophecy*, p. 30.

[36]Gregory K. Beale, *The Book of Revelation* (Grand Rapids, MI: Eerdmans, 1999), p. 62.

[37]Beate Kowalski, "Das Verhältnis von Theologie und Zeitgeschichte in den Sendschreiben der Johannes-Offenbarung," in *Theologie als Vision: Studien zur Johannes-Offenbarung*, K. Backhaus, ed. (Stuttgart: Katholisches Bibelwerk, 2001), pp. 54-76; Heinz

no question that Sunday became known as "the Lord's day" during the late second century A.D.[38] However, the question is whether Sunday was known as "the Lord's day" during the first century A.D. and whether John meant Sunday when he used this phrase. The fact is that there is no first-century biblical or extra-biblical evidence to support the interpretation of "the Lord's day" as Sunday. On the contrary, the New Testament consistently refers to Sunday as "the first day of the week"[39] and not as "the Lord's day." The Gospel of John specifically refers to Sunday as "the first day of the week." Thus, it would have been strange if "the Lord's day" meant Sunday in the book of Revelation.

2. *The Emperor's Day*. A second interpretation holds that "the Lord's day" refers to the Roman emperor's day.[40] Inscriptions confirm that the Roman emperor claimed the title *kurios* ("lord") and had a day devoted to imperial honor. However, the question is whether John would refer to the emperor's day as "the Lord's day" during a time when Christians were persecuted for refusing to call the emperor *kurios* or to worship him.[41] One interpretation that could justify "the Lord's day" as referring to the Roman emperor's day would be to see literary features such as irony and parody utilized in the book of Revelation in order to destabilize and demystify the oppressive social and religious order of the ancient Roman Empire.[42] However, this interpretation implies that the phrase "the Lord's day" would then occur in the book of Revelation to divert attention from the emperor cult, whose day of worship was Sunday, and to point deliberately to the Sabbath as "the Lord's day" of worship instituted in creation and promoted by the law of God (Exod 20:8-11).

3. *Easter Sunday*. A third interpretation views "the Lord's day" as Easter Sunday, an annual event.[43] However, the evidence for this interpreta-

---

Giesen, *Die Offenbarung des Johannes* (Regensburg: Pustet, 1997), p. 85.

[38] "The Gospel of Peter," in *New Testament Apocrypha*, vol. 1, Wilhelm Schneemelcher, ed., (Philadelphia, PA: Westminster, 1963-1966), p. 224.

[39] Matt 28:1; Mark 16:2; Luke 24:1; John 20:1, 19; Acts 20:7; 1 Cor 16:2.

[40] James Moffat, "The Revelation of St. John the Divine," in *The Expositor's Greek Testament*, vol. 5 (Grand Rapids, MI: Eerdmans, 1961), p. 342; Robert H. Charles, *The Revelation of St. John*, vol. 1 (Edinburgh: Clark, 1920), p. 23; George R. Beasley-Murray, *The Book of Revelation* (Grand Rapids, MI: Eerdmans, 1981), p. 65.

[41] Ranko Stefanovic, *Revelation of Jesus Christ: Commentary on the Book of Revelation* (Berrien Springs, MI: Andrews University Press, 2002), p. 90.

[42] Harry O. Maier, *Apocalypse Recalled: The Book of Revelation after Christendom* (Minneapolis, MN: Fortress, 2002), pp. 166, 181.

[43] For a discussion of this possibility see, Lawrence T. Geraty, "The Pascha and the Origin of Sunday Observance," *AUSS* 3 (1965): 85-96; and Kenneth A. Strand, "Another

tion does not derive from the biblical text but from the writings of the church fathers of the second century A.D. when Easter Sunday was designated as "the Lord's day." Reading back into Revelation practices from the second century is methodologically not sound.

4. *The Eschatological Day of the Lord.* A fourth interpretation comes to the conclusion that Rev 1:10 speaks of the eschatological "day of the Lord" of the Hebrew Bible (e.g., Joel 2:11, 31; Amos 5:18-20; Zeph 1:14; and Mal 4:5).[44] It has been suggested that "John was led in vision to witness the eschatological time of God by observing the events in history . . . leading toward the climactic event of the Second Coming."[45] David Aune questions this interpretation by asking why the author did not use the more common expression *hēmera tou kuriou*, which occurs frequently in the LXX and refers to the eschatological day of the Lord, instead of *tē kuriakē hēmera*.[46]

5. *The Sabbath.* The interpretation of "the Lord's day" as the seventh-day Sabbath is supported by the fact that the Sabbath is designated by the Lord as "my holy day" and "the holy day of the Lord" (Isa 58:13; cf. Exod 16:25; 20:10). Furthermore, the expression "the Lord's day" sounds very similar to Jesus' words in all three of the Synoptic Gospels: "The Son of Man is Lord of the Sabbath" (Matt 12:8, NIV; Mark 2:27-28; Luke 6:5), signifying the seventh-day Sabbath. In this regard, Josephine Ford comes to the conclusion that, in John's time, "most probably the Christians would still be keeping the Sabbath, the seventh day."[47]

The reference to the Sabbath in Rev 1:10 validates the use and presence of Sabbath theology throughout the book. In other words, since the vision was received during the Sabbath, it would not be strange at all for the message of the book to be developed against the background of Sabbath theology. This Sabbath consciousness on the part of the author provided the conceptual structure for the book based on the number seven. Besides, the explicit reference to the Sabbath in that verse makes it unnecessary for the biblical writer to explicitly mention the Sabbath again. One could even suggest that the literal Sabbath mentioned at the

---

Look at 'Lord's Day' in the Early Church and in Rev. 1.10," *NTS* 13 (1966–1967): 174-181.

[44]William Milligan, *The Book of Revelation* (Cincinnati, OH: Jennings & Graham, 1889), p. 13; Samuele Bacchiocchi, *From Sabbath to Sunday: A Historical Investigation of the Rise of Sunday Observance in Early Christianity* (Rome: Pontifical Gregorian University, 1977), pp. 123-131.

[45]Stefanovic, *Revelation of Jesus Christ*, p. 91.

[46]David E. Aune, *Revelation 1–5* (Waco, TX: Nelson, 1997), p. 84.

[47]Josephine Massyngberde Ford, *Revelation* (New York: Doubleday, 1975), p. 384.

beginning of the book points to the coming re-creation—the new heaven and new earth (21:1)—recorded at the end of the book. The one does not exclude the value and significance of the other.

The Sabbath Allusion in Revelation 14:7

Jon Paulien suggests that "at the decisive centerpoint of Revelation's description of the final crisis is a direct allusion to Exod 20."[48] To substantiate this point, he identifies verbal, thematic, and structural parallels between Rev 14:7 and the Sabbath commandment in Exod 20:8-11. Acknowledging that the linguistic connection could also be to Ps 146:6, he rejects this possibility on the grounds of thematic parallel. Exod 20 and Rev 14:6 provide a reason for obedience. According to Exod 20:1, obedience is a response to God's redemption from Egypt. In Rev 14:6, the motivation is the eternal gospel. Another motivation for obedience is judgment, referred to in Exod 20:5 and Rev 14:7. Finally, there is the motivation that results from knowing that God is our Creator. This is provided by the Sabbath commandment itself (Exod 20:11) and by the allusion to it in Rev 14:7. Then there are the structural parallels within Rev 12–14 with a particular emphasis on the commandments of God.[49] We can safely conclude that "there is no direct allusion to the Old Testament in the book of Revelation that is more certain than the allusion to the fourth commandment in Rev 14:7."[50] According to Rev 12:17 and 14:12, the remnant are identified as those who keep the commandments of God. The allusion to the Sabbath commandment in 14:7 indicates that they also pay particular attention to the seventh-day Sabbath.

III. Summary and Conclusions

The Sabbath commandment is never mentioned in Revelation, but its theological content seems to be present in its sevenfold division that culminates in the vision of the New Jerusalem. Also relevant is the chiastic structure of the book, having at its center an allusion to the Sabbath commandment (Rev 14:7), as well as the prominent use of the number seven as a number of completeness and sabbatical fulfillment, and specific Sabbath language and allusions. Reading this material through the lens of the Sabbath is not speculative because of the explicit reference to

---

[48] Jon Paulien, "Revisiting the Sabbath in the Book of Revelation," *JATS* 9 (1998): 183.
[49] Ibid., pp. 183-185.
[50] Ibid., p. 185.

the Sabbath in Rev 1:10 and the direct allusion to it in Rev 14:7. The chiastic structure focusing on the Sabbath of the fourth commandment makes clear that the issue marks the fundamental crisis of humanity in relation to its Creator. The focal point of the book of Revelation is an angel's call for a change in perspective, for a transformation of the heart in harmony with the spirit of the Sabbath. Here the Sabbath reveals divine law and divine love in the context of the everlasting gospel proclaimed by God's end-time remnant people.

CHAPTER VIII

IDENTIFYING MARKS OF THE END-TIME REMNANT IN THE BOOK OF REVELATION

Gerhard Pfandl
Associate Director
Biblical Research Institute
Silver Spring, MD

The existence of an end-time remnant is clearly taught in Rev 12. The chapter provides an overview of the history of God's faithful followers, symbolized by a woman who goes to the wilderness for a period of 1260 days or three and a half times. There she is cared for and nourished spiritually by God (vv. 6, 14). Using the historicist method of interpretation,[1] Seventh-day Adventists believe that the 1260 prophetic days refer to the period of papal supremacy from the sixth to the end of the eighteenth century (A.D. 538–1798),[2] during which many of God's people were oppressed, persecuted, and killed. In Rev 12:17, after the fulfilment of the prophetic period of 1260 days, i.e., in the nineteenth century,[3] Satan is described as directing his attack at the remnant of the woman's seed— the end-time remnant people of God.[4]

---

[1] See William H. Shea, *Selected Studies on Prophetic Interpretation* (Silver Spring, MD: Biblical Research Institute, 1992), pp. 67-110; Alberto Timm, "Miniature Symbolization and the Year-Day Principle of Prophetic Interpretation," *AUSS* 42.1 (Spring 2004): 149-167; Gerhard Pfandl, "The Pre-Advent Judgment: Fact or Fiction?" (Part 1), *Ministry* (Dec 2003): 20-23.

[2] See F. D. Nichol, ed., "Revelation," in *AdvBibComm*, vol. 7, p. 809; C. Mervyn Maxwell, *God Cares*, vol. 2 (Nampa, ID: Pacific Press, 1985), p. 328; William H. Shea, "Time Prophecies of Daniel 12 and Revelation 12–13" in *Symposium on Revelation—Book I*, Frank B. Holbrook, ed. (Silver Spring, MD: Biblical Research Institute, 1992), p. 360.

[3] The time frame of Revelation 12 is explained by Ekkehardt Mueller, "The End-Time Remnant in Revelation" *JATS* 11/1-2 (2000): 196-197.

[4] See Gerhard F. Hasel, "The Remnant in Scripture and the End Time," *AdvA* (Fall 1988): 5-12, 62-64; Gerhard Pfandl, "The Remnant Church and the Spirit of Prophecy" in *Symposium on Revelation—Book II*, Frank B. Holbrook, ed. (Silver Spring, MD: Biblical Research Institute, 1992), pp. 295-333; *idem*, "The Remnant Church," *JATS* 8/1-2 (1997): 19-27; Ranko Stefanovic, *Revelation* (Berrien Springs, MI: Andrews University Press, 2002), p. 395.

I. Essential Characteristics of the Remnant

Several specific and essential identifying marks of the end-time remnant are found in Rev 12–14: (1) They keep the commandments of God (12:17); (2) they have the testimony of Jesus (12:17); (3) they are a persevering people (14:12); (4) they have the faith of Jesus (14:12); and (5) they proclaim a specific message—the three angels' messages.[5] We will explore the significance of those characteristics in detail.

Keep the Commandments of God

The word *entolē* (commandment) is primarily used in the New Testament for divine commandments. There are only a few cases in which it refers to human commandments (Luke 15:29; John 11:57; Acts 17:15; Col 4:10; Titus 1:14). Outside of Scripture *entolē* is generally used for the command of a king.[6] In a number of New Testament texts, *entolē* clearly refers to the Ten Commandments (e.g., Matt 15:3, 6; 19:17; Mark 10:19; Rom 7:8-13). In the book of Revelation, *entolē* appears only twice (12:17; 14:12).[7] The immediate context in both chapters refers to God's people as "those who keep the commandments of God." While we are not told which commandments they keep, we can hardly go wrong in concluding that the Ten Commandments are primarily in view in both passages.[8]

We should add that in Rev 14:7, to "fear God and give glory to Him" implies a right relationship with God and obedience to His commandments. Fearing God leads one to repentance (16:9; cf. 11:3). In the Scripture, the fear of the Lord is related not only to the worship of God but also to obedience to His commandments. In other words, those who fear God are those who keep His commandments (e.g., Deut 10:12-13, 20; 11:1, 13, 22; 30:6, 16). In fact, in the Old Testament, "fear as worshipful reverence and as obedience are inseparable."[9] Thus to fear God is to take Him seriously, make a decisive turnaround in life, enter into a relationship

---

[5]The description of the 144,000 in Revelation 14:1-5 provides additional information about the remnant (see Mueller, "Remnant," p. 201, and Lehmann, "The Remnant in the Book of Revelation," in this volume.)

[6]See G. Schrenk, "*Entellomai, entolē*," *TDNT*, vol. 2, p. 546.

[7]The *Textus Receptus* has one more occurrence in Revelation 22:14, "Blessed are those who do His commandments" (KJV, NKJV) instead of "Blessed are those who wash their robes" (RSV, NIV).

[8]See Johannes Kovar, "The Remnant and God's Commandments," in this volume.

[9]Harold C. Washington, "Fear," *NIDB*, vol. 2, p. 141.

with Him, and be totally committed. God is then glorified through a life characterized by obedience to His commandments.[10]

The Decalogue, "as a summary of the Torah, defined the quality of a sanctified life before God. The Sabbath commandment, in turn, is the sign of a proper awareness of sanctification."[11] Thus, the first identifying mark of the end-time remnant is their loyalty to God's commandments. In the time of the apostles, (the early church), keeping the Sabbath would not have been a special mark because they all kept the Sabbath;[12] today, when most Christians keep Sunday, keeping the Sabbath commandment has indeed become a distinguishing mark. Simon Kistemaker has aptly said:

> The divine commands are summarized in the Decalogue and fully revealed in the Scriptures of the Old and New Testaments. As the world increasingly turns away from the divine commands and considers them obsolete, Christians are told to keep them. They know that in observing them is a great reward (Ps 19:11). God's law endures throughout the ages, need not be amended, is relevant in all cultures, and will never be repealed.[13]

The Testimony of Jesus

The second identifying mark of God's end-time remnant is the testimony of Jesus. The phrase "the testimony of Jesus" (*tēn marturian Iēsou*) occurs six times in the book of Revelation (1:2, 9; 12:17; 19:10 [twice]; 20:4). Two grammatically possible explanations concerning its meaning have been put forward. The first view takes the last word in the phrase *tēn marturian Iēsou* as an objective genitive and interprets it as our witness to Christ.[14] Thus, the war mentioned in 12:17 refers to the

---

[10]Stefanovic, *Revelation*, p. 443.

[11]Mario Veloso, "The Law of God" in *Handbook of Seventh-Day Adventist Theology*, Raoul Dederen, ed. (Hagerstown, MD: Review and Herald, 2000), p. 463.

[12]See Walter Specht, "The Sabbath in the New Testament" in *The Sabbath in Scripture and History*, Kenneth A. Strand, ed. (Washington, DC: Review and Herald, 1982), pp. 114-129. Samuel Bacchiocchi, in his book *From Sabbath to Sunday* (Rome: Pontifical Gregorian University, 1977), has shown that it is not until the second century A.D. that we find any references to Sunday-keeping in the Christian church (see pp. 305-309).

[13]Simon J. Kistemaker, *Revelation* (Grand Rapids, MI: Baker, 2001), p. 413.

[14]M. E. Osterhaven, "Testimony," *ZPEB*, vol. 5, p. 82. See also Osborne, *Revelation*, p. 678; John J. Walvoord, *The Revelation of Jesus Christ* (Chicago: Moody Press, 1966), p. 41; Petros Vassiliades, "The Translation of *Marturia Iēsou* in Revelation," *BT* 36 (1985): 129-34; David Aune, *Revelation 17–22* (Nashville, TN: Thomas Nelson Publishers, 1998),

"persecutions against all individuals of the church who keep the commandments of God and bear testimony to Jesus."[15] This is grammatically possible, but its viability would have to be evaluated on other grounds.[16]

The second view takes *tēn marturian Iēsou* ("the testimony of Jesus") as a subjective genitive and understands the "testimony of Jesus" as the self-revelation of Jesus that moves the Christian prophets[17] or as "the truths He taught that are revealed in the New Testament."[18] Commenting on Revelation 1:2, A. A. Trites says:

> Similarly in 1:9 and 12:17 it makes excellent sense to take the genitives as subjective genitives. "The word of God and the testimony of Jesus" would then mean "the word spoken by God and the testimony borne by Jesus" (1:9), and "the commandments of God and the testimony of Jesus" would imply "the commandments of God and the testimony borne by Jesus" (12:17). The subjective genitive interpretation receives further confirmation in the explanatory words appended by the seer in 19:10: "For the testimony borne by Jesus is the spirit which inspires the prophets" (independent translation).[19]

---

pp. 1038-1039; Matin Rist, "Revelation," in *Interpreter's Bible*, vol. 12, G. A. Buttrick, ed. (Nashville, TN: Abingdon, 1957), p. 459; Morris Ashcraft, "Revelation," in *Broadman Bible Commentary*, vol. 12 (Nashville, TN: Broadman, 1972), p. 312; G. R. Beasley-Murray, *The Book of Revelation* (Grand Rapids, MI: Wm. B. Eerdmans, 1978), p. 206; Stephen S. Smalley, *The Revelation to John* (Downers Grove, IL: InterVarsity, 2005), p. 334.

[15]Ray F. Robbins, *The Revelation of Jesus Christ* (Nashville, TN: Broadman, 1975), p. 154.

[16]This interpretation is based partly on the view that by the time the book of Revelation was written, the word *marturia* had acquired the technical meaning of martyrdom; see Vassiliades, "Translation," p.131; William Henry Simcox, *Revelation of St. John the Divine* (Cambridge: Cambridge University, 1898), p. 117. We know that in the letter written from the Smyrnaeans to the Church of Philomelium in Phrygia in the second half of the second century A.D., called *The Martyrdom of Polycarp*, the term *martus* ("witness") was used as an equivalent to "martyr." There is no indication that such was the case when the book of Revelation was written; see J. Massyngberde Ford, *Revelation* (New York: Doubleday, 1975), p. 374; and A. A. Trites, "*Martus* and Martyrdom in the Apocalypse," *NovT* 15 (1973): 80. On the topic of *martus* and "martyrs," see F. Kattenbusch, "Der Märtyrertitel" *ZNW* 4 (I903): 111-127; T. W. Manson, "Martyrs and Martyrdom," *BJRL* 39 (1956–1957): 463-484; Ernst Lohmeyer, "Die Idee des Martyriums im Judentum und Urchristentum," *ZST* 5 (1927–1928): 232-249.

[17]James Moffatt, "Revelation of St. John the Divine," in *Expositor's Greek Testament*, vol. 5, W. Robertson Nicoll, ed. (Grand Rapids, MI: Eerdmans, 1980), p. 465. See also Stefanovic, *Revelation*, pp. 392-393.

[18]John MacArthur, *Revelation 12–22* (Chicago, IL: Moody, 2000), p. 34.

[19]Trites, "Martyrdom," p. 75.

Finally, we note that many commentators do not take an either/or position. Rather, they consider *tēn marturia Iēsou* in some texts to be an objective genitive and in other texts a subjective genitive,[20] or as a combination of both.[21]

Use of *Marturia* in John's Gospel and in His Epistles

To determine the correct meaning of the phrase *tēn marturian Iēsou*, it would be helpful to ascertain how John used the word *marturia* in his Gospel and in his letters. The scriptural evidence clearly indicates the following:[22]

1. *Marturia* is used 21 times in John's Gospel and in his epistles. It is used 14 times in a genitive construction, and in all of them, it is a subjective genitive.
2. John never uses the noun *marturia* ("testimony, witness") with an objective genitive construction by itself to express the idea of "witness about/to." The objective idea is consistently expressed in the Gospel of John and in his epistles through the combination of the verb *martureō* ("to witness, to testify") plus the preposition *peri* ("about, concerning").[23] For example:

> To bear *witness* to the light [*martureō + peri*] (John 1:7).
> If I bear *witness* to myself [*martureō + peri*] (5:31).
> Who bears *witness* to me [*martureō + peri*] (5:32).
> He has born *witness* to his Son [*martureō + peri*] (1 John 5:9).[24]

---

[20] J. Massyngberde Ford, "For the Testimony of Jesus Is the Spirit of Prophecy," *ITQ* 42 (1975): 285; Albert Barnes, *Revelation* (Grand Rapids, MI: Baker, 2001), pp. 37, 316, 411; R. H. Charles, *Revelation of St. John*, vol. 2 (Edinburgh: T. and T. Clark, 1920), p. 7; G. E. Ladd, *A Commentary on the Revelation of John* (Grand Rapids, MI: Eerdmans, 1972), p. 265; Beasley-Murray, *Revelation*, pp. 206, 276.

[21] Louis A. Brighton, *Revelation* (St. Louis, MO: Concordia, 1999), pp. 502-503; M. Eugene Boring, *Revelation* (Louisville, KY: John Knox, 1989), p. 194; G. K. Beale, *The Book of Revelation* (Grand Rapids, MI: Eerdmans, 1999), p. 679.

[22] The term *marturia* is found in the following passages: John 1:7, 19; 3:11, 32-33; 5:31-32, 34, 36; 8:13-14, 17; 19:35; 21:24; 1 John 5:9 [three times], 10 [two times], 11; 3 John 12.

[23] A similar genitive construction is the phrase "the word of God" (*ho logon tou theou*) (John 10:35; 1 John 2:14), which always means what God Himself says, not what men say about Him.

[24] Other texts using *peri* ("about, concerning") are John 1:8, 15; 2:25; 5:36-37, 39, and 1 John 5:9-10.

3. It would be natural to expect to find in the book of Revelation the same use of *marturia* as in John's Gospel and epistles.

Marturia Iēsou in Revelation[25]

In Rev 1:2, 9; 12:17; and 20:4, the expression "testimony of Jesus" is symmetrically balanced each time with the expression "the Word of God" or the phrase "the commandments of God." In each text the genitive *tou theou* ("of God") is a subjective genitive. "The Word of God" is what God has said; "the commandments of God" are God's commandments. In the phrase "the testimony of Jesus" the genitive "of Jesus," therefore, should also be a subjective genitive.[26]

The parallelism between the "Word of God" or "the commandments of God" and "the testimony of Jesus" is vital for an understanding of the latter expression. "The Word of God" in John's time referred to the Old Testament, and the "testimony of Jesus" to what Jesus had taught in the gospels and through His prophets, such as Peter and Paul. Thus, both genitives should be taken as subjective genitives. That explains why, in Rev 19:10 John writes, "For the testimony of Jesus is the spirit of prophecy."

What is "the spirit of prophecy?" This phrase occurs only once in the Bible. Its closest parallel is found in 1 Cor 12:8-10, where Paul indicates that the Holy Spirit gives the gift of prophecy as one of the spiritual gifts. The person who receives this gift is called a prophet (1 Cor 12:28; Eph 4:11). Just as in 1 Cor 12:28, those who have the gift of prophecy are called prophets (cf. v. 10), so in Rev 22:8-9, those who have the Spirit of prophecy are called prophets (19:10).

---

[25]The linguistic differences between the Gospel and letters of John on the one hand and the Apocalypse on the other hand have led many scholars to posit a different John as the writer of the Apocalypse. The Greek of the Gospels and letters is relatively simple and normally correct, whereas in the Apocalypse, the law of concord is often disregarded. We find mixed-up genders, numbers, and cases, as well as several unusual constructions. For exhaustive examples see Charles, *Revelation*, vol. 1, pp. XXIX-XXXVII. Yet in spite of these differences, the Apocalypse has a closer affinity to the Greek of the other Johannine books than to any other New Testament book. The linguistic differences may be due to the fact that Revelation was probably written when John was alone on Patmos, whereas the Gospels and letters were written with the help of one or more fellow believers at Ephesus. See Donald Guthrie, *New Testament Introduction* (Leicester, England: InterVarsity, 1976), pp. 934-942.

[26]Massyngberde Ford, "Testimony of Jesus," p. 285. See also Isabelle Donegani, "*A Cause de la parole de Dieu et du témoignage de Jésus . . . :*" *Le témoignage selon l'Apocalypse de Jean* (Paris: J. Gabalda, 1997), pp. 360-364, 377-378.

19:10 (NKJV)	22:8-9 (NKJV)
And I fell at his feet to worship him.	I fell down to worship before the feet of the angel who showed me these things.
But he said to me, "See that you do not do that! I am your fellow servant, and of your brethren who have the testimony of Jesus. Worship God." For the testimony of Jesus is the spirit of prophecy.	Then he said to me, "See that you do not do that! For I am your fellow servant, and of your brethren the prophets, and of those who keep the words of this book. Worship God."[27]

The situation in both passages is the same. John falls at the angel's feet to worship. The words of the angel's response are almost identical, yet the difference is significant. In 19:10, the brethren are identified by the phrase "who hold [have] the testimony of Jesus." In 22:9, the brethren are simply called "prophets." Scripture is interpreting itself; therefore, the comparison should lead to the conclusion that "the spirit of prophecy" in 19:10 is not the possession of all church members in general, but only of those who have been called by God to be prophets.[28]

---

[27]Some may argue that "those who keep the words of this book" must be included in the group of those who have the testimony of Jesus. In other words, all believers have the testimony of Jesus. Some later manuscripts even omit the *kai* ("and") and link the prophets with those who keep the words of this book. In response it needs to be said that while the two passages are parallel, they are not identical. In 19:10, the angel tells John that he is his fellow servant and of the brethren who have the testimony of Jesus; i.e., the prophets like John himself. In 22:9, the angel repeats what he said in 19:10, but adds that he is also a fellow servant of those who keep the words of this book. While the genitive constructions are the same for "the prophets" (*tōn adelphōn*) and for "those keeping the words of this book" (*tōn tērountōn* . . .), there is no grammatical necessity to link the latter group with "the testimony of Jesus" in 19:10. In 22:8-9 two groups are mentioned: the prophets who, according to 19:10, have "the testimony of Jesus," and the rest of the believers who "keep the words of this book." The two groups, the prophets and the rest of the saints, are also mentioned in Rev 11:18; "Your servants the prophets and the saints;" and in 16:6 and 18:24, "the blood of saints and prophets" (see Hermann Strathmann, "Martus," *TDNT*, vol. 4, p. 501).

[28]This interpretation is sustained by some non-Adventist scholars. For example, the Lutheran scholar Hermann Strathmann says: "According to the parallel 22:9 the brothers referred to are not believers in general, but the prophets. Here, too, they are characterized as such. This is the point of verse 10c. If they have the *marturia Iēsou*, they have the spirit of prophecy, i.e., they are prophets, like the angel, who simply stands in the service of *marturia Iēsou*" ("*Martus*," p. 501; see also Richard Bauckham, *The Climax of Prophecy* [Edinburgh: T. and T. Clark, 1993], p. 162). Similarly, James Moffatt explains: "'For the

The Witness of the Targumim[29]

Jewish readers in John's day knew what was meant by the expression "spirit of prophecy." They would have understood the expression as a reference to the Holy Spirit, who imparts the prophetic gift to humans. Rabbinic Judaism equated the Old Testament expressions "Holy Spirit," "Spirit of God," and "Spirit of Yahweh" with "the spirit of prophecy."[30] This can be seen in the frequent occurrence of this phrase in the Targumim:

> Thereupon the Pharaoh said to his servants, "Can we find a man like this in whom there is *the spirit of prophecy from before the Lord?* (Gen 41:38).[31]

> Now two men had remained behind in the camp—one's name was Eldad; the other's name was Medad, yet *the spirit of prophecy* rested upon them though they were listed [among the elders], but they had not gone out of the tent and prophesied in the camp (Num 11:14-15).

> Then the Lord said to Moses, "Take Joshua, son of Nun, a man who has within himself the *spirit of prophecy*, and lay your hand on him" (Num 27:18).[32]

---

testimony or witness of (i.e., borne by) Jesus is (i.e., constitutes) the spirit of prophecy.' This prose marginal comment specifically defines the brethren who hold the testimony of Jesus as possessors of prophetic inspiration. The testimony of Jesus is practically equivalent to Jesus testifying (xxii. 20). It is the self-revelation of Jesus (according to 1:1, due ultimately to God) which moves the Christian prophets (Moffat, "Revelation," vol. 5, p. 465). Donegani, *Témoingnage de Jésus*, p. 380, concludes that the phrase "Spirit of prophecy" refers to the Spirit that inspired the prophets (p. 360), but extends its meaning to include not only the Christian prophets but also the collective testimony of the Christian church (p. 380). As we will show, her ecclesiological interpretation cannot be supported by the use of the verb "have" or by the use of the phrase "Spirit of prophecy" in other extra-biblical literature.

[29]Targumim is the plural of targum, an Aramaic term meaning "translation, interpretation." It refers specifically to the Aramaic translations of the Old Testament which came into use after the Babylonian exile, when Hebrew was no longer understood by many Jews.

[30]E. Sjöberg, "*Rûaḥ* in Palestinian Judaism," *TDNT*, vol. 6, p. 382.

[31]Bernard Grossfeld, *Targum Onqelos to Genesis*, The Aramaic Bible, vol. 6, K. Cathart, M. Maher, M. McNamara, eds. (Collegeville, MN: Liturgical, 1988), p. 138.

[32]*Idem*, *The Targum Onqelos to Leviticus and the Targum Onqelos to Numbers*, The Aramaic Bible, vol. 8, K. Cathart, M. Maher, M. McNamara, eds. (Collegeville, MN: Liturgical, 1988), pp. 102, 145 (italics in the original). Other occurrences of the term

Sometimes the term "spirit of prophecy" simply refers to the Holy Spirit, but in many cases it refers to the gift of prophecy given by the Holy Spirit. This is particularly the case in the Old Testament. Commenting on the use of this expression in the Targumim, J. P. Schäfer says:

> Thence, first of all it proves that the term "Spirit of prophecy" is closer to the MT than the term "Holy Spirit." Moreover an examination of the verses where TO [Targum Onqelos] uses the term "Spirit of prophecy" shows that in almost all cases there is a direct relationship to the prophecy in the biblical context. The translation "Spirit of prophecy," although not in the strictest sense literal, is almost always stipulated through the MT (Gen. 41:38—Joseph had the "Spirit of prophecy" because he was able to interpret Pharaoh's dream; Num. 11:25—The Spirit that settled on the 70 Elders, according to the MT, brought about "prophesying"; Num. 24:2—Bileam prophesied concerning Israel). In other words, the term "Spirit of prophecy" describes a clearly delineated situation, namely, the Holy Spirit sent from God who imparts the prophetic gift to man.[33]

F. F. Bruce comes to the same conclusion, saying:

> The expression "the Spirit of prophecy" is current in post-biblical Judaism: it is used, for example, in a targumic circumlocution for the Spirit of Yahweh which comes upon this or that prophet. Thus the Targum of Jonathan renders the opening words of Isaiah 61:1 as "The Spirit of prophecy from before the Lord God is upon me." The thought expressed in Revelation 19:10 is not dissimilar to that already quoted from 1 Peter 1:11, where "the Spirit of Christ" is said to have borne advanced testimony in the Old Testament prophets. There too Jesus is the theme of the witness borne by the prophetic Spirit; the prophets did not know who the person was or what the time would be, but at last the secret is out: the person is Jesus; the time is now.

"spirit of prophecy" are found in the Targumim of Num 11:25; 24:2; Judg 3:10; 1 Sam 10:6; 19:20, 23; 2 Sam 23:2; 1 Kgs 22:24; 2 Chr 15:1; 18:22-23; 20:14; 24:20; Ps 51:13; Isa 11:2; 40:13; 61:1; Ezek 11:5, 24; 37:1; Mic 3:8 (Hermann L. Strack and Paul Billerbeck, *Kommentar zum Neuen Testament aus Talmud und Midrasch*, 2 vol. [München: Beck'sche Verlagsbuchhandlung, 1924], p. 129).

[33] J. P. Schäfer, "Die Termini 'Heiliger Geist' und 'Geist der Prophetie' in den Targumim und das Verhältnis der Targumim zueinander," *VT* 20 (1970): 310 (my translation).

In Revelation 19:10, however, it is through Christian prophets that the Spirit of prophecy bears witness. What the prophets of pre-Christian days foretold is proclaimed as an accomplished fact by the prophets of the new age, among whom John occupies a leading place.[34]

Thus we can say that in Rev 12:17, the second mark of the remnant church is "the testimony of Jesus," which is the spirit of prophecy or the prophetic gift. This gift is present among the end-time remnant.[35]

The Meaning of *echō*

This interpretation is strengthened by a study of the Greek word *echō*, meaning "to have" or "to hold." The question is, what is "the testimony which they held"? Is it the witness they received and held onto under adverse circumstances,[36] or is it the witness they bore under the same circumstances?[37] Those who accept the latter interpretation usually think it refers to all martyrs (Christian or pre-Christian). But can the phrase be interpreted to mean "bear testimony"?

The lexical meaning of *echō* in its active transitive form is "to have, to hold, to have as one's possession."[38] Further it can mean to bring about, cause, consider or "have the possibility, can, be able, be in a position."[39] The middle participle of *echō* in the New Testament means "to hold oneself fast, to cling to."[40] The closest we come to the idea of "bearing some-

---

[34] F. F. Bruce, *The Time is Fulfilled* (Grand Rapids, MI: Eerdmans, 1978), pp. 105-106.

[35] Ellen G. White also interprets the phrase "the testimony of Jesus" in terms of "the spirit of prophecy" but places the emphasis on its content; see Rodríguez, "The Testimony of Jesus in the Writings of Ellen G. White," in this volume.

[36] Wilhelm Bousset, *Die Offenbarung des Johannes* (Göttingen: Vandenhoeck and Ruprecht, 1906), p. 270; Friedrich Düsterdieck, *Critical and Exegetical Handbook to the Revelation of John* (New York: Funk and Wagnalls, 1887), p. 229; I. T. Beckwith, *The Apocalypse of John* (Eugene, OR: Wipf and Stock, 2001), p. 526; Robert H. Mounce, *The Book of Revelation* (Grand Rapids, MI: Eerdmans, 1977), p. 158; Charles, *Revelation*, vol. 1, p. 174; Simcox, *Revelation*, p. 44; Ladd, *Revelation*, p. 104.

[37] NEB, Berkeley, REB, and the Jerusalem Bible translate it this way, and several commentators adopt this reading, e.g., Barnes, *Revelation*, p. 316; A. Plummer, *Revelation* (London: Funk and Wagnalls, n. d.), p. 188; Martin Kiddle, *The Revelation of St. John* (London: Hodder and Stoughton, 1940), p. 118; Beasley-Murray, *Revelation*, p. 135; Massyngberde Ford, *Revelation*, p. 96.

[38] Walter Bauer, Wm. F. Arndt, F. Wilbur Gingrich, and William Danker, *A Greek-English Lexicon of the New Testament and Other Early Christian Literature* (Chicago, IL: University of Chicago, 2000), pp. 420-422.

[39] Ibid.

[40] Ibid., p. 422.

Identifying Marks of the End-Time Remnant in the Book of Revelation 149

thing" is when the verb is used to mean "wearing clothing/weapons/covering" (Matt 3:4; 22:12; 1 Cor 11:4; Rev 9:9, 17; John 18:10). Even in those cases the basic idea is that of having.[41]

In Rev 6:9, *echō* is written in the imperfect tense, active voice, third person plural. The meaning, therefore, can be only "to have" or "to hold," not "to bear." For it to mean "they bore their own testimony," we would expect the verb *martureō* ("to witness, testify") or some compound form of it.[42] Since this is not the case, we conclude that their "testimony was not primarily their witness about Jesus but the witness they had received from Him (cf. 12:17; 20:4)."[43] They had accepted it, they refused to give it up, and, consequently, they were put to death. The "testimony," no less than the "word," was an objective possession of the martyrs.[44]

This interpretation is in harmony with the parallelism of "the Word of God" and "the testimony of Jesus" found in other places:

Rev 1:2: "Who bore witness to *the word of God*, and to *the testimony of Jesus Christ*, to all things that he saw."

Rev 1:9: "I, John, both your brother and companion in the tribulation and kingdom and patience of Jesus Christ, was on the island that is called Patmos for the *word of God* and for *the testimony of Jesus Christ*."

---

[41]Henry G. Liddell and Robert Scott, *A Greek-English Lexicon*, rev. ed. (Oxford: University Press, 1958), pp. 749-750, give hundreds of references for the active transitive form of *echō* with the same meaning as given by Bauer, Arndt, Gingrich, and Danker, *A Greek-English Lexicon*. In the middle form they give four references where *echō* means "to bear" or "to hold for oneself" something concrete; for example, a shield (pp. 749-750). Liddell and Scott (pp. 750-751) also cite a second word *echō* which is found in a Cyprian inscription which mentions an offering that is "brought" (*echō*). Nowhere do we find *echō* with the abstract meaning "to bear a testimony." David Hill comments, "If *he marturia Iēsou* means 'witness to Jesus,' the verb *echō* is a quite unusual one (even in the Greek of this book) to connote the bearing of that witness by Christians" ("Prophecy and Prophets in the Revelation of St. John," *NTS* 18 [1971–1972]: 411).

[42]For example, *summartureō* "to testify" or "bear witness."

[43]Mounce, *Revelation*, p. 158.

[44]Charles, *Revelation*, vol. 1, p. 174. See also Bousset, *Offenbarung*, p. 270. In his book *Light for the Last Days* (Nampa, ID: Pacific Press, 1999), Hans K. LaRondelle argues that the witness which the martyrs had (*echō*) in Rev 6:9 is identical to the "testimony of Jesus" in Rev 12:17 (pp. 180-181), but this is incorrect. In 6:9, the martyrs have their own testimony which they hold; in 12:17, the remnant has (*echō*) the "testimony of Jesus" (subjective genitive). Revelation 12:17 does not refer to the remnant's testimony but to Jesus' testimony to the remnant.

Rev 20:4: "And I saw the souls of those who had been beheaded because of *the testimony of Jesus* and because of *the word of God*, and those who had not worshiped the beast or his image, and had not received the mark upon their forehead and upon their hand; and they came to life and reigned with Christ for a thousand years." (NKJV; emphasis mine)

This interpretation is also in harmony with the grammatical sense of *echō* ("to have, to hold"). In Rev 12:17, the remnant church has "the testimony of Jesus"; in 17:1 and 21:9, the seven angels have or hold "the seven bowls"; and in 19:10 the fellow servants of the angel also have "the testimony of Jesus." Throughout the book of Revelation, the verb *echō* always means "to have" or "to hold."

A Persevering People
The third characteristic of the remnant church is that they have "the patience (*hupomonē*) of the saints (*tōn hagiōn*)" (Rev 14:12, NKJV). Revelation 14 can be divided into four sections:

1. God's redeemed people (14:1-5)
2. The three angels' messages (14:6-2)
3. The voice from heaven and a blessing (14:13)
4. The harvest of the earth at the Second Coming (14:14-20)

Revelation 14 begins with John's vision of the remnant standing on Mount Zion. They follow the Lamb wherever He goes (v. 5). Then John is taken back in time to the events that lead up to what he has seen (vv. 1-5), the proclamation of the three angels' messages (vv. 6-12) and the Second Coming (vv. 14-20). In verse 12 he provides another outstanding characteristic of the remnant, namely, that they have the "patience" (*hupomonē*) of the saints.

In classical Greek the word *hupomonē* ("patience") described one of the Greek virtues and meant "to hold out," or to show "courageous endurance which manfully defies evil."[45] In the Old Testament, however, the focus of endurance is not so much on evil powers but on God. In the LXX, therefore, where the noun *hupomonē* appears 25 times and the verb *hupomenō* about 80 times,[46] the word is primarily used to express

---

[45] F. Hauck, "*Hupomonē*," *TDNT*, vol. 4, pp. 581-582.

[46] This includes the apocryphal books in the LXX. In the canonical books the noun *hupomonē* appears only 9 times and the verb *hupomenō* about 60 times.

the idea of waiting for God. The righteous wait upon the Lord (Pss 36:9; 37:9; Isa 8:17; 40:31; Micah 7:7); He is "the hope [Heb. *miqweh*] of Israel" (Ezra 10:2; Jer 14:8; 17:13), "the hope [Heb. *tiqwāh*] of man" (Job 14:19; Ps 9:18; Jer 31:17). "Surrounded by unrighteousness and much inward distress, the righteous know that they are protected by God and that they have only to wait for His liberating action which will bring an alleviation of their situation."[47] Thus Micah, for example, says that although "the faithful man has perished from the earth, and there is no one upright among men . . . I will look to the LORD; I will wait for the God of my salvation; My God will hear me" (7:2, 7).

In the New Testament *tēn hupomonēn tou Christou*, "the patience of Christ" (2 Thess 3:5)[48] understood as an objective genitive, continues to describe the basic attitude of the righteous exhibited in the Old Testament—they wait patiently for the coming of Christ. This would agree well with the major theme of the two letters to the Thessalonians and with 1 Thess 1:3 in particular, where Paul speaks of "your . . . patience [*hupomonē*] of hope in our Lord Jesus Christ."

If the genitive construction is taken as a subjective genitive, as most commentators understand it, then "the patience of Christ" is a reference to Christ's perseverance "who endured [*hupomonē*] the cross" and "who endured [*hupomonē*] such hostility from sinners against Himself" (Heb 12:2-3). The thought would then parallel the preceding reference to the "love of God" (*tēn agapēn tou theou*) understood as God's love for the Thessalonians. "All these things considered, the prayer most likely was a request for the Lord to guide the Thessalonians to exhibit the same perseverance Christ exhibited when He suffered persecution."[49]

The primary meaning of *hupomonē* and *hupomenō* in the New Testament, similar to the understanding of the word in classical Greek, is the steadfast endurance of the Christian under difficulties (2 Cor 1:6; 2 Thess 1:4; 2 Pet 1:6). "Unbreakable and patient endurance in face of the evil and injustice of the world is the true attitude of the Christian (1 Cor 13:7)."[50] Thus Paul rejoices in tribulation, "knowing that tribulation produces perseverance [*hupomonē*]" (Rom 5:3). In his response to the false teachers (2 Cor 1:17; 5:12), Paul commends himself as a minister of God

---

[47] Hauck, "*Hupomonē*," p. 584.

[48] The *Textus Receptus* has a similar genitive construction in Rev 1:9: *hupomonē Iēsou Christou*; the Nestle-Aland Greek text, however, reads *hupomonē en Iēsou*.

[49] D. Michael Martin, *1, 2 Thessalonians* (Nashville, TN: Broadman & Holman Publishers, 2002), p. 268.

[50] Hauck, "*Hupomonē*," p. 586.

in "much patience [*hupomonē*], in tribulations, in needs, in distress" (2 Cor 6:4). Repeatedly in 2 Corinthians Paul refers to the hardships he faced (4:8-9; 6:4-5; 11:23-29; 12:10).

The patience, endurance, or perseverance of the saints is one of the primary themes in the book of Revelation, where we have seven references to *hupomonē* (1:9; 2:2-3, 19; 3:10; 13:10; 14:12). In his introduction John describes himself as a fellow partaker in the suffering of the Christians in Asia Minor which they are able to endure in Jesus (*en Iēsou*).[51] The repetition of "in . . . in" ("in tribulation," "in Jesus") "stresses the New Testament teaching that all Christian suffering was interpreted in the early church as a participation 'in Christ' (cf. Rom. 8:17; 2 Cor. 1:5; 4:10; Phil. 3:10; Col. 1:24; 1 Pet. 4:13)."[52]

In the letters to the seven churches, *hupomonē* appears four times (Rev 2:2-3, 19; 3:10). Ephesus, Thyatira, and Philadelphia are commended for their patience and endurance. There are vertical and horizontal aspects of *hupomonē* in the messages to these churches. The vertical aspect is their faithfulness to God, in that they wait patiently upon God; the horizontal aspect is their standing up to the temptations of this world and their "patient endurance of evil."[53] In the message to Philadelphia, Christ's endurance[54] becomes the model for the endurance of the Philadelphians in their own trials (3:10).

The last two occurrences of *hupomonē* in Revelation are clearly referring to the same situation (13:10; 14:12). Both chapters deal with end-time events and describe God's people in their final struggle with God's enemies. In chapter 13, all who dwell on the earth worship the beast except those whose names are found in the book of life (v. 8); they are like their Lord, who, "when they hurled their insults at him, he did not retaliate; when he suffered, he made no threats. Instead, he entrusted himself to him who judges justly" (1 Pet 23:23, NIV).

The saints of Rev 14:12 are the same as those of Rev 13:7 against whom the satanic trinity wages war and who are called the remnant of the woman's seed (12:17). In Rev 14:12, the saints are contrasted with those who worship the beast and his image. The saints are not deceived by the miraculous phenomena associated with the worship of the beast.

---

[51]The Textus Receptus reads *hupomonē Iēsou Christou* "patience of Jesus Christ," but the Nestle-Aland text has *hupomonē en Iēsou*.

[52]Osborne, *Revelation*, p. 81.

[53]Ibid., p. 80.

[54]While some translations see *mou* as the governing "word" or "command" of Christ (NKJV, NIV), most translations understand *mou* to govern *hupomonē* rather than *logos*.

Identifying Marks of the End-Time Remnant in the Book of Revelation   153

"They are resolute in their convictions, not swayed by persuasion or coercion; above all they are loyal to their God, prepared to suffer loss, physical hardship, and even death itself to maintain their relationship with Him."[55] They patiently await the return of their Lord. *Hupomonē* in this context may best be translated as "endurance."

> Although the coming of Jesus seems delayed, although doubts and fears assail, His people never lose hope. They endure to the end. They know that He who promised is faithful and one day He will return. Buffeted by false ideas, assaulted by religious confederacy, threatened by the civil powers, they keep on waiting with steadfast loyalty.[56]

The message of these texts is clear. Satan and his demonic hosts may have their hour, but God controls the future, and believers belong to Him as long as they put their trust in Him and persevere in living out their faith by keeping God's commandments.

Keep the Faith of Jesus

The fourth mark of God's remnant people discussed in this chapter is that they keep the faith of Jesus (*tērountes . . . tēn pistin Iēsou*). The genitive "faith of Jesus" in Rev 14:12 can again be understood in two ways. If it is taken to be an objective genitive, as most commentators seem to do,[57] the meaning is that the saints remain "faithful to Jesus."[58] It is interesting to note that the first part of this text appears also in 13:10 (NKJV): "Here is the patience and the faith of the saints." If "the faith of Jesus" in 14:12 is an objective genitive (meaning "faith in Jesus"), then 13:10 and 14:12 are saying basically the same thing.

---

[55]William G. Johnsson, "The Saint's End-Time Victory Over the Forces of Evil," in *Symposium on Revelation—Book II*, p. 38.

[56]Ibid., p. 39.

[57]See Aune, *Revelation 6–16*, p. 838; Charles, *Revelation*, vol. 1, p. 369; MacArthur, Jr., *Revelation 12–22*, p. 103; Moffatt, "Revelation," p. 439; Mounce, *Revelation*, p. 277; Osborne, *Revelation*, p. 544; Pierre Prigent, *Commentary on the Apocalypse of St. John* (Tübingen: Mohr, 2004), p. 445; Smalley, *Revelation*, p. 369; Stefanovic, *Revelation*, p. 454; Beckwith, *Apocalypse*, p. 659; Philip E. Hughes, *The Book of Revelation* (Leicester, England: InterVarsity, 1990), p. 164; Margaret Barker, *The Revelation of Jesus Christ* (London: T. and T. Clark, 2000), p. 250; Robert W. Wall, *Revelation* (Peabody, MA: Hendrickson, 1991), p. 186; Alan Johnson, "Revelation," in *Expositor's Bible Commentary*, vol. 12, Frank E. Gaebelein, ed. (Grand Rapids, MI: Zondervan, 1981), p. 542.

[58]The NEB translates it, "remaining loyal to Jesus."

As a subjective genitive "the faith of Jesus" has been interpreted in various ways. According to some, *tēn pistin Iēsou* "refers first of all to *his* faithfulness, then also to the believers' faith in Jesus."[59] In contrast to the majority of interpreters, William G. Johnsson says:

> This expression does not mean that the people of God have faith in Jesus (although they do), because the faith of Jesus is something they keep. "The faith" probably refers to the Christian tradition, the body of teachings that center in Jesus. Jude 3 may provide a parallel: "the faith which was once delivered to the saints." When God's loyal followers keep the faith of Jesus they remain true to basic Christianity—they "keep the faith."[60]

Similarly, G. K. Beale calls this genitive a "genitive of source" and translates *tēn pistin Iēsou* as "faith from Jesus." He identifies the "faith of Jesus" as "the objective gospel traditions having their origin in Jesus, since it is parallel with the preceding 'commandments from God.'"[61] He further argues "that *pistis* refers to the doctrinal content of the Christian faith (cf. Jude 3) is further evident from [Rev] 2:13, where the word occurs with the same meaning."[62]

In the LXX[63] the noun *pistis* and the adjective *pistos* are used primarily to translate the Hebrew words *'emûnāh*[64] ("faithfulness, truth, faith"—1 Sam 26:23; Prov 12:17; Jer 5:1; Hab 2:4)[65] and *'āman* ("faithful, reliable"—Num 12:7; Deut 7:9; Isa 15:18), characterizing the relationship between human beings and God.[66] However, these Hebrew words do not occupy the central position that *pistis, pistos,* and *pisteuein* do in the New Testament. "Faith" is a key word in the New Testament which describes the relationship into which the gospel calls men and women—that of trust in God through Jesus Christ.

---

[59]Brighton, *Revelation*, p. 385.
[60]Johnsson, "End-Time Victory," pp. 38-39. See also Kistemaker, *Revelation*, p. 413.
[61]Beale, *Revelation*, p. 766.
[62]Ibid. This meaning is also apparent in Gal 1:23 and 1 Tim 4:1, 6.
[63]The word *pistis* appears about 60 times in the LXX (37 times in the canonical books) and more than 240 times in the New Testament.
[64]*'emûnāh* usually refers to the faithfulness of God.
[65]The verb *pisteuō* is used to translate the stem *'mn*, which in *niphal* often carries the meaning of "faithful" and in hiphil means "believe, think."
[66]Twice each *pistis* translates the word *ṣaddîq* "righteous" (Job 17:9; Prov 11:21) and *ᵉmet* "true" (Prov 14:25; Jer 42:5).

Faith or trust in God presupposes some knowledge about Him. Throughout Scripture, trust in God rests on the belief of what He has revealed concerning His character and purposes. J. I. Packer explains:

> In the NT, where faith in God is defined as trust in Christ, the acknowledgement of Jesus as the expected Messiah and the incarnate Son of God is regarded as basic to it. The writers allow that faith in some form can exist where as yet information about Jesus is incomplete (Acts 19:1 ff.), but not where his divine identity and Christhood are consciously denied (1 John 2:22 f.; 2 John 7-9); all that is possible then is idolatry (1 John 5:21), the worship of a man-made unreality.[67]

Paul repeatedly depicts faith as knowing, believing, and obeying "the truth" (Titus 1:1; 2 Thess 2:13; Rom 2:8, etc.), indicating that he regarded orthodoxy as a fundamental ingredient of faith. But faith in the New Testament is not primarily knowledge about God; rather, it is a divine gift (Eph 2:8; 2 Peter 1:1; Acts 18:27; Phil 1:29), freely given to all who are willing to receive it (Rom 8:32; 1 Cor 2:12). Human beings cannot comprehend divine realities and come to trust God without the drawing and enlightening of the Holy Spirit (John 6:44, 65; 16:13).

Most commentators simply assume that *tēn pistin Iēsou* is an objective genitive without further investigation or justification. David Aune is an exception. He admits that the phrase *tēn pistin Iēsou* in Rev 14:12 is grammatically awkward if interpreted as "faithful to Jesus" because *tērountes* "must then be understood to have two simultaneous meanings, 'obey' with *tas entolas*, 'the commandments,' and 'remain, maintain' with *tēn pistin*."[68] Nevertheless, because the phrase *pistin tērein* ("to keep faith, to remain loyal") was a common Greek expression,[69] he interprets the word "Jesus" in *tēn pistin Iēsou* as an objective genitive, so that the entire phrase means "[their] faithfulness to Jesus."[70]

While the phrase *pistin tērein* does generally have the meaning of "keeping faith" or "being loyal" to people, it also can have the more abstract meaning of keeping faith with an institution. In Polybius, for example, the Iberian commander Andobales, who revolted against the

---

[67] James I. Packer, "Faith," *BDTh*, p. 209.
[68] Aune, *Revelation 6–16*, p. 837.
[69] Polybius, *Histories* 6.56.13; 10.37.9; Josephus, *JW* 2.121; 6.345.
[70] Aune, *Revelation 6–16*, p. 838.

occupying force of the Carthaginians, is trying to convince the Roman general Scipio of his loyalty to the Roman State.[71] Thus to understand "keeping the faith" in Rev 14:12 as remaining true to Christianity is not out of harmony with the idiomatic use of the phrase "keeping faith." Therefore the phrase can be understood objectively as being faithful to Christianity and subjectively as keeping to the doctrines of Jesus. In support of the latter, there is a pronounced parallelism between Rev 12:17 and 14:12:

Rev 12:17	Rev 14:12
The remnant people	The saints
keep the commandments of God	keep the commandments of God
they have the testimony of Jesus	they keep the faith of Jesus
(subjective genitive)	(subjective genitive)

Therefore, we concur with Johnsson and Beale that "the faith of Jesus" refers primarily to the doctrinal content of the Christian faith[72] which is centered in Jesus, rather than to faith in Jesus which is usually expressed with *pisteuō* and *en*[73] or *eis*,[74] "believe in." This is also the position taken in the explanation of the Seventh-day Adventist fundamental beliefs. Referencing the term "the faith of Jesus," it says, "God's remnant people are characterized by a faith similar to that which Jesus had. . . . Their faith encompasses all the truths of the Bible—those which Christ believed and taught."[75]

The saints in Rev 14:12 in the final crisis remain firm in their loyalty to God and His Word. As Jesus kept the commandments of God by faith in Him, so His remnant will obey by faith in Jesus and keep "the faith of Jesus," i.e., they will teach what He taught, they will say what He said, and they will do what He did; they will hold firm to the faith once delivered to the saints (Jude 1:3).

---

[71] Polybius, *Histories* 10.37.9. Similarly, government employees in Greece do not "keep faith" with their government, whereas the Romans do (*Histories* 6.56.13).

[72] See the discussion in Rodríguez, "The Testimony of Jesus in the Writings of Ellen G. White" in this volume.

[73] Mark 1:15; John 1:12.

[74] Matt 18:6; Mark 9:42; John 3:18.

[75] *Seventh-day Adventists Believe* (Silver Spring, MD: Ministerial Association, General Conference of Seventh-day Adventists, 2005), p. 191.

The Message of the Remnant[76]

Finally, the remnant is characterized by proclaiming the message found in Rev 14:6-12, namely the "three angels' messages." Through it God addresses the satanic deceptions that will exist in the world prior to the closing of the cosmic conflict. The message is anchored in the eternal good news of salvation through Christ—the eternal gospel (Rev 14:6). Its proclamation occurs shortly before the return of the Lord and is directly connected to the last judgment,[77] which, according to Paul, is part of the gospel (Rom 2:16). For believers, that judgment is good news because Christ is their high priestly Mediator before the Father.

The human race is invited to worship God rather than the beast and its image (Rev 14:7; 13:12-15). At a time when the Christian world has by and large accepted the theory of natural evolution, the remnant is calling upon humanity to "worship Him who made heaven and earth, the sea and the springs of water" (14:7).

The proclamation of the eternal gospel takes place in the context of the last work of deception of the dragon, the beast, and the false prophet. When the apocalyptic apostasy is reaching its climax, the remnant alerts the world concerning that act of rebellion and announces the fall of spiritual Babylon—the embodiment of that apostasy. Adventists, like the Reformers, have identified the presence of apostasy within Christianity. We anticipate that this apostasy will reach new dimensions. It is therefore important to announce the demise of spiritual "Babylon." The remnant also announces the final extermination of the unholy trinity and those who identified themselves with its program (14:9-11). Their message is God's final appeal to every nation, tribe, tongue, and people to prepare for the final judgment. Unquestionably, God has His people in all churches, but He is calling them through His remnant to come out of Babylon in preparation for the Second Advent (Rev 18:4).

II. Summary and Conclusion

The remnant church in Rev 12–14, which according to Rev 12:17 appeared after the 1260-day period (i.e., after 1798), has several specific identifying marks: They keep the commandments of God, including the Sabbath commandment; they have the testimony of Jesus, which is the

---

[76] See Rodríguez, "Concluding Essay," in this volume.

[77] The Greek word *krisis*, used in Rev 14:6, refers primarily to the act of judging (see Bauer, Arndt, Gingrich, Danker, *Greek-English Lexicon*, p. 569), not to the sentence of judgment which is generally expressed by *krima* (ibid., p. 567).

spirit of prophecy or the prophetic gift; they are a persevering people, i.e., they have the patience/endurance which Paul says is the result of Christ's presence in our tribulations (Rom 5:3-4); they keep the faith of Jesus, i.e., they are faithful to what Jesus believed and taught; and they proclaim the three angels' messages which prepare God's people for the Second Advent.

Revelation 14:6-12 spells out the message that the remnant is proclaiming at the time of the end. Those who are part of God's remnant people will warn the world that the hour of God's judgment has arrived and will call those who are willing to prepare to meet the Lord at His second coming. The characteristics of the remnant challenge us both to study and to exemplify them in our lives.

CHAPTER IX

THE REMNANT IN CONTEMPORARY ADVENTIST THEOLOGY

Frank M. Hasel
Dean
Bogenhofen Seminary
Austria

The biblical concept of the remnant is central to the self-understanding of Seventh-day Adventists and has played a significant role in our mission and message.[1] The importance of the remnant image in Adventism goes back to the very beginnings of the movement. Over the years, Sabbatarian Adventists have considered themselves God's prophetic end-time remnant people.[2] "The phrase *the remnant church* has become the definite, self-proclaimed mark of Seventh-day Adventists."[3] This understanding is still maintained in official church documents,[4] standard Seventh-day Adventist reference works,[5] and other representative publications.[6]

---

[1] According to Ángel Manuel Rodríguez, there is an almost unconscious feeling among Seventh-day Adventists "that if we lose the idea of the remnant we would lose, as a church, our purpose, our reason for existence" ("The Remnant and the Adventist Church" [Silver Spring, MD: Biblical Research Institute, unpublished paper, Oct 2002], p. 1).

[2] Alberto Timm, *The Sanctuary and the Three Angels' Messages, 1844–1863: Integrating Factors in the Development of Seventh-day Adventist Doctrines* (Berrien Springs, MI: Adventist Theological Society, 1995), pp. 240-242. Cf. P. Gerard Damsteegt, *Foundations of the Seventh-day Adventist Message and Mission* (Grand Rapids, MI: Eerdmans, 1977), pp. 146, 168, 185, 191, 244; and C. Mervyn Maxwell, "The Remnant in SDA Thought," *AdvA*, 2/2 (1988): 13-20.

[3] Clifford Goldstein, *The Remnant: Biblical Reality or Wishful Thinking?* (Boise, ID: Pacific Press, 1994), p. 11.

[4] Cf. *AdvChManual*, p. 33, and "The Remnant and Its Mission," in *Seventh-day Adventists Believe* (Silver Spring, MD: Ministerial Association, General Conference of Seventh-day Adventists, 2005), p. 181.

[5] "Remnant Church," in *AdvEnc*, vol. M-Z, pp. 434-435; and *AdvBibCom*, vol. 7, pp. 813-815.

[6] *Seventh-day Adventists Believe*, pp. 181, 190-197; and Hans K. LaRondelle, "The Remnant and the Three Angels' Message," in *A Handbook of Seventh-day Adventist Theology*, Raoul Dederen, ed. (Hagerstown, MD: Review and Herald, 2000), pp. 857-892.

The issue of the remnant raises a number of important questions for the Seventh-day Adventist Church, such as: What is the relationship of the remnant to other Christian churches and to the "universal church"? Can the concept of the remnant be applied to sincere, committed Christians in other churches? What is the relationship of the remnant to other religions? Is the remnant visible or invisible? Is the church a visible or invisible entity? Can the remnant be identified in terms of an ecclesiastical institution, or is it to be defined without such a reference? What are the implications of our understanding of the remnant for the ecclesiology, message, and mission of the Seventh-day Adventist Church? In this chapter, we will touch on some of these and similar issues. Further detailed discussions of some of them are found in the rest of this volume.

I. Seventh-day Adventist History and the Remnant Identity

To better understand the significance and the implication of the remnant concept for the Seventh-day Adventist Church, we should examine the use of this concept in the self-understanding of the Adventist church from its historic beginnings. This will enable us to evaluate more recent attempts to redefine the concept that have far-reaching implications for our ecclesiology and mission.

Even before the Seventh-day Adventist Church was formally organized in 1863, early Adventists called themselves a "remnant." The earliest known use of the term to designate Adventists can be traced back to April 1846, when Ellen G. White wrote a brochure entitled "To the Little Remnant Scattered Abroad."[7] While the understanding of the pioneers of being the remnant was closely linked to their personal experience in the Millerite movement up to 1844, Sabbatarian Adventists considered themselves as God's end-time remnant primarily because they were convinced they fulfilled the biblical description of the remnant in Rev 12:17.[8] Based on a historicist methodology and in line with the biblical call to sanctification,

---

[7]This account of her first vision, written on Dec 20, 1845, was originally a personal letter she sent to Enoch Jacobs. He took the liberty to publish it in *The Day-Star*, Jan 24, 1846. It was subsequently published in a pamphlet entitled *A Word to the Little Flock*, dated April 1847. See "Remnant Church," *AdvEnc*, vol. M-Z, p. 435.

[8]Timm, *Sanctuary*, pp. 240-242, with further primary sources. This will be further developed by Pfandl, "Identifying Marks of the Remnant in the Book of Revelation," and Rodríguez, "Concluding Essay," in this volume.

Sabbatarian Adventists saw the personal covenant-commitment of the whole life to God as a basic characteristic of the true remnant. This was considered as implying a personal relationship with God and as obeying God's will as expressed in Scripture. Nobody could keep a covenant relationship with God, according to Sabbatarian Adventists, while consciously disregarding the abiding teachings of the Scriptures.[9]

This included obedience to the fourth commandment as well as the affirmation of the prophetic gift within their ranks.[10]

As early as 1849, Joseph Bates used the key text of Rev 12:17 to describe Adventists as the remnant.[11] In Rev 12:17, with its identification of the remnant as those who "keep the commandments of God and have the testimony of Jesus," early Sabbath-keeping Adventists recognized the clearest reference to the end-time remnant.[12] Since 1849, the term was used regularly for and by them. In 1874, George I. Butler commented on Rev 12:17 that "Seventh-day Adventists . . . have everywhere claimed to be the 'remnant' church for the last twenty-five years."[13] W. H. Littlejohn wrote in 1883:

> Be it known, therefore, that Seventh-day Adventists claim to be the ones whom John saw in vision, and whom he styled the "remnant

---

[9]Timm, *Sanctuary*, p. 241, with further primary sources. Among early Adventists "the concept of the remnant was applied exclusively to those whose lives had been dedicated to God" (ibid.).

[10]While the early Adventists in their proclamation focused on distinctive biblical truths that distinguished them from other denominations and that were significant to their new theological identity, their proclamation and biblical conviction was nevertheless based on a sincere and genuine love for God's Word, for each other, and for a perishing world. This is indicated in the following statement by James White: "As a people we are brought together from divisions of the Advent body [the Millerites], and from the various denominations, holding different views on some subjects; yet thank Heaven the Sabbath is a mighty platform on which we can all stand united. And while standing here, with the aid of no other creed than the Word of God, and *bound together by the bonds of love—love for the truth, love for each other, and love for a perishing world*—'which is stronger than death,' all party feelings are lost. We are united in these great subjects: Christ's immediate personal second Advent, and the observance of all the commandments of God, and the faith of his Son Jesus Christ, as necessary to a readiness for his Advent" (James White, *RH*, Aug 11, 1853, p. 53, emphasis added).

[11]Joseph Bates, *A Seal of the Living God. A Hundred Forty Four Thousand of the Servants of God Being Sealed* (New Bedford, MA: by the author, 1849), pp. 45-46.

[12]Maxwell, "Remnant," p. 14.

[13]George I. Butler, "Visions and Prophecy," in *RH*, June 2, 1874, p. 193.

who keep the commandments of God, and have the testimony of Jesus Christ." As it regards the two prominent points of the faith of the remnant church spoken of by John, it is well-known that Seventh-day Adventists claim to hold and practice both of them.[14]

The same identification of the remnant with the Seventh-day Adventist Church can be found in the writings of Ellen G. White,[15] many pioneers,[16] and Adventist thought leaders throughout Adventist history up to the present.[17]

The previous discussion has shown that from early in their history, Adventists called themselves "the remnant" without hesitation and had no reservations in identifying the Seventh-day Adventist Church with the remnant of end-time Bible prophecy. They did so because it "reflected the idea that they were a small group who remained loyal to the Advent hope, that they were the last group of God's chosen people prior to the

---

[14]W. H. Littlejohn, "Seventh-day Adventists and the Testimony of Jesus Christ," *RH*, Aug 14, 1883, p. 14. When the Adventist pioneers were considering the choice of a name for their new church, the name "The Remnant" was considered (*RH*, Sept 25, 1860, p. 148).

[15]See Rodríguez, "The Remnant in the Writings of Ellen G. White," in this volume.

[16]Cf. Uriah Smith and James White, who published articles pointing to Rev 12:17 and Joel 2:28-32, noting that Seventh-day Adventists fulfill the conditions outlined in these texts: they keep the commandments of God and have the faith of Jesus (Uriah Smith, *RH*, Feb 28, 1856; James White, *RH*, Jan 8, 1857). Uriah Smith, *Synopsis of the Present Truth* (Battle Creek, MI: Seventh-day Adventist Publishing Association, 1884), pp. 302-303, refers to Rev 12:17 and then comments on it: "By the woman we are to understand the church; by her seed, the members of the church throughout this dispensation. Therefore the remnant of her seed can refer to only one body of people, the last generation of Christians upon the earth. These are characterized by keeping the commandments of God, and having the testimony of Jesus Christ. In Rev 19:10 we have the definition of what is here called 'the testimony of Jesus Christ.' Said the angel to John, 'the testimony of Jesus is the spirit of prophecy.' This the reader will at once recognize as one of the gifts in the church. . . . That the gift of prophecy is manifested, according to the Scriptures, in connection with the third angel's message, we refer the reader to works published at the *Review and Herald* office, entitled the 'Spirit of Prophecy' and the 'Testimony to the Church.'" For other references to pioneers, see Maxwell, "Remnant," pp. 13-20; and Gerhard Pfandl, "The Remnant Church and the Spirit of Prophecy" in *Symposium on Revelation—Book II*, Frank B. Holbrook, ed. (Silver Spring, MD: Biblical Research Institute, 1992), pp. 323-326.

[17]Cf. Goldstein, *Remnant*; Gerhard F. Hasel, "The Remnant in Scripture and the End Time," *AdvA* 2/2 (1988): 5-12, 62; *idem*, "Who are the Remnant?" *AdvA* 7/2 (1993): 5-13, 31; Maxwell, "Remnant," pp. 13-20. See also "Remnant Church," *AdvEnc*, vol. M-Z, pp. 434-435; *Seventh-day Adventists Believe*, pp. 153-169, 190-197; LaRondelle, "Remnant," pp. 857-892.

coming of Christ, and that they alone were complying with the conditions specified in Rev 12:17."[18]

Adventists have seen "themselves as a fulfillment of apocalyptic prophecy, a prophetic movement called to prepare a people in all parts of the earth to be ready for Christ's appearance."[19] They still believe they have a sacred and unique responsibility in that they have been divinely commissioned to proclaim to the world God's last message of grace—the eternal gospel—prior to Christ's second advent.[20] This is an essential part of the three angels' messages of Revelation 14. Seventh-day Adventists are convinced that "they alone among the bodies of Christendom are giving this message."[21] Thus Adventists believe "the term 'remnant' to be an appropriate designation of themselves in their role as God's appointed witness to earth's last generation."[22] Hence, the remnant is an identifiable and visible Christian movement.[23]

II. Contemporary Adventist Thinking on the Remnant

The application of the remnant concept to the Adventist church has at times produced strong reactions from other Christian communities against it. These groups have claimed that the remnant concept fosters an arrogant,[24] exclusivist,[25] and judgmental attitude toward the spirituality of others.[26] The force of such criticism appears to have been stronger in the context of inter-confessional conversations. While inter-confessional contacts in and of themselves are not necessarily the cause for this chal-

---

[18]"Remnant Church," in *AdvEnc*, vol. M-Z, p. 435.

[19]LaRondelle, "Remnant," p. 887.

[20]"Remnant," *AdvEnc*, vol. M-Z, p. 434.

[21]Ibid., p. 434.

[22]Ibid.

[23]Note that the profession of faith that candidates for baptism affirm when they join the Seventh-day Adventist Church identifies the Adventist church with the remnant. Baptismal Vow No. 13 reads: "Do you accept and believe that the Seventh-day Adventist Church is the remnant church of Bible prophecy and that people of every nation, race, and language are invited and accepted into its fellowship? Do you desire to be a member of this local congregation of the world church?" (*AdvChManual*, p. 33).

[24]See the discussion in Richard Lehmann, "Die Übrigen und ihr Auftrag," in *Die Gemeinde und ihr Auftrag*, Johannes Mager, ed. (Lüneburg: Saatkorn-Verlag, 1994), p. 73.

[25]Walter R. Martin, *The Truth About Seventh-day Adventism* (Grand Rapids, MI: Zondervan, 1960), p. 212.

[26]Ibid., p. 213. For a good response to some challenges leveled against an exclusive concept of the remnant, see Goldstein, *Remnant*.

lenge, it is a fact that in such settings, the Adventist self-understanding can quickly be perceived by others as maintaining that Adventists are the only true Christians. This concern has had an impact on some Adventists who have attempted to redefine their understanding of the concept of the remnant. We will explore and evaluate this theological debate.[27]

The Remnant Includes Other Christians

In the context of the creation of the World Council of Churches and the ecumenical movement, a series of dialogues took place between Adventists and Evangelicals in the mid 1950s. It has been suggested that "it is to those dialogues that we can trace the seeds of the first divergence from the Adventist Church's self-understanding as the remnant church."[28] The effort to present the Adventist understanding of biblical truth and to correct misconceptions culminated in the preparation of a nearly 700-page book—*Seventh-day Adventists Answer Questions on Doctrine*.[29] In response to question number 20 ("Who constitutes the Remnant Church?"), the answer given does not vary much from those of the early Adventist pioneers. Seventh-day Adventists, in a spirit of deep humility, apply Rev 12:17 to the Advent movement and its work.[30]

It has been pointed out, however, that, regarding the remnant, the book introduces a subtle shift of meaning. It is now also used to designate non-Adventists:

> Seventh-day Adventists firmly believe that *God has a precious remnant*, a multitude of earnest, sincere believers, *in every church*, not excepting the Roman Catholic communion, who are living up to all the

---

[27]A helpful overview of different approaches can be found in Rodriguez, "Remnant" and in Samuel Garbi, "The Seventh-day Adventist Church as the Remnant Church: Various Views over 150 Years of Denominational History" (unpublished M.Div. project, Andrews University Theological Seminary, 1994). The most complete discussion of the theological debate among Adventists is found in Carmelo L. Martines, "El concepto del remanente en la iglesia Adventista del Séptimo Día: Razones subyacentes en el debate contemporáneo" (Tesis Doctoral de Teología, Universidad Adventista del Plata, Argentina, 2002), pp. 153-372. This doctoral dissertation is very useful and contains the most complete Adventist bibliography on the topic.

[28]Garbi, "Remnant Church," p. 32.

[29]For a convenient and helpful introduction and background to this book, see George R. Knight, "Historical and Theological Introduction to the Annotated Edition" in *Seventh-day Adventists Answer Questions on Doctrine: Annotated Edition* (Berrien Springs, MI: Andrews University Press, 2003), xiii-xxxvi.

[30]*Questions on Doctrine*, p. 191.

light God has given them. The great Shepherd of the sheep recognizes them as His own, and He is calling them into one great fold and one great fellowship in preparation for His return.[31]

The term "remnant" is now applied to sincere Christians anywhere in the world.[32] In fact, it comes very close to defining the remnant as an invisible group of God's faithful servants among Christians.[33] Evangelicals commented that such a statement is "in contradistinction to some early writers in the movement who maintained that the term 'remnant' applied only to Seventh-day Adventists."[34] Furthermore, the book states as a summary conclusion: "We believe that through all the ages God has had His elect, distinguished by their sincere obedience to Him in terms of all the light revealed to them. These constitute what may be described as the church invisible."[35] It is here that the issue of the nature of an invisible church and its relationship to the remnant is brought up and will surface in later discussions on the remnant.

This shift in the understanding of the remnant could have far-reaching consequences for the Seventh-day Adventist ecclesiological identity and mission. If other Christians are already part of God's end-time remnant, on what ground is that determined and in what sense can the term be applied to them? Do they bear the marks of the remnant mentioned in Revelation? If so, why do we have to invite them to become part of God's (visible) remnant church?[36]

---

[31] Ibid., p. 192, emphasis added.

[32] A more recent example of such a revisionist interpretation of the remnant concept that follows the shift in *Questions on Doctrine* can be found in the exposition of Fundamental Belief No. 13 (new sequence) by Rolf J. Pöhler, " 'Der Herr kennt die Seinen' 'Die Übrigen' und die anderen," *Adventecho* 104 (3/2006): 21-24, esp. pp. 23-24, and more recently in Rolf J. Pöhler, *Hoffnung die uns trägt: Wie Adventisten ihren Glauben bekennen* (Lüneburg: Saatkorn-Verlag, Abt. Advent-Verlag, 2008), pp. 86-91, esp. p. 90.

[33] Rodríguez, "Remnant," p. 5.

[34] Walter Martin, "The Truth about Seventh-day Adventism: Adventist Theology vs. Historic Orthodoxy," *Eternity*, January 1957, pp. 12-13.

[35] *Questions on Doctrine*, p. 195.

[36] Cf. Maxwell, "Remnant," p. 13; and Rodriguez, "Remnant," p. 5. Ellen G. White acknowledges the fact that "there are many true Christians not of our faith, with whom we come in contact, who live according to the best light that they have, and they are in greater favor with God than are those who have greater light but who have not improved it by showing corresponding works" (*Counsels on Sabbath School Work* [Washington, DC: Review and Herald, 1938], p. 85). She also states: "All in the world are not lawless and sinful. God has many thousands who have not bowed the knee to Baal. There are God-fearing men in the fallen churches. If this were not so, we should not be given the

The Remnant Includes Non-Christians

It has been pointed out that missiological concerns have encouraged certain Seventh-day Adventists to modify the Adventist understanding of the remnant.[37] The mission among Muslims has received a new force through those who have come to the conclusion that Mohammed could be seen as a God-led reformer.[38] This approach has become a major missiological issue in the church.[39] It is suggested by some that we should

---

message to bear, 'Babylon the great is fallen, is fallen. . . . Come out of her, My people'" (*Evangelism* [Washington, DC: Review and Herald, 1946], p. 559; cf. also *Prophets and Kings* [Mountain View, CA: Pacific Press, 1917], pp. 188-189). Those God-fearing persons are invited to join the remnant church. In fact, Ellen G. White is very sensitive to those Christians "who have conscientiously withdrawn from other churches for the truth's sake" (*Evangelism*, p. 351). Inasmuch as these genuine Christians authentically live their faith to the best of their knowledge, the concept of the remnant does not automatically preclude the salvation of anyone or even everyone who is not part of the Seventh-day Adventist Church.

[37]So Garbi, "Remnant Church," p. 39, referring to Gottfried Oosterwal, *Mission Possible: The Challenge of Mission Today* (Nashville, TN: Southern Publishing Association, 1972). For some reason Martines, "Concepto del remanente," did not include a discussion of the theological reasons underlying the debate over the remnant among those who are interested in reaching the non-Christian religions.

[38]A basic assumption of this position is "that God has been at work in all cultures to preserve a measure of true spirituality" (Jerald Whitehouse, "Contextual Adventist Mission to Islam: A Working Model," in *The Three Angels and the Crescent: A Reader*, Jonquil Hole and Borge Schantz, eds. [Newbold College: Global Centre for Islamic Studies, 1993], p. 257; similarly Peter Roennfeldt, "Faith Development in Context – An Overview," in *Faith Development in Context: Presenting Christ in Creative Ways*, Bruce L. Bauer, ed. [Berrien Springs, MI: Department of World Mission, 2005], p. 41) and that the original intent of Islam has in God's purpose contributed to the restoration of certain important truths. This raises important questions such as: Is the Qur'an just as inspired as the Bible? Is Mohammed a God-sent and divinely-used prophet? Is the teaching of the Qur'an in harmony with God's will as revealed in Scripture? Does the Qur'an leave room for the authority of the Bible? Is God indeed using different religions to restore certain important truths? Does not true conversion and acceptance of biblical truth necessarily result in a shift of spiritual identity? (On the last question see John Kent, "Issues of Identity," in *Faith Development in Context*, p. 131.) It has been pointed out that "this assumption also provides the foundation for a remnant within Hinduism, Buddhism, and virtually within any religious or secular movement where 'kernels of truth' may be found" (Carlos Martin, "C-5 Churches, C-5 Missionaries, or C-5 Strategies?" *JATS* 17/2 [2006]: 131).

[39]Stefan Höschele, *From the End of the World to the Ends of the Earth: The Development of Seventh-day Adventist Missiology* (Nürnberg: Verlag für Theologie und Religionswissenschaft, 2004), p. 36. For a critical response to this new approach in Muslim missions, see the article by Borge Schantz, "'Political Correctness' in Muslim Evangelism?" *Ministry*, 76/6 (June 2004): 12-13; *idem*, "What do Adventists and Muslims *Really* Share?" *Spectrum*, May 24, 2006; and Kent, "Issues in Identity," pp. 128-133; as well as Robert M. Johnston, "Kingdom and Church," in *Faith Development in Context*, pp. 135-146, esp. p.

use Muslim terminology and ideas from the Qur'an to close, as much as possible, the gap between Muslims and Seventh-day Adventists.[40] More recently the idea of engaging in deep religious search together with Muslims has brought forth "a movement of Muslims who speak of themselves as 'followers of Isa [Jesus]' but remain culturally Muslims."[41] It has been pointed out that a "distinct group among these 'Jesus Muslims' observes the Sabbath and considers itself as a part of the end-time 'remnant' that believes in Jesus as mediator and keeps God's commandments."[42] This movement has been described as a "remnant of God within Islam."[43] They

---

144. The same principles that are applied to Muslim mission can be extended to other religions and to secularized people as well.

[40] One of the first to promote such ideas seems to have been Robert C. Darnell in the 1960s (cf. Stefan Höschele, *Missiology*, p. 35; and Peter Roennfeldt, "Faith Development in Context – An Overview," in *Faith Development in Context*, pp. 33-36, 43-44). Others have followed this new approach that utilizes Qur'anic thought patterns to explain biblical truths (cf. Whitehouse, "Mission to Islam," p. 253). According to Whitehouse, a significant contribution to the theological foundation of this new missiological approach is found in Alden Thompson's understanding of inspiration that sees the Bible as casebook rather than codebook (cf. Jerald Whitehouse, "Contextualization and Mission II: The Prophetic Model for Mission," unpublished paper, Andrews University, Adventist Heritage Center, 1992, p. 15). The new missiological approach also seems to be influenced by Charles H. Kraft, *Christianity in Culture: A Study in Dynamic Biblical Theologizing in Cross-Cultural Perspective* (Maryknoll, NY: Orbis Books, 1990). For a concise analysis and criticism of Kraft's position, see Carl F. H. Henry, "The Cultural Relativizing of Revelation" in *Biblical Authority and Conservative Perspectives*, Douglas Moo, ed. (Grand Rapids, MI: Kregel Publications, 1997), pp. 166-177, 237-240. For a balanced critique of the use of the Qur'an in sharing the biblical faith, see Ganoune Diop, "The Use of the Qur'an in Sharing the Gospel: Promise or Compromise?" in *Faith Development in Context*, pp. 151-179.

[41] Höschele, *Missiology*, p. 36. The question is how one can live legally, socially, and culturally within the community of Islam and not compromise with Islamic religious practices if one not only speaks, eats, talks, feels, dresses, rejoices, gives, and honors as a Muslim does, but also thinks, marries, prays, worships, and grows spiritually as a Muslim (cf. Roennfeldt, "Faith Development in Context," p. 38).

[42] Höschele, *Missiology*, p. 36. See Jon Dybdahl, "Mission Faces the Twenty-first Century," in *Re-Visioning Adventist Mission in Europe*, Erich Baumgartner, ed. (Berrien Springs, MI: Andrews University Press, 1998), p. 55, who speaks of over 1,500 individuals involved in this "remnant" group in 1997.

[43] See Whitehouse, "Mission to Islam," p. 253. This reform movement of true believers in Islam is called *Hanif*. According to a number of Qur'anic verses, the followers of the true religion of Abraham are called *Hanif* (ibid., p. 258). The *Hanif* are "God's faithful remnant . . . in the Islamic community" (ibid., p. 251, cf. pp. 257-258). While the term *Hanif* continues to be used (cf. Jerald Whitehouse, "Communicating Adventist Beliefs in the Muslim Context," *JAMS* 2/2 [2006]: 75, 77-78), more recently the preferred terminology for the approach to such believers in various religions is "Faith Development in Context"

are trying to develop an understanding of themselves as "God's remnant people and [are] able to relate to the larger body of Christ."[44] One challenging aspect of this remnant among the Muslims is the fact that they "continue attendance at the mosque," practice "fasting during Ramadan," and "observe the feast of sacrifice."[45] It has been pointed out that this Muslim Jesus movement "tries to interpret the Bible for a Muslim worldview, thus avoiding controversial doctrinal elements such as the Trinity."[46]

This Muslim-remnant group is organizationally independent from the Seventh-day Adventist Church, although it resulted from Adventist

---

(FDIC). See Bruce L. Bauer, "Introduction," in *Faith Development in Context*," p. vii-viii and passim. Sometimes they are also called "special affinity groups."

[44]Whitehouse, "Mission to Islam," pp. 248, 251, 253. Yet it has been pointed out that "in most Muslim countries those coming to faith in Christ within the Muslim context often do not know they have any connection with the Adventist Church" (Bruce L. Bauer, "Maintaining Unity with Parallel Structures," in *Faith Development in Context*, p. 268).

[45]Whitehouse, "Mission to Islam," p. 254. The crucial question is not that of culturally remaining a Muslim but of not compromising the biblical faith by accommodating Islamic religion. How much contextualized theologizing can we allow without being in danger of developing a theological pluralism that leads to a relativization of Adventism? (cf. Ángel Manuel Rodríguez, "Dealing with Syncretism in Insider Movements," in *Faith Development in Context*, pp. 252-258; cf. Jerald Whitehouse, "Communicating Adventist Beliefs," p. 75). Hence "the struggle in which the church is engaged today is between making mission primary or maintaining unity in belief–orthodoxy" (Jerald Whitehouse, "Responses to *Questions on C-5*," *JAMS* 1/2 [2005]: 44). This raises the question: "Which is better–no syncretism and no progress toward Christianity, or some syncretism and movement toward the biblical faith?" (Bruce Bauer, "Bounded and Centered Sets: Possible Applications for Adventist Mission," *JAMS* 3/1 [2007]: 72). If Islamic religious practices, such as repeating in the mosque "several times a day that 'Mohammed is the Prophet of God'" or attending the mosque on a regular basis where the divinity of Christ is consistently denied, or participating in the Muslim "feast of the sacrifice," continue to be alive in the new believers, we clearly face the challenge of religious syncretism (cf. Carlos Martin, "Questions on C-5" *JAMS* 1/2, [2005]: 36-38). Some believe that "syncretism is always the unintended consequence of a healthy desire to make the gospel relevant" (Jon Paulien, "Dealing with Syncretism in Insider Movements," in *Faith Development in Context*, p. 219). This has been controversial in the larger evangelical world (cf. Phil Parshall, "Danger! New Directions in Contextualization," *EvMisQ* 34/4 [1998]: 404-410).

[46]Höschele, *Missiology*, p. 37. Borge Schantz has pointed out some difficulties with such a contextualized approach when he writes: "Attempts have been made to equate the Allah of the Koran with the God in the Bible. Despite some superficial commonalities, the comparison is invalid. When Christians talk about God, we talk about a Trinity: Father, Son, and Holy Spirit. To the Muslim, that is blasphemy – and polytheism." Furthermore, there are "three very significant attributes that Christians ascribe to God [that] are absent in Islam. Allah is never called Father, never called Love, never called Spirit" (Schantz, "Political Correctness," p. 12).

missionary activities.⁴⁷ Using the same hermeneutical presuppositions, similar missionary methods have also been developed by Seventh-day Adventists for Buddhism,⁴⁸ and there are attempts to establish similar "remnants" in the Hindu community as well.⁴⁹ Thus, according to this position, there are "various remnants in other communities . . . yet we are all part of God's larger remnant which will be united when He reconciles all things unto Himself at His coming."⁵⁰ It is no longer true that the term "remnant" is applied only to believers in other Christian communities; it is now applied to groups among non-Christian religions who have an incomplete understanding of the message and mission of the end-time

---

⁴⁷See Jerald Whitehouse, "Adventist Christians, Cultural Muslims," *Spectrum* 22/4 (1992): 25-32, and Höschele, *Missiology*, p. 36. These Muslim remnant believers are at times baptized with no knowledge of the Seventh-day Adventist Church or even without understanding that they are becoming Christians (cf. Carlos Martin, "Questions on C-5," *JAMS* 1/2 [2005]: 37). Proponents of this new approach admit that "institutionalizing the project into the traditional church structure would compromise many of the key principles and strategies of the project. It would also threaten the security of the existing church" (Whitehouse, "Adventist Mission," pp. 258-259). This raises the pertinent question: "What should be the administrative relationships? . . . Must we always work through the local existing church? Or is there a place for a functionally separate mission body to assume and address these special mission challenges? . . . What structure should this contextual ministry develop?" (ibid., p. 259). Lowell C. Cooper has aptly pointed out that "for Seventh-day Adventists, missiology and ecclesiology cannot be completely separated. . . . [M]ission needs to embrace a particular view of the church. For Seventh-day Adventists, the pursuit of mission cannot be accompanied by a fluctuating view of a remnant body of believers" ("Response: Maintaining Unity with Parallel Structures," in *Faith Development in Context*, p. 276). It has been said that "with the existence of baptized believers who have not reached a complete awareness of the Adventist faith and have not developed a full fellowship with other sister communities in the world, the stage has been set for a fragmented world church" (Carlos Martin, "Questions on C-5" *JAMS* 1/2 [2005]: 38-39).

⁴⁸There are contextualized Buddhist Adventist Church services in Yangon, Myanmar, where Psalm 23 mantra sheets are being distributed and a "meditation house" is being built in Burma, and Burmese gospel paintings are being used to explain the Christian gospel to Buddhists (Höschele, *Missiology*, pp. 37-38).

⁴⁹Whitehouse, "Mission to Islam," p. 257.

⁵⁰Ibid., p. 258. More recently it has been stated that the mission of the Seventh-day Adventist Church "is bigger than itself. It is a prophetic role within all peoples. It is *a role and mission that takes precedence over institution building or sectarian agendas*. It is to carry a warning message to prepare a people from among all peoples for the coming of Jesus. It is based on the understanding that God is using the Advent movement to prepare *a larger remnant that we are certainly a part of, but we are not the whole. The final remnant is larger than Seventh-day Adventists alone*. This understanding forms the basis for my relationship with Muslims" (Jerald Whitehouse, "New Directions in Adventist-Muslim Relations" *Spectrum* 34/3 [2006]: 56, emphasis added).

remnant. This usage of the term weakens the nature of the end-time remnant as described in the book of Revelation.

The Remnant as an Invisible Entity

Others have recently argued that the remnant is by its very nature invisible. Noting that Seventh-day Adventists have traditionally been very much opposed to the ecumenical movement, it has been argued that we cannot afford to ignore a new ecumenism that is sweeping through much of the Christian world.[51] This new spiritual ecumenicity reconnects "Christians and all who acknowledge the Lordship of Christ *outside* Christianity to a common core"[52] that is not institutional. It is argued that "this movement is directly connected to the 'Charismatic renewal'"[53] and calls us to quit debating differences and to renounce our sectarian mentality. Rather than thinking of ourselves as God's chosen people, it has been suggested that we should start recognizing the existence and ministry of God's chosen *peoples*.[54] Thus, we are called to "cease to think or speak of ourselves as the remnant church and see ourselves as a part of God's larger remnant."[55] Such a position requires a rejection of the Adventist institutional and denominational identity. The remnant has at best only an invisible spiritual identity.

Others have come very close to the idea of an invisible remnant by claiming that "neither in Scripture nor in the writings of Ellen G. White is the remnant directly equivalent to an institutional structure, church organization, or denominational entity."[56] According to this voice, "remnant people are those who are never satisfied with the status quo but want to examine, learn, grow, and gather those 'scattered gems.'"[57] While it is certainly laudable to have an open and teachable spirit that is willing to learn and grow, the position just described seems to question the connection between a visible church organization and the remnant and instead appears to express the idea that the remnant is scattered throughout

---

[51]Steve Daily, *Adventism for a New Generation* (Portland, OR: Better Living Publishers, 1994), p. 312.

[52]Ibid., p. 313, emphasis supplied.

[53]Ibid.

[54]Ibid., p. 314.

[55]Ibid., p. 315.

[56]Jon Dybdahl, "It is God's Call: What It Means to be the Remnant," *AdvR*, May 9, 1996, p. 14. For a corrective to this view, see Rodríguez, "The Remnant in the Writings of Ellen G. White," in this volume.

[57]Ibid.

Christianity and at the present time is invisible. One can detect here a growing discontinuity with the traditional biblical-Adventist position and a redefinition of our understanding of the remnant. Other studies in this volume have shown that the remnant is identifiable and that organization is an essential part of it.[58]

The Remnant as a Future Reality

Some have suggested that the remnant of Revelation is yet to appear and conclude that it is almost perverse for the church to call itself "the remnant church" because the remnant is more than an institution.[59] The remnant is redefined in terms of a quality of life and faith and not in terms of membership in an ecclesiastical organization. Recognizing that the remnant motif is very important for the Adventist church, it is then suggested that even though the remnant is still in the future, the Adventist church may refer to itself as "a proleptic remnant" in the sense that its members will be absorbed into a final remnant, the true remnant of God.[60] This effectively denies the idea that the Seventh-day Adventist Church is God's end-time remnant and re-interprets Rev 12:17 as prophecy that is still to be fulfilled. This view assigns to the church the role of a prophetic minority, meaning that like a prophet, it cries out for reform and change in the world, thus preparing the way of the Lord.[61]

The Remnant as a Movement for Social Justice

Some seek to re-interpret the remnant concept along socio-political lines. Prompted by the social evils in the world, it is proposed that, foremost the role of the remnant is to address social and political issues and to promote reform in these areas.[62] Others have gone even further and have divested the remnant concept of almost any religious content. Instead, the remnant has been transformed into a social movement of reform in opposition to social abuse and oppression, largely to the neglect

---

[58]See for instance Richard Lehmann, "The Remnant in the Book of Revelation."

[59]Jack W. Provonsha, *A Remnant in Crisis* (Hagerstown, MD: Review and Herald, 1993), p. 35.

[60]Ibid., p. 163.

[61]Jack W. Provonsha, "The Church as a Prophetic Minority," *Spectrum* 12/1 (1981): 18-23.

[62]Cf. Charles Scriven, "The Remnant and the Church: A Reconsideration," unpublished paper, Andrews University, Heritage Room, 1984; *idem*, "The Real Truth About the Remnant," *Spectrum* 17/1 (1986): 6-13.

of its clearly religious dimensions.⁶³ While the remnant should have some social impact and must condemn evil in all its forms, this new approach radically redefines the concept along sociological lines and neglects the fact that the biblical remnant is fundamentally a religious entity.⁶⁴ As described in the apocalyptic literature of the Bible, the final conflict is a religious conflict whose central issue is loyalty to God and true worship.

The above discussion has shown that, among some Adventists, there is a tendency to modify or even redefine the concept and theology associated with the Adventist view of the end-time remnant. While the term is still used, "the ways in which the content is presented raises questions of whether the same biblical message as previously understood is being communicated in a new context or if there is a failure to reassert, or even a conscious desire to have as little as possible to do with it."⁶⁵ In other words, the traditional terminology of the remnant is used, but it is infused with a new meaning that, in some cases, contradicts it or is incompatible with it. In spite of those attempts to introduce change, the church has officially retained, throughout the world, its biblical self-understanding as God's end-time remnant. This makes it necessary to raise the question of the relationship of the Adventist church to other Christian churches and the so-called invisible church.

III. Seventh-day Adventists and Other Christian Churches

We will first consider how Seventh-day Adventists have seen other churches and the relationship of the remnant to other Christian believers.

The Remnant and Other Christian Churches

As already indicated, Seventh-day Adventists have never been reluctant to identify themselves unambiguously as God's visible end-time

---

⁶³Cf. Charles W. Teel, Jr., "Growing Up With John's Beasts: A Rite of Passage," *Spectrum* 21/3 (1991): 25-34; also *idem*, "Remnant," in *Remnant and Republic: Adventist Themes for Personal and Social Ethics*, Charles W. Teel, Jr., ed. (Loma Linda, CA: Center for Christian Bioethics, 1995), pp. 1-35.

⁶⁴Cf. Rodríguez, "Remnant," p. 7. The question is one of presuppositions and a proper hermeneutical starting point: does the remnant, because of its basic religious character, also have a legitimate concern for social reform and justice, or is the basic understanding of the remnant a social and political movement that in its socio-political activity gains a quasi-religious quality?

⁶⁵Garbi, "Remnant Church," p. 28. Garbi raises the question "whether the 'Adventism for a new generation' is still any Adventism at all?" (p. 37).

remnant church. Such "identification with the remnant church of prophecy (Rev 12:17; 14:6-12) offers no ground for a spirit of exclusivism or triumphalism."[66] Instead, it serves to heighten a sense of responsibility and self-criticism that holds the remnant church fully accountable to Christ.[67] Thus, Adventists have repeatedly expressed great respect for other faithful Christians in the Christian world. They believe "that various Protestant groups served as Heaven's appointed harbingers of truth, point by point restoring the gospel to its pristine purity."[68] While it is true that "one by one these groups became satisfied with their partial concept of truth and failed to advance as light from God's Word increased,"[69] Adventists nevertheless sincerely believe "that God's faithful ones are now scattered among all who purpose to order their lives in harmony with all His revealed will."[70] This important distinction between the remnant church on the one hand and faithful believers in every land on the other hand[71] can help to maintain a balance between a particular ecclesiology and the acknowledgment that it is not an organization that saves.

Thus, even though Adventists apply Rev 12:17 to themselves, this "does not imply in any way that we believe we are the only true Christians in the world, or that we are the only ones who will be saved."[72] Ellen G. White affirms that "from the beginning, faithful souls have constituted the church on earth. In every age the Lord has had His watchmen, who have borne faithful testimony to the generation in which they lived."[73] This attitude is in harmony with what early Adventists affirmed: "We attach great importance to the doctrines which we cherish; but we have ever held that God has true people wherever men are found who are obeying what light they have."[74]

This position has found entrance into the official *Working Policy* guidelines regulating the relationship of the Adventist church with other Chris-

---

[66] LaRondelle, "Remnant," p. 888.

[67] Ibid.

[68] "Remnant," *AdvEnc*, vol. M-Z, p. 434.

[69] Ibid.

[70] Ibid., p. 435.

[71] Ellen G. White, *Prophets and Kings*, p. 188.

[72] *Questions on Doctrine*, pp. 191-192.

[73] Ellen G. White, *The Acts of the Apostles*, p. 11. This statement seems to imply that the church is a visible entity because it consists of faithful people who bear faithful testimony.

[74] J. N. Andrews and J. H. Waggoner, "The Articles of Eld. T. M. Preble," *RH*, Feb 15, 1870, p. 60.

tian churches and religious organizations. There, among other things, it is stated:

> To avoid creating misunderstanding or friction in our relationships with other Christian churches and religious organizations, the following guidelines have been set forth:
>
> 1) We recognize those agencies that lift up Christ before men as a part of the divine plan for evangelization of the world, and we hold in high esteem Christian men and women in other communions who are engaged in winning souls to Christ.
>
> 2) When interdivision work brings us in contact with other Christian societies and religious bodies, the spirit of Christian courtesy, frankness, and fairness shall prevail at all times.
>
> 3) We recognize that true religion is based on conscience and conviction. It is therefore to be our constant purpose that no selfish interest or temporal advantage shall draw any person to our communion and that no tie shall hold any member save the belief and conviction that in this way the true connection with Christ is found. If a change of conviction leads a member of our church to feel no longer in harmony with Seventh-day Adventist faith and practice, we recognize not only the right but also the responsibility of that member to change, without opprobrium, religious affiliation in accord with belief. We expect other religious bodies to respond in the same spirit of religious liberty.[75]

In Fundamental Belief No. 12, on "The Church," Adventists state that "in continuity with the people of God in Old Testament times, we are called out of the world" and that God at His return in triumph "will present her to Himself a glorious church, the faithful of all the ages, the purchase of His blood."[76] Once again there is continuity with the people of God in the Old Testament and the faithful ones of all ages. In Fundamental Belief No. 13, on the remnant and its mission, it is explicitly stated that "the

---

[75] "O 110 Relationships with Other Christian Churches and Religious Organizations," in *Working Policy of the General Conference of Seventh-day Adventists 2006-2007* (Hagerstown, MD: Review and Herald, 2006), p. 482.

[76] *Seventh-day Adventist Yearbook* (Silver Spring, MD: General Conference of Seventh-day Adventists, 2008), p. 6.

universal church is composed of all who truly believe in Christ, but in the last days, a time of widespread apostasy, a remnant has been called out to keep the commandments of God and the faith of Jesus."[77] Commenting on this Fundamental Belief, the book *Seventh-day Adventists Believe: An Exposition of the Fundamental Beliefs of the Seventh-day Adventist Church* states: "God has His children in all churches, but through the remnant church He proclaims a message that is to restore His true worship by calling His people out of the apostasy and preparing them for Christ's return."[78] This raises the question of the relationship between those believers in all churches and the remnant.

Universal Church and the Remnant

It is customary for many to speak about the "invisible church" in ecclesiological discussions. It should be carefully noted that Adventists talk about a *universal church* composed of all who truly believe in Christ[79] but do not consider the church to be essentially invisible. Indeed, Adventists acknowledge that different groups have arisen throughout Christian history with a burden to draw the people of their day back to a more scriptural faith. They have been called "in a sense remnant groups."[80] "Although Seventh-day Adventists differ from these groups in various respects regarding doctrine and practice, they have in common with them the image of the remnant in the sense of bringing their contemporaries to a faith closer to the Scriptures."[81] Adventists have traditionally listed among them the Waldenses, the Anabaptists, the Puritans, the German Pietists, the Methodists, and the Millerite Revivalists.[82] These were visible entities.

The concept of an invisible church was an apologetic device of the Reformers, especially of Luther,[83] to comply with the creeds' statements

---

[77]Ibid.

[78]*Seventh-day Adventists Believe*, p. 197.

[79]See Rodríguez, "Concluding Essay," in this volume.

[80]LaRondelle, "Remnant," p. 880. The *AdvEnc*, vol. M-Z, "Remnant," says more explicitly: "The Protestant churches of the Reformation era may be considered God's faithful remnant after more than a millennium of papal apostasy" (p. 434).

[81]LaRondelle, "Remnant," p. 880.

[82]Ibid., pp. 880-883; perhaps one could also add the early Ethiopian and Abyssinian Churches in Africa, as well as some ancient churches in Africa and Asia; cf. Ellen G. White, *The Great Controversy*, pp. 577-578; cf. also Werner Vyhmeister, "The Sabbath in Egypt and Ethiopia" in *The Sabbath in Scripture and History*, Kenneth A. Strand, ed. (Washington, DC: Review and Herald, 1982), pp. 169-189, and *idem*, "The Sabbath in Asia," in *Sabbath in Scripture*, pp. 151-168.

[83]According to R. Seeberg, Martin Luther was the first to make the distinction between

concerning a "catholic church" and was based on a particular conception of unconditional election.[84] It has been stated that Luther sometimes repeated "the traditional Augustinian idea of a 'church of the predestined,' known only to God."[85] Although Lutherans regard the church as "the assembly of all believers, among whom the gospel is preached in its purity and the holy sacraments are administered according to the gospel,"[86] they appear to consider the church itself more as the spiritual communion of all who believe in Christ and thus, it is essentially invisible.[87] Similarly, Reformed theology with its "doctrine of divine election had as its corollary that one must leave to God alone the knowledge of his church, for its foundation was his secret election."[88]

Luther's "insistence on the invisibility of the Church served the purpose of *denying* that the Church is *essentially* an *external society with a visible head* and of affirming that the essence of the Church is to be found in the sphere of the invisible: in faith, communion with Christ, and in participation in the blessings of salvation through the Holy Spirit."[89] Since the church is an object of faith, it is not visible, for what is believed is not bodily, nor visible.[90] Thus,

> Luther argues for an essential invisibility of faith together with the hiddenness of the true church against Rome's hierarchical claims to rule Christendom and particularly to exclude people from it through

---

the visible and invisible church (quoted in Louis Berkhof, *The History of Christian Doctrines* [Grand Rapids, MI: Baker, 1937], p. 236).

[84] So Randall Otto, "The Remnant Church," *JCThR* 7 (2002): 15, 16.

[85] Jaroslav Pelikan, *The Christian Tradition: A History of the Development of Doctrine, Vol. 4: Reformation of Church and Dogma (1300–1700)* (Chicago, IL: University of Chicago Press, 1984), p. 173.

[86] Ibid.

[87] On Luther and his understanding of the remnant, see the insightful discussion in Rico Javien, "The Remnant Theology of Martin Luther," *AASS* 7 (2004): 113-124.

[88] Pelikan, *Christian Tradition*, p. 174, writes, "Therefore the church was indeed the communion of saints, but with the important proviso that 'the church is hidden, and the saints are concealed.'"

[89] Berkhof, *Christian Doctrines*, pp. 236-237.

[90] Reinhold Seeberg, *Text-Book of the History of Doctrines*, vol. 2 (Eugene, OR: Wipf & Stock, 1997), pp. 292-293. On Luther's concept of the church, see also Paul Althaus, *The Theology of Martin Luther* (Philadelphia, PA: Fortress Press, 1966), pp. 287-293. This same church, however, becomes visible and can be known, not by the headship of the pope, nor by the rule of the cardinals and bishops, but by the pure administration of the Word and the sacraments (Berkhof, *Christian Doctrine*, p. 237).

excommunication. No earthly power can draw the boundaries of the church and decide who belongs to it and who does not.[91]

Simply stated, God has predestined those who shall be saved from before the foundation of the world, and only those divinely predestined and elected constitute the true church.[92] The invisible church, then, is:

> the totality of the elect according to the divine decree without regard to time, place, or even personal existence, while embracing within the visible church the totality of those in time and space who personally profess faith in Jesus as Lord and Savior. . . . The priority given to the invisible church, based on the divine decree before creation, challenges the historical reality of the church, notwithstanding verbal affirmations of the visible church's present existence.[93]

The underlying philosophy of such an ecclesiology eventuates in an historical state of being, for if the true church is already made up in an inscrutable divine predestination where all the (invisible) elect, regardless of their temporal existence, are present, then what happens on earth in the human response to God's revelation appears inconsequential.[94] The inscrutability of divine election necessitates an invisible church and makes election secret and ultimately incapable of outward validation. The Bible, however, teaches that our election has discernible outward signs. Thus the biblical exhortation is to "make every effort to add to your faith" the

---

[91]Althaus, *Martin Luther*, p. 292. It has been said that "Luther's doctrine of the church is his weakest point" and that his "distinction between the visible and the invisible church is one of the most difficult things to understand" (Paul Tillich, *A History of Christian Thought* [New York: Simon and Schuster, 1968], pp. 251-252). For Luther the church is not a hidden reality in every sense of the word and can be recognized by the administration of baptism, the bread, and, most importantly, the gospel. Ecclesiastical discipline can exclude from the community of the outward church but never from the inward, spiritual, invisible community in the heart which is given together in faith (cf. Althaus, *Martin Luther*, pp. 289, 292).

[92]Javien has pointed out the significance of the idea of predestination for Luther, who believed that salvation was limited only to the elect who had been predestined from eternity (cf. Javien, "Remnant Theology," p. 122). Thus for Luther "the remnant became the remnant not by exercising free choice or free will but by God's election of grace" (Ibid., p. 123; cf. *LW*, 17:276 on Mic 5:17-18, delivered April 7, 1525). It is not explicitly clear whether Luther equated the remnant with the true church (Javien, "Remnant Theology," p. 124).

[93]Otto, "Remnant Church," pp. 15-16.

[94]Ibid., p. 16.

virtues of goodness, knowledge, self-control, perseverance, godliness, brotherly kindness, and love "to make your calling and election sure. For if you do these things, you will never fall, and you will receive a rich welcome into the eternal kingdom of our Lord and Savior Jesus Christ" (2 Pet 1:10-11, NIV).

In light of these problems, it has been said that the reformed distinction between a visible and an invisible church needs to be revised, if not rejected, for a "biblical theology does not allow for an 'invisible church,' but only a 'remnant church.'"[95] The Bible underscores a visible covenant community. Just as there is one people of God in the Old Testament, so in the New Testament there is one people of God gathered visibly at the end of time. There is no instance in the New Testament where the term *ekklesia* ("church") requires the meaning of an invisible assembly or congregation. While there are genuine believers in other churches, the remnant will always be a visible entity that can be joined by all those who are willing to be faithful to all of God's commandments and to His leading.[96] It is therefore better to say that the visibility of the church is a reality in the remnant.[97] While there is a visible and recognizable fold, there are "other sheep, which are not of this fold" (John 10:16, NASB). According to Jesus, there are "other sheep," but there is only one true Shepherd and there is only "*one* flock with *one* shepherd" (John 10:16, NASB, emphasis supplied). This one flock is characterized by obedience to the Word of God ("they will hear my voice" [John 10:16, NASB]). Thus, it seems that Jesus is not endorsing multiple flocks existing simultaneously as a legitimate expression of the remnant.

The fact that there are true believers in the universal church allows us to pinpoint some commonalities between the remnant and believers in the universal church.[98] Believers in both the remnant church and the universal church are open to truth. Openness to truth, rather than fullness of truth, seems to be one common bond that characterizes both. This openness to truth is accompanied by a sincere desire to follow the truth and a deliberate effort to implement God's truth in one's personal

---

[95]Ibid.

[96]The remnant is an entity that faces the wrath of the dragon and against whom the dragon wages war. This too implies a visible entity.

[97]Ellen G. White supports the idea of a visible true church when she writes: "All who believe are to be gathered into one church" (*The Acts of the Apostles*, p. 28). Here she acknowledges the existence of believers who are not yet belonging to the church and who are to be gathered into one church.

[98]For more on this see Rodríguez, "Concluding Essay," in this volume.

life. This openness to truth and the willingness to follow truth might also apply to non-Christian individuals, where the Holy Spirit works on the individual heart and awakens a genuine interest in God's truth. Such openness to truth will lead to a fuller and more comprehensive understanding of truth and to the acceptance of new light. The faithfulness in all believers will be discernible. The individual desire to be faithful to God and His Word will be the basis for joining the eschatological remnant. This eschatological remnant is historically connected to the revelation of God's truth in the Judeo-Christian tradition and does not exist in other religions. As such the eschatological remnant is an extension of the true church of God through the centuries and stands on the shoulders of its faithful predecessors.

IV. Implications and Conclusion

In baptism a believer joins the fellowship of other believers, i.e., the body of Christ (1 Cor 12:13). The remnant concept emphasizes that God has a people who are united to Christ by faith and who demonstrate this by living in submission to God, by worshiping Him, and by a loving service to others. While there are "other sheep" (John 10:16) who truly believe in Christ[99] according to the light they have received (the universal church), there will be a remnant of Bible prophecy in the last days. This remnant has a specific prophetic task to fulfill: To preach the eternal gospel to all people and to prepare the whole world for the soon coming of Jesus Christ.

Furthermore, this eschatological remnant is connected to the Christian church, which is built upon the Israel of faith as described in the Old and New Testaments. It has a global mission whose target is every nation, tribe, and people. Such a universal commission cannot be fulfilled by one or two individuals. A genuine Adventist ecclesiology will assign a high priority to the fulfillment of its prophetic mission and will maintain adequate organizational structures to be able to fulfill its worldwide missionary mandate. The mission of the church is closely bound to the content of that which is proclaimed and gains credibility if it is authentically lived.

While our proclamation of the eternal gospel will be adapted to the context and audience we are addressing, the theology of our proclamation must be firmly grounded in the written Word of God, the totality of the Scripture (*tota scriptura*), as authoritative for faith and praxis. It is there that we find the basis for the unity of the church. Hence, an Adven-

---

[99] See Fundamental Belief No. 12. Cf. also the Summary of Doctrinal Beliefs, nos. 21, 22, and 28 in the *AdvChManual*, pp. 212-213.

tist ecclesiology and missiology must be faithful to the Word of God and should inform, direct, and guide the missionary activity of the church.

Almost by necessity, the biblical-prophetic understanding of the remnant concept, implies a minority, even though it is a great multitude from all corners of the earth. This minority remains politically powerless but does rely on God and His intervention. Therefore, a separation of church and state and the principle of liberty of conscience are integral aspects of the remnant church. The idea of the remnant church does not square well with a state-church model. Any ecclesiological model that makes recourse to the remnant concept needs to reflect these aspects in its structure and organization. Adventists respect religious liberty and the religious convictions of others. The very remnant concept stands in strong contrast to any form of coercion or feeling of superiority.

The biblical concept of a visible end-time remnant provides Seventh-day Adventists with a more distinct understanding of the nature of the church than is present in any other Protestant church. Adventists believe that the church is not essentially invisible, but rather that it is a reality represented worldwide and inclusive of all nations, peoples, and tongues. Thus it is "catholic" in the truest sense of the word.[100]

---

[100]The word "catholic" is derived from the Greek word *katholikos,* meaning "general" or "universal."

CHAPTER X

THE REMNANT PEOPLE OF GOD IN THE WRITINGS OF ELLEN G. WHITE

Ángel Manuel Rodríguez
Director
Biblical Research Institute
Silver Spring, MD

The term "remnant" is employed by Ellen G. White in a variety of ways, but the predominant ones are religious and theological. The non-religious use designates "what remains" or "is left" of something. For instance, she writes about "the remnant of an abused life,"[1] "the remnant" of a day,[2] "the remnant" of one's energy,[3] "the remnant" of financial resources,[4] "the last remnant of time,"[5] etc. When "remnant" carries a religious connotation, in most cases one finds synonymous expressions that accentuate the religious content. For instance, the remnant is contextually defined as "faithful ones"[6] or "faithful children of God,"[7] "people of God,"[8] "those who maintain their loyalty to God,"[9] "a little company,"[10] "this [Adventist] movement,"[11] "the saints,"[12] and so on. "Remnant" itself is often qualified by terms or expressions such as "the remnant *church*,"[13] "the remnant *of the people of God*," "the rem-

---

[1] *Testimonies for the Church*, vol. 3 (Mountain View, CA: Pacific Press, 1948), p. 165.
[2] *The Desire of Ages* (Mountain View, CA: Pacific Press, 1898), p. 527.
[3] *Gospel Workers* (Washington, DC: Review and Herald, 1948), p. 196.
[4] *The Adventist Home* (Nashville, TN: Southern Publishing Association, 1952), p. 389.
[5] *The Great Controversy* (Mountain View, CA: Pacific Press, 1911), p. 562.
[6] *The Acts of the Apostles* (Mountain View, CA: Pacific Press, 1911), p. 535.
[7] *Testimonies for the Church*, vol. 5, p. 475.
[8] Ibid., vol. 9, p. 231.
[9] *Prophets and Kings* (Mountain View, CA: Pacific Press, 1917), p. 245.
[10] *Testimonies for the Church*, vol. 9, p. 231.
[11] Ibid., p. 154.
[12] Letter 1, 1897, Sunnyside, Cooranbong, New South Wales, Australia, April 22, 1897, Church in Adelaide.
[13] "The Return of the Exiles," *RH*, Jan 9, 1908.

nant *people of God*,"[14] "*faithful* remnant,"[15] "*despised* remnant,"[16] "*godly* remnant,"[17] and others. Of those, the most common usages are "remnant people" and "remnant church."[18] All of these suggest that we are dealing with an important topic in the thinking of Ellen G. White.

In this paper we will discuss the religious use, particularly Ellen G. White's understanding of the end-time remnant people of God. We should make clear that this is a study of the use and presence of the term "remnant" in the writings of Ellen G. White. The concept of the remnant is present in many places where Ellen G. White does not explicitly use the term itself, but we have abstained from exploring those cases. Such a study would have required a full exploration of her eschatology rather than a single aspect of it. Another limitation is that this is not an historical study but a theological one. Our approach is synchronic rather than diachronic. We did not find a significant development in Ellen G. White's use of the term "remnant." We recognize that in some of the usages, she was addressing specific historical situations, but we have found that in most of those cases, she was drawing implications of a more general nature that help us to create a profile of her understanding of the remnant. Those limitations provide a frame of reference for our study.

I. Nature of the Remnant

Ellen G. White's conception of the remnant is determined by her reading of the Scriptures and is framed within her understanding of the cosmic conflict between God and Satan. In that conflict the revelation of the character of God and His saving design for sinful human beings are of paramount importance. God's saving purpose is fulfilled through a remnant. It was through the prophets that God made known His "eternal purpose on behalf of mankind. In the teachings of the prophets, His love for the lost race and His plan for their salvation are clearly revealed."[19] The remnant designates those through whom God carries out "the plan of the ages" and "to whom are to be fulfilled all the covenant promises."[20]

---

[14]*Testimonies for the Church*, vol. 9, p. 274.

[15]Ibid., vol. 5, p. 524.

[16]Ibid., p. 475.

[17]*Prophets and Kings*, p. 22.

[18]There are 139 hits in the Ellen G. White CD-ROM for "remnant people" and 92 for "remnant church." We did not make any attempt to eliminate repetitions.

[19]*Prophets and Kings*, p. 22.

[20]Ibid.

Referring to the northern kingdom of Israel shortly before its fall, she commented,

> Never was the kingdom of Israel to be left without noble witnesses to the mighty power of God to save from sin. Even in the darkest hours some would remain true to their divine Ruler and in the midst of idolatry would live blameless in the sight of a holy God. These faithful ones were numbered among the goodly remnant through whom the eternal purpose of Jehovah was finally to be fulfilled.[21]

This eternal purpose was to be fulfilled through them not only in the sense that the Messiah would come from among them, but also in that they were the beneficiaries of the divine saving design.

Closely related to what we just said, Ellen G. White suggests that the remnant is directly related to the preservation of the human race. That is the ultimate and central purpose of God's loving and saving plan. The cosmic conflict threatened the existence of the human race. The importance of the remnant hinges on the fact that if Satan "could blot them from the earth, his triumph would be complete."[22] This explains Satan's opposition to God's remnant throughout history. In that conflict, even when the enemy may appear to have the upper hand, God has always preserved a remnant people through whom He will protect the human race from spiritual and natural extinction. Their preservation occurred through Christ, who took their place to forgive their sins.[23] They accepted Christ's offer of salvation.[24] The remnant is an inclusive group formed by individuals gathered from every nation, people, and tongue.[25]

The remnant is also God's instrument for the preservation of God's revelation. It is because of them that "the true faith revealed to His prophets . . . will not become extinct."[26] The implication is that God has always

---

[21] Ibid., p. 108.

[22] *Testimonies for the Church*, vol. 9, p. 231.

[23] *Thoughts From the Mount of Blessing* (Mountain View, CA: Pacific Press, 1956), p. 116; she is quoting Mic 7:18.

[24] *Testimonies for the Church*, vol. 5, p. 470. According to her, they are "bound up together with Christ in God! They are His chosen ones, His children, heirs of God and joint heirs with Jesus Christ, redeemed to Himself by the blood of the Lamb. They are His remnant people, in whose hearts is His law" (Manuscript 51, 1890, Danvers, MA, Dec 1890, Diary, Labors at Danvers, MA).

[25] *Prophets and Kings*, p. 299.

[26] *Patriarchs and Prophets* (Mountain View, CA: Pacific Press, 1958), p. 125.

"preserved a remnant to serve Him" and thus "preserved from age to age the precious revealing of His will."[27] Abraham became "the inheritor of this holy trust"[28] and to him God gave "a distinct knowledge of the requirement of His law and of the salvation that would be accomplished through Christ."[29] That holy trust was preserved through God's remnant people. Concerning the remnant of Israel that returned from exile, Ellen G. White pointed out that although they were a feeble people, "through them God purposed to preserve in the earth a knowledge of Himself and of His law. They were the guardians of the true worship, the keepers of the holy oracles."[30]

II. God's Remnant in History

For Ellen G. White "the remnant" is a designation not only for the end-time remnant people mentioned in Rev 12:17; it also refers to His faithful people throughout the course of history. As we indicated already, God always "preserved a remnant to serve Him."[31]

Remnant in the Old Testament

Most of the references to the remnant in Old Testament times found in Ellen G. White's writings are related to the time of Isaiah, Jeremiah, and the exilic and post-exilic periods. It was during that time that the existence of the people of God was most seriously threatened. Her use of remnant language is basically the same as we find in the Old Testament itself. Before the fall of the northern kingdom of Israel, God sent prophets like Hosea and Amos, and as a result of their ministry, some "remained true to their divine Ruler and in the midst of idolatry lived a blameless life."[32] This was a small and faithful remnant. After the fall of the kingdom, "a feeble remnant" continued a form of government in the land, but without power.[33] We refer to it as an historical remnant.

---

[27]Ibid.

[28]Ibid.

[29]Ibid.

[30]*Prophets and Kings*, p. 677.

[31]*Patriarchs and Prophets*, p. 125. The full quotation reads, "But the true faith was not to become extinct. God has ever preserved a remnant to serve Him. Adam, Seth, Enoch, Methuselah, Noah, Shem, in unbroken line, had preserved from age to age the precious revealings of His will."

[32]*Prophets and Kings*, p. 108.

[33]Ibid., p. 284. Later the remnant of the 10 tribes rejected Hezekiah's invitation to

Judah also moved toward apostasy; consequently, the "forces of good were rapidly diminishing."[34] This led Isaiah to say, "Except the LORD of hosts had left unto us a very small remnant we should have been as Sodom, and . . . Gomorrah" (Isa 1:9, KJV).[35] Indeed, there was a "goodly remnant," and the prophet continued to encourage and to challenge them to constant reformation.[36] Jeremiah also foresaw the fall of Judah, the scattering of the people, and the gathering of a remnant.[37] Before the fall there was a "faithful remnant" in the city, and the prophet encouraged them with messages of salvation and forgiveness.[38] The term "remnant" is also applied by Ellen G. White to the historical remnant that was taken into captivity[39] and to those who were left in the land.[40]

During the exile, there was "a remnant who resolutely withstood the evil influences surrounding them, and maintained their allegiance to Jehovah. These were constantly growing in courage and true godliness. They clung to the Lord more firmly as they saw the apostasy of their brethren. Their faith grew stronger with every conflict."[41] This obviously points to the endurance of the faithful remnant and to the depth of their commitment to the Lord. Finally a remnant chose to return from Babylon.[42] This was not an exclusive remnant. "God gave every captive Israelite in Babylon an opportunity to form a part of this remnant."[43] Among the remnant that returned under Cyrus were those who had found salvation in the midst of their afflictions during the exile.[44] Unfortunately, "many of the remnant who returned to Judea, had fallen into a backslidden condition"[45] and had stopped rebuilding the temple. Under the leadership of Zerubbabel and Joshua and at the urging of Haggai and Zechariah, they repented and finished the temple.

---

repent (ibid., p. 291).

[34] Ibid., p. 324.

[35] Ibid.; the passage is quoted by her.

[36] Ibid., p. 333.

[37] Ibid., p. 426.

[38] Ibid., p. 466.

[39] Ibid., p. 453.

[40] Ibid., p. 460.

[41] "Idolatry Punished," *ST*, June 9, 1881.

[42] *Prophets and Kings*, p. 268.

[43] "The Return of the Exiles—No. 11: In the Days of Queen Esther," *RH*, Jan 23, 1908.

[44] *Prophets and Kings*, p. 598.

[45] "Return of the Exiles."

Ellen G. White also found an eschatological remnant in a number of passages from the Old Testament (e.g., Hos 2:18-23; Isa 10:20).[46] This eschatological remnant will include non-Israelites from all the nations.[47] These prophecies addressing God's people in the Old Testament will find their fulfillment in the end-time remnant of the Christian church.[48]

Remnant in the New Testament

Ellen G. White does not develop the concept of the remnant in the New Testament. Apart from her discussion of the remnant in the book of Revelation, she makes comments on the remnant of Israel mentioned by Paul in Rom 11. She identifies the Jews who accepted Jesus as the Messiah as the faithful Jews who listened to and received the message of John the Baptist and who had been studying messianic prophecies. They constituted the Christian church.[49] They belonged to the true stock of Israel, namely. "the remnant who had remained true to the God of their fathers."[50] To them and to the Gentiles who joined them belonged the blessings of Israel.[51]

During the time of the apostle John, Ellen G. White writes that many Christians were being martyred. In that context she indicates that "the remnant of believers was facing fierce opposition."[52] These were the faithful believers who were still alive.

Remnant in Church History

Ellen G. White applies the term "remnant" to groups of believers who experienced oppression and persecution for their faith. At the end of the persecution against the Protestant Bohemians in 1470, she writes that "a goodly remnant" of them were left.[53] We can refer to them as a faithful and historical remnant. She also describes the Waldenses as a remnant of the apostolic church of Italy.[54] The faith of the remnant is in continuity with the apostolic faith. The term is also applied to those who, after the

---

[46] *Prophets and Kings*, p. 299.

[47] Ibid., pp. 376-378.

[48] Ibid., pp. 300, 727-728.

[49] *The Acts of the Apostles*, p. 377.

[50] Ibid., p. 378.

[51] Ibid., p. 379.

[52] Ibid., p. 581.

[53] *The Great Controversy*, p. 119.

[54] *Historical Sketches of the Foreign Missions of the Seventh-day Adventists* (Basel: Imprimerie Polyglotte, 1886), p. 239.

Millerite disappointment, continued to wait for the coming of Christ but who were forbidden to speak about it in their churches.[55] This remnant was again an historical and faithful remnant. Through Bible study, they discovered the truths of Christ's work in the heavenly sanctuary and the permanent validity of the Ten Commandments, including the seventh-day Sabbath.[56]

Her discussion of the witness of God's remnant throughout history highlights several important elements related to the remnant itself. First, in a number of cases, the emphasis is on an historical remnant who survived a national life-threatening experience but whose spiritual commitment was practically non-existent. Second, more often the remnant is a faithful remnant that is not only encouraged by God's prophets but who, in the midst of apostasy, also practiced and preserved the messages and the truth coming from the Lord. Third, the remnant suffered oppression and even persecution, yet they remained loyal to the Lord under very adverse circumstances. These aspects of the remnant will be accentuated by Ellen G. White in her discussion of the end-time remnant.

III. End-Time Remnant

Since God has always had a remnant, it is to be expected that at the close of the cosmic conflict, He will also have a remnant people. Ellen G. White explicitly states, "As the end of all things earthly should approach, there would be faithful ones able to discern the signs of the times. While a large number of professing believers would deny their faith by their works, there would be a remnant who would endure to the end."[57] This conviction is based on the apocalyptic prophecies of the book of Revelation, particularly Rev 12:17 and 14:12.[58]

Characteristics of the Remnant

The fundamental characteristics of the eschatological remnant in the

---

[55] *Early Writings* (Washington, DC: Review and Herald, 1882), p. 247. See P. Gerard Damsteegt, *Foundations of the Seventh-day Adventist Message and Mission* (Grand Rapids, MI: Eerdmans, 1977), p. 147.

[56] *Early Writings*, p. 255.

[57] *The Acts of the Apostles*, pp. 535-536.

[58] E.g., *The Desire of Ages*, p. 398; *Manuscript Releases*, vol. 13 (Silver Spring, MD: Ellen G. White Estate, 1993), p. 69. Those two passages describe the character and the work of the remnant (Manuscript 18, 1904, St. Helena, CA, Feb 3, 1903, "The World to Be Warned").

writings of Ellen G. White are basically developed along the lines of what Revelation says about them. In her view, two passages provide the essential characteristics that reveal the distinctiveness of the remnant. The first is Rev 14:12, where they are identified as those who keep the commandments of God and the faith of Jesus.[59] According to her, the commandments of God involve all of the Ten Commandments, including the seventh-day Sabbath.[60] The remnant is identified by their obedience to the law of God (12:17).

The remnant is also characterized by keeping "the faith of Jesus."[61] Ellen G. White understood this phrase in two complementary ways. First, it refers to "all the teachings of Jesus in the New Testament."[62] The remnant is not only loyal to the law of God but also to the teachings of Jesus. In fact, she emphasizes that there is a close connection between the remnant and the Word of God. God has always had "a remnant who trusted in the Word of God."[63] Scripture defines and identifies who they are.[64] They are diligent students of it[65] and have been called "to proclaim his Word in all lands."[66] They are faithful to the Word of God under the most difficult conditions and have made it "their shield and buckler."[67]

At times she interprets the phrase "faith of Jesus" as "faith in Jesus," suggesting that the remnant "have faith in Jesus."[68] Consequently, she

---

[59]"Humility and Faithfulness in Laborers," *RH*, April 8, 1884; "Build the Old Waste Places," *RH*, June 12, 1893.

[60]*Prophets and Kings*, p. 768.

[61]For further discussion of this phrase in her writings, see Rodríguez, "The Testimony of Jesus in the Writings of Ellen G. White," in this volume.

[62]*Manuscript Releases*, vol. 5, p. 290.

[63]"They Shall be Mine, Saith the Lord of Hosts," *RH*, Nov 23, 1904.

[64]"Humility and Faithfulness in Laborers," *RH*, April 8, 1884; *Manuscript Releases*, vol. 5, p. 53.

[65]*Counsels on Sabbath School Work* (Washington, DC: Review and Herald, 1938), p. 34.

[66]"The Return of the Exiles," *RH*, Feb 27, 1908.

[67]*Manuscript Releases*, vol. 5, p. 51. She emphasizes the fact that "God will have a people upon the earth to maintain the Bible, and the Bible only, as the standard of all doctrines, and the basis of all reforms. The opinions of learned men, the deductions of science, the creeds or decisions of ecclesiastical councils, as numerous and discordant as are the churches which they represent, the voice of the majority,—not one or all of these should be regarded as evidence for or against any point of religious faith. Before accepting any doctrine or precept, we should demand a plain 'Thus saith the Lord' in its support" (*The Great Controversy*, p. 595).

[68]*Testimonies to Ministers and Gospel Workers* (Mountain View, CA: Pacific Press, 1923), p. 58.

interprets the full phrase "keep the commandments of God and have the faith of Jesus" as a reference to the law and the gospel. The remnant do not pull apart the gospel and the law but proclaim both in their proper theological balance. According to Ellen G. White, the Adventist people are "the only people who are fulfilling the description given of the remnant people, who keep the commandments of God and have faith in Jesus."[69]

Revelation 12:17 defines the end-time remnant as those who keep the commandments of God and "have the testimony of Jesus." When that last phrase is used in conjunction with the commandments of God, Ellen G. White interprets it to mean that the remnant "keep the commandments of God and the testimony of Jesus."[70] She seems to suggest that Rev 12:17 affirms that the remnant are those who practice the truth.[71] When that phrase is used in conjunction with the term "remnant," she does not clearly define its meaning. In most cases she is simply quoting Rev 12:17.[72] She states that "the faith of Jesus and the testimony of Jesus are blended. They are to be clearly presented to the world."[73] "Blended" seems here to mean that they are proclaimed together, each one perhaps carrying a particular emphasis.

Based on Rev 14:12—"they have the patience of the saints"—Ellen G. White comments that the remnant are end-time believers who love God and endure and are faithful to the end.[74] They are firmly committed to divine truth under adverse circumstances, but at the same time, they are open to more divine biblical truth.[75] Finally, the remnant are not only the bearers of biblical truth in the midst of apostasy but also worshipers

---

[69]Ibid.

[70]*Testimonies for the Church*, vol. 2, p. 105.

[71]"God's Standard of Character," *RH*, May 3, 1898.

[72]See, for instance, *Testimonies to Ministers*, p. 133; *Testimonies for the Church*, vol. 8, p. 117; vol. 5, p. 449.

[73]*PH086—Special Testimony to Battle Creek Church* (1898), p. 6.

[74]*The Acts of the Apostles*, p. 536; *Early Writings*, p. 66.

[75]She specifically wrote, "New light will ever be revealed on the word of God to him who is in living connection with the Sun of Righteousness. Let no one come to the conclusion that there is no more truth to be revealed. The diligent, prayerful seeker for truth will find precious rays of light yet to shine forth from the word of God. Many gems are yet scattered that are to be gathered together to become the property of the remnant people of God. But light is not given simply to be a strength to the church, but to be shed upon those who are in darkness" (*Counsels on Sabbath School Work*, p. 34). She then adds, "Great truths which have been neglected and unappreciated for ages, will be revealed by the Spirit of God, and new meaning will flash out of familiar texts. Every page will be illuminated by the Spirit of truth" (p. 35).

of the Creator of heaven and earth (14:7).[76] According to Ellen White, it should be clear that the obedience of the remnant and their commitment to God are not the grounds for their acceptance before God. They "stand before the world as monuments of God's mercy."[77] Divine mercy constituted them in what they are.

There is one last characteristic of the remnant that Ellen G. White emphasizes in a particular way, namely, the unity of God's remnant people. Their oneness and unity have a profound persuasive power upon the world concerning their claims and identity as God's end-time remnant.[78] Such deep union and oneness "disconcert the enemy, and he is determined that it shall not exist."[79] It is a unity based on biblical truth that is to be accepted and appropriated by believers.

Mission of the Remnant

Since the end-time remnant will be gathered by God from all over the world, the message they proclaim has to be global in nature. The members of the remnant church are exhorted "to go into all the world with the gospel message."[80] In other places Ellen G. White indicates that the remnant are to "call attention to the commandments of God and the faith of Jesus."[81] The emphasis on the commandments of God and the faith of Jesus, understood by her to designate the teachings of Jesus and the faith we place on Him as our Savior, is determined by her understanding that the Christian church rejected, altered, or neglected important biblical truths. She sees the movement toward apostasy as an important element in the cosmic conflict.[82]

Because biblical truth has been distorted, Ellen G. White considers God's end-time remnant people to be reformers and their mission to restore biblical truth. She finds a parallel between the work of the Israelites who returned from exile and the work and mission of the eschatological remnant. The work of the returnees was one of restoration and reform and illustrates "a work of spiritual restoration that is to be wrought in the

---

[76] *Prophets and Kings*, p. 300.

[77] Ibid.

[78] *Testimonies for the Church*, vol. 1, p. 327.

[79] Ibid.

[80] "The Great Commission: A Call to Service," *RH*, March 24, 1910.

[81] *The Desire of Ages*, p. 398.

[82] For a fuller discussion of these issues see *The Great Controversy*, pp. 49-60. Her views are based on the prophecies of Daniel and Revelation interpreted from an historicist perspective.

closing days of this earth's history."[83] As reformers, the remnant will show that the law of God should be the foundation of all true reformation, that the Sabbath is a memorial of the creative power of God, and that God expects obedience to His law.[84] What propels the mission of the remnant is not a legalistic concern that undermines the freedom of the gospel of salvation. "Constrained by the love of Christ, they are to co-operate with Him in building up the waste places. They are to be repairers of the breach, restorers of paths to dwell in."[85] What they do is a genuine expression of love to Christ as their dear Savior. They consider the gospel to be at the very heart of their message ("I saw another angel . . . proclaiming the eternal gospel" [Rev 14:6]), but not in opposition to obedience to the Decalogue. As we already indicated, it is to this delicate balance that Ellen G. White refers through the phrase "keep the commandments of God and have faith in Jesus." She applies Isa 58:13-14 to the remnant and concludes that "in the time of the end every divine institution is to be restored. The breach made in the law at the time the Sabbath was changed by man, is to be repaired."[86] This work of restoration and reformation cannot be separated from the gospel.[87]

The messages of the three angels of Rev 14:6-12 place the gospel at the center and alert humanity to satanic deception. Therefore, it is indispensable for the remnant to proclaim them.[88] They proclaim "the last message of warning, the last invitation to the marriage supper of the Lamb."[89] Their mission is to prepare the world for the coming of the Lord.[90] That last message is to be proclaimed with a loud cry and "will go

---

[83]*Prophets and Kings*, p. 677.

[84]Ibid., p. 678.

[85]Ibid.

[86]*Prophets and Kings*, p. 678.

[87]This work of reformation also applies to the private lives of believers and includes, among many other things, health reform. Ellen G. White promoted a return to the diet that God gave to Adam and Eve (vegetarianism) and encouraged the remnant to abstain from harmful food. She specifically mentions flesh meats, tea, and coffee. See *Counsels on Diet and Foods* (Washington, DC: Review and Herald, 1938), pp. 380-382.

[88]"A Present Help in Every Time of Trouble," *RH*, July 16, 1901; and *Ellen G. White: 1888 Materials* (Washington, DC: Ellen G. White Estate, 1987), p. 724.

[89]*Prophets and Kings*, p. 87.

[90]"The Need of Love," *RH*, Aug 28, 1888. She exhorts every believer, saying: "As humble, faithful soldiers of Jesus Christ, you are to stand in the world, breasting its opposition,—a little remnant to clear the King's highway. You want to exert such an influence that men will be drawn to give their heart's affections to God, and to take the requisite steps in faith, repentance, conversion, and baptism."

forward with increasing importance till the close of the time."[91] In other words, the message will become more and more relevant and will result in polarizing the human race: "Two parties will exist at the appearing of our Lord and Savior Jesus Christ."[92] The remnant will be characterized by a childlike faith and "as a child lost weeps and longs for home, so did the remnant long to see Him who their souls loveth, their Deliverer, Him on whom their hope of eternal life was centered. Pilgrims and strangers amidst labors, sorrows, and conflicts, they turn the eyes of faith heavenward, exclaiming, 'Come, Lord Jesus, and come quickly.' "[93]

Opposition to the Remnant

Apocalyptic prophecies indicate that satanic powers will be angered with the end-time remnant and will oppose them (Rev 12:17). Ellen G. White often alerts believers concerning the wrath of the dragon against them and reveals to them elements of his plan of deception. He will work with cunning to "wrest from Christ the remnant of the children of men who have accepted His salvation."[94] In that effort, Satan will attempt to bring false doctrines among God's remnant people to unsettle their faith in the "old landmarks."[95] She comments that Satan will suggest "doubts as to whether we are really the people whom God is leading, whom by tests and provings he is preparing to stand in the great day," but that we should "be ready to meet his insinuations by presenting the clear evidence from the word of God that this is the remnant people who are keeping the commandments of God and the faith of Jesus."[96]

The dragon will also attempt to bring division among God's remnant people. "As we near the close of time, Satan comes down with great power knowing his time is short. Especially upon the remnant will his power be exercised. He will war against them, he will seek to divide and scatter them, that they may grow weak and be overthrown."[97] She exhorts the people of God to "be of the same mind, of the same judgment."[98] But satanic deception will fail. Then he will direct his efforts to blot them from

---

[91] *Testimonies for the Church*, vol. 9, p. 154.

[92] *PH086—Special Testimony to Battle Creek Church* (*1898*), p. 31.

[93] Manuscript 16, 1884, "Satan's Last Deception."

[94] *Testimonies for the Church*, vol. 5, p. 470.

[95] Ibid., p. 295.

[96] "Humility and Faithfulness in Laborers," *RH*, April 8, 1884.

[97] *Spiritual Gifts*, vol. 4b, (Battle Creek, MI: Steam Press, 1864), p. 45.

[98] Ibid.

the earth in order for his triumph to be complete.[99] In that endeavor he will gain the support of civil powers and apostate Christendom.[100]

Condition and Experience of the Remnant

God's remnant people will go through a diversity of experiences as they fulfill their mission. To better understand the significance of those experiences, we will suggest that Ellen G. White appears to distinguish between the condition and experience of the remnant in the present—as it is fulfilling the mission—and their experience at the very close of the conflict. We can perhaps refer to the first as the historical and faithful remnant, and the second as not only historical and faithful but also eschatological. She does not employ that terminology, but it could be useful to us in analyzing what she has to say.

Faithful and Historical Remnant

For Ellen G. White, the term "remnant" is a collective designation that allows for the presence of defective elements within it. This seems to be supported by the following statement: "I saw that there was too little glorifying God, too little childlike simplicity among the remnant."[101] It is not that these are characteristics of the remnant but that some within the remnant lack a spirit of Christian joy and gratitude. In other cases she condemns a spiritual condition that seems to be prevalent among the remnant people. For instance, they need to wake from spiritual sleep and walk in the light they have.[102] In a particular case she wrote, "I saw that the remnant were not prepared for what is coming upon the earth. Stupidity, like lethargy, seemed to hang upon the minds of most of those who profess to believe that we are having the last message."[103]

With prophetic voice she condemns sin and indifference in the remnant and exhorts them to loyalty. She specifically condemns the waning of love,[104] indifference to the needs of a perishing world,[105] selfishness

---

[99] *Testimonies for the Church*, vol. 5, p. 450.

[100] "The Seal of God—No. 2," *ST*, Nov 8, 1899. Satan and his angels will inspire "the world, the church, and state against them" (Manuscript 16, 1884, "Satan's Last Deception").

[101] *Manuscript Releases*, vol. 5, p. 238.

[102] *Testimonies for the Church*, vol. 1, p. 263.

[103] *Early Writings*, p. 119.

[104] *Selected Messages*, Book 1 (Washington, DC: Review and Herald, 1958), p. 387.

[105] *Testimonies to the Churches*, vol. 8, p. 24.

and pride,[106] and a spirit of fanaticism among the remnant.[107] She mentions cases of persons who, although part of the remnant people of God, were acting independent of the body of believers and causing division.[108] There was a time when some were not involved in the proclamation of the gospel but were depending on ministers for the fulfillment of that task.[109] She exhorts the remnant people to walk closely with the Lord[110] and to fully surrender their wills to Him so as not to be trapped by the enemy.[111] Her exhortation to loyalty and to a full commitment to the Lord on the part of the remnant appears to be grounded on her conviction that Satan was trying to undermine that commitment and distract them from proclaiming the message in an effort to destroy their effectiveness. In those cases the term "remnant" is practically used as a synonym for "Adventists." Yet the theological content of the term is not absent.

Historical, Faithful, and Eschatological Remnant

Ellen G. White says that for God to accomplish His purpose through the remnant, He will pass them through a purifying process, or a shaking. The church will remain,

> while the sinners in Zion will be sifted out—the chaff separated from the precious wheat. This is a terrible ordeal, but nevertheless it must take place. None but those who have been overcoming by the blood of the Lamb and the word of their testimony will be found with the loyal and true, without spot or stain of sin, without guile in their mouths. . . . The remnant that purify their souls by obeying the truth gather strength from the trying process, exhibiting the beauty of holiness amid the surrounding apostasy.[112]

The experience the remnant will go through will result in a faithful and purified people of God. It is their unbending obedience to the truth that

---

[106]*Early Writings*, p. 119.

[107]*Selected Messages*, Book 2, p. 46.

[108]*Selected Messages*, Book 3, p. 23.

[109]"The Great Commission: A Call to Service," *RH*, March 24, 1910.

[110]*Historical Sketches*, p. 156.

[111]*Life Sketches of Ellen G. White* (Mountain View, CA: Pacific Press, 1915), p. 323.

[112]*Maranatha: The Lord is Coming* (Washington, DC: Review and Herald, 1975), p. 203. This indicates that for Ellen G. White, the end-time remnant is the last remnant in human history; another remnant will not come out of it. It is God's "last church" (Manuscript 40, 1887, "Peril of Doubt and Unbelief").

purifies their souls.[113] She further comments, "As the storm approaches, a large class who have professed faith in the third angel's message, but have not been sanctified through obedience to the truth, abandon their position and join the ranks of the opposition."[114] At the same time, the call to come out of Babylon will go out and "all who are honest will leave the fallen churches, and take their stand with the remnant."[115]

The remnant people of God will confront the wrath of the dragon in an almost unprecedented way. They will be brought into great trial and distress and will feel the wrath of their enemy.[116] They will "have to meet the constant and most powerful masterly workings of the power of darkness for this last time."[117] The nations of the earth will unite "in making void God's law."[118] But there "will be a remnant of the righteous that will be obedient to God's requirements."[119] They will be required to obey human laws, but they will resist the supremacy of the evil powers.[120] They will be betrayed by relatives and friends, but their "greatest trials will come from those who profess holiness . . . from those who profess to be their brethren."[121]

The experience of the eschatological remnant will be similar to that of God's people during the time of Esther. Through the support of apostate religious powers and governments, the enemy will be able to decree

---

[113] *Manuscript Releases*, vol. 12, p. 325.

[114] *The Great Controversy*, p. 608.

[115] *Early Writings*, p. 261; *The Great Controversy*, p. 608. She interprets Rev 18:4—"Come out of her [Babylon] my people"—to mean that many of God's people will be found in apostate Christendom.

[116] *Testimonies for the Church*, vol. 8, p. 231.

[117] Letter 60, 1893, Wellington, New Zealand, July 20, 1893, to Elder I. D. Van Horn, Charlotte, Michigan.

[118] *Testimonies for the Church*, vol. 5, p. 524. She wrote, "The dignitaries of church and state will unite to bribe, persuade, or compel all classes to honor the Sunday. The lack of divine authority will be supplied by oppressive enactments. Political corruption is destroying love of justice and regard for truth; and even in free America, rulers and legislators, in order to secure public favor, will yield to the popular demand for a law enforcing Sunday observance. Liberty of conscience, which has cost so great a sacrifice, will no longer be respected. In the soon-coming conflict we shall see exemplified the prophet's words: 'The dragon was wroth with the woman, and went to make war with the remnant of her seed, which keep the commandments of God, and have the testimony of Jesus Christ.' Revelation 12:17" (*The Great Controversy*, p. 592).

[119] "Preparation for the Testing Time," *ST*, April 22, 1889.

[120] *Testimonies for the Church*, vol. 9, p. 231.

[121] "Our Present Position," *RH*, Aug 28, 1883.

the extermination of God's remnant people.[122] They will be threatened with death, and they will be unable to defend themselves (Rev 13:13-18).[123] The divine promise is that during that time of trouble, the Lord will provide bread and water for them.[124] Under these stressful conditions, their faith will grow even stronger,[125] and they will find in God their refuge and hope and will find in prayer their only defense.[126] They will particularly pray "for pardon and deliverance through their Advocate."[127] In response, God will assure them that they have received the robe of Christ's righteousness and that their names remain in the book of life, eternally secure.[128]

God's remnant people will be scattered all over the world, exiled, pursued, and persecuted by the forces of evil.[129] But God will gather "the remnant church from among the nations of the earth," and they will shout for joy as they see their Savior coming in glory to deliver them.[130] This eschatological remnant will be formed by those who have come out of Babylon and by the faithful remnant who have passed through a cleansing experience. They will overcome "by the blood of the Lamb and the word of their testimony."

IV. A Remnant Outside the Remnant

The term "remnant" is used by Ellen G. White to designate individuals who love the Lord but who are not members of God's end-time remnant people. We should examine this particular usage so as not to confuse the two. She writes, "In the cities and nations of our world, there will be found among unbelievers a remnant who will appreciate the blessed Word, and who will receive the Saviour. Christ will give men and women power to become the sons and daughters of God."[131]

---

[122]*Prophets and Kings*, pp. 605-606. This is based on the end-time death decree predicted in Rev 13:15.

[123]*Christian Experience and Teachings of Ellen G. White* (Mountain View, CA: Pacific Press, 1922), p. 188.

[124]*The Story of Redemption* (Washington, DC: Review and Herald, 1947), p. 129.

[125]*Testimonies for the Church*, vol. 5, p. 524.

[126]Ibid.; *Prophets and Kings*, p. 588.

[127]*Prophets and Kings*, p. 588.

[128]Ibid., p. 591.

[129]*That I May Know Him* (Washington, DC: Review and Herald, 1964), p. 360.

[130]*Prophets and Kings*, p. 727.

[131]"The Power of the Word of God," *RH*, Nov 10, 1904.

It is clear that she is not using the term "remnant" to designate the end-time eschatological people of God. Here "remnant" seems to mean "a minority" or "a small group." This specific "remnant" is found among unbelievers and is defined by her as people who will listen to God's Word and who will accept Christ as their Savior. They are sincere and open to biblical truth. We find a similar usage in another of her statements:

> The world is preparing for the last great conflict, nation rising against nation. The vast majority of human beings are taking their stand against God. But in every age the Lord Jesus has had His witnesses,— a remnant who trusted in the Word of God. And today, in every place, there are those who hold communion with God. A vital undercurrent of influence is leading them to the light, and when the question comes to them, "Who is on the Lord's side?" they will take their position for Him. Their characters have been molded after the divine similitude, because they have read and practiced the teachings of His Word.
>
> Many in retired homes are God's hidden ones, serving Him according to the light they have received. These hidden ones greatly delight in the Word of God. His precepts are appreciated and treasured by them, and many are the works of love that they do for Christ's sake.[132]

The term is apparently being applied to individuals who are not yet part of God's end-time eschatological remnant, but who serve God according to the knowledge of Him that they have.[133] At the moment when

---

[132] "'They Shall be Mine,' Saith the Lord of Hosts," *ST*, Nov 23, 1904.

[133] Ellen G. White has commented on the idea that even non-Christians who are living up to the light they have are accepted by God. For instance, she writes, "Our standing before God depends, not upon the amount of light we have received, but upon the use we make of what we have. Thus even the heathen who choose the right as far as they can distinguish it are in a more favorable condition than are those who have had great light, and profess to serve God, but who disregard the light, and by their daily life contradict their profession" (*The Desire of Ages*, p. 239). Even more direct is the following statement: "Those whom Christ commends in the judgment may have known little of theology, but they have cherished His principles. Through the influence of the divine Spirit they have been a blessing to those about them. Even among the heathen are those who have cherished the spirit of kindness; before the words of life had fallen upon their ears, they have befriended the missionaries, even ministering to them at the peril of their own lives. Among the heathen are those who worship God ignorantly, those to whom the light is never brought by human instrumentality, yet they will not perish. Though ignorant of the written law of God, they have heard His voice speaking to them in nature, and have done the things that the law required. Their works are evidence that the Holy Spirit has

the message of the biblical eschatological remnant reaches them, they will take their stand with them. This is a unique usage of the term "remnant" in the writings of Ellen G. White and points in a particular way to the inclusive nature of the remnant. According to her, God is also active outside the end-time remnant, working in the hearts of humans all over the planet. She explicitly states:

> Among earth's inhabitants, scattered in every land, there are those who have not bowed the knee to Baal. Like the stars of heaven, which appear only at night, these faithful ones will shine forth when darkness covers the earth and gross darkness the people. In heathen Africa, in the Catholic lands of Europe and of South America, in China, in India, in the islands of the sea, and in all the dark corners of the earth, God has in reserve a firmament of chosen ones that will yet shine forth amidst the darkness, revealing clearly to an apostate world the transforming power of obedience to His law.[134]

Although the specific term "remnant" is not used by her in that statement, we do find an equivalent expression, "a firmament of chosen ones." The clear implication is that, for her, the people of God include many more than those who are now part of the end-time remnant church.

V. Conclusion

The concept of the remnant in the writings of Ellen G. White is firmly grounded in the Scriptures and placed by her within the frame of reference of the cosmic conflict. She defines the remnant as those through whom God fulfills His saving design for the human race and to whom are fulfilled the covenant promises. They accepted the salvation provided to them through the Son of God. It is through them that God preserves His self-revelation, given to humans by means of His prophets.

According to Ellen G. White, God has always preserved a faithful remnant for Himself. This was the case in the Old and New Testaments and

---

touched their hearts, and they are recognized as the children of God" (Ibid., p. 638). That is only possible through the work of Christ: "As through Christ every human being has life, so also through Him every soul receives some ray of divine light. Not only intellectual but spiritual power, a perception of right, a desire for goodness, exists in every heart" (*Education* [Mountain View, CA: Pacific Press, 1903], p. 29). She never defined Adventism as an exclusive religious movement.

[134]*Prophets and Kings*, pp. 188-189.

throughout the history of the Christian church. This will also be the case at the end of the cosmic conflict, when the world will be characterized by apostasy and rebellion against God's will. Ellen G. White argues that this remnant is clearly identified in the book of Revelation and that its members have a mission to the world. At the center of the message they proclaim, we find the gospel and the law of God. The remnant people are reformers, called by God to restore biblical truth that has been displaced by human traditions. They have become the object of the wrath of evil powers who will try to deceive them and finally to exterminate them with the support of human instrumentalities. Consequently, the remnant will go through very trying circumstances and through a cleansing experience. Many will leave the remnant, but many from Babylon will join them.

In two cases Ellen G. White refers to sincere believers who are still in Babylon as a remnant. This usage should be distinguished from that of the end-time remnant people of God. The remnant who believe will come out of Babylon and will join God's eschatological remnant. These remnant people "are not only pardoned and accepted, but honored. 'A fair miter' is set upon their heads. They are to be as kings and priests unto God. While Satan was urging his accusations and seeking to destroy this company, holy angels, unseen, were passing to and fro, placing upon them the seal of the living God. These are they that stand upon Mount Zion with the Lamb, having the Father's name written in their foreheads. They sing the new song before the throne . . ."[135]

---

[135] *Testimonies for the Church*, vol. 5, pp. 475-476.

CHAPTER XI

CONCLUDING ESSAY: GOD'S END-TIME REMNANT AND THE CHRISTIAN CHURCH

Ángel Manuel Rodríguez
Director
Biblical Research Institute
Silver Spring, MD

This closing chapter will attempt to integrate the main theological emphases of the previous ones, further develop some of them, and introduce new ones so as to clarify as much as possible the Adventist understanding of the remnant as an ecclesiological self-designation. We have already indicated that Adventist ecclesiology is fundamentally expressed through the biblical concept of the remnant. Previous chapters in this volume have demonstrated how pervasive the concept of the remnant is in the Scriptures, thus indicating its centrality in biblical thinking and its direct connection with God's plan for the human race. Since the concept runs through both Testaments, it provides a high level of continuity to the biblical concept of the people of God. Consequently, it can be of great value in the formulation of a biblical ecclesiology that addresses issues related to the very life and experiences of God's people throughout history. The concept is used in the Bible to establish distinctions that contribute to a clearly defined mission of the remnant.

I. Christological Focus of the Concept of the Remnant

As has been pointed out, in the Old Testament the motif of the remnant is employed to address the fundamental question of life and death.[1] When confronted with a mortal threat, the family, the tribe, or the nation asked whether life would be extinguished or whether some, a remnant, would survive. The remnant became a sign of hope, because as survivors the members carried with them the potential to preserve the life of

---

[1] See the discussion in Tarsee Li, "The Remnant in the Old Testament," in this volume. Also, Gerhard F. Hasel, "Remnant," *ISBE*, vol. 4, p. 132; *idem*, "Remnant," *IDBSup*, p. 735.

their group. In them the possibility for its restoration was real.² From that broad non-religious usage, the term "remnant" developed a theological content closely related to God's activity within salvation-history. The remnant became the center or nucleus of God's true people, through whom God's redemptive work will succeed in spite of threats, obstacles, and opposition.³ Situations arise in history that would oppose God's sovereign purpose, threatening His people and the realization of His plans for the human race, but God has always preserved a remnant through which His willingness to save the human race from extinction was to be fulfilled. For this "believing minority"⁴ there is a future, and through it, a future for the human race. Therefore, the concept is of profound theological significance and illustrates God's unbending determination to preserve the human race from extinction in spite of the presence of sin and evil in the world.

If the divine intention is to preserve the human race through a remnant, then it is obvious that the concept of the remnant is to be deeply connected to the person of Christ, who is God's instrument for the salvation of sinners. It could even be affirmed that, theologically speaking, Jesus Christ is the truest "remnant." In Him we finally find a person who was absolutely faithful to God under the most difficult circumstances and who was able to overcome the forces of evil (e.g., Heb 3:2; 2:14-15). In His life and ministry, Jesus recapitulated the experiences not only of Adam but also of the people of God. Where Adam failed, Jesus overcame. He was the only one who remained absolutely loyal to God and to His plan on earth; He was the Servant of the Lord par excellence. In His own person and through His sacrificial death, God was to preserve for Himself a remnant. Since Christ permanently took upon Himself human nature, we could argue that even if the totality of the human race were to reject the salvation He obtained for them, the race would not be extinguished from the universe. God would have preserved it in the person of His Son as a human being (cf. 1 Cor 15:22-28; 1 Tim 2:5).

If Christ is to be identified as the true and faithful remnant, then the identity of the eschatological remnant is fundamentally related to the person and work of Christ. This remnant constitutes the true people of God by virtue of their union with Him. Therefore, the remnant not only

---

²See, R. E. Clements, "*Šā'ar*," *TDOT*, vol. 14, p. 285.
³G. Hasel, "Remnant," *IDBSup*, p. 736.
⁴Clements, "*Šā'ar*," p. 274.

owes its existence to Him, but He also shared with it His victory over evil.[5] The remnant people have joined Christ in the realization of the divine plan for the preservation of the human race and, empowered by the Spirit, they participate in His mission. It has been through Christ that God has preserved the remnant and used it to His glory.

II. Adventist Appropriation of the Remnant Motif

Indeed, God always has had a remnant through which He has fulfilled His purposes for humanity. This has also been the case in the history of the Christian church. The book of Revelation places the existence of the remnant at the close of the cosmic conflict, shortly before the return of the Lord in glory (12:17). Adventists have found their self-identity and mission in the nature and role of the end-time remnant described in the book of Revelation.

Appropriation Based on the Historicist Interpretation of Rev 12–14

To comprehend the nature and role of the end-time eschatological remnant and its appropriation by Adventists, it is necessary to understand the Adventist interpretation of Rev 12–14.[6] Revelation 12 provides a sum-

---

[5]The close connection between the end-time remnant and Christ is suggested by a comparison between Rev 12:17 and 12:5 (the parallel between the two passages is pointed out by Ekkehardt Mueller, "The End Time Remnant in Revelation," *JATS* 11.1, 2 [2000]: 191, but not developed). In 12:5 Christ is the son of the woman dressed with the sun. He is her male child, the descendent promised to her in Gen 3:15. In 12:17, the remnant is specifically called "the rest of her offspring." They also are descendents of the woman, and consequently they are related to Christ. The dragon fought against Him at the beginning of and during His earthly ministry, and now at the end he is ready to make war again against Christ and the rest of the descendents of the woman. They, like Christ, are obedient to the will of God under the most difficult and trying circumstances (Matt 26:39; Rev 14:12). On the allusion to Gen 3:15 in Rev 12:17, see David E. Aune, *Revelation 6–16* (Nashville, TN: Thomas Nelson, 1998), p. 708.

[6]Here we cannot provide a detailed exegesis of those chapters. The reader is referred to the following Adventist sources: Ranko Stefanovic, *Revelation of Jesus Christ: Commentary on the Book of Revelation* (Berrien Springs, MI: Andrews University Press, 2002), pp. 377-465; Jacques B. Doukhan, *Secrets of Revelation: The Apocalypse Through Hebrew Eyes* (Hagerstown, MD: Review and Herald, 2002), pp. 107-139; Jon Paulien, *What the Bible Says About the End-Time* (Hagerstown, MD: Review and Herald, 1994), pp. 105-129; William G. Johnsson, "The Saints' End-Time Victory over the Forces of Evil," in *Symposium in Revelation—Book II*, Frank B. Holbrook, ed. (Silver Spring, MD: Biblical Research Institute, 1992), pp. 3-40; Herbert Kiesler, "Étude exégétique d'Apocalypse 14," in *Études sur l'Apocalypse: Signification des messages des trois anges aujourdhui*, vol. 1 (France: Institut Adventiste du Saleve, 1988), pp. 76-103; and C. Mervyn Maxwell, *God*

mary of the conflict between Christ and Satan which is further developed in chapters 13–14. Chapter 13 describes the historical instruments used by the dragon to persecute the people of God—the beast from the sea and the beast from the earth. In Rev 13:1-10, there is a description of an attack against the church that parallels and develops 12:6, 13-16. The attack against the remnant mentioned in 12:17 is particularly developed in 13:11-18.[7] The beast from the sea is mortally wounded, but after gaining the support of the beast from the earth, its wound is healed. Under the influence of the dragon, they form a coalition against the remnant (cf. 16:12-14). Revelation 14:1-5 is a description of the remnant gathered with the Lamb on Mount Zion, protected from the attack of the dragon and its instruments.[8]

Cares, Volume 2: The Message of Revelation for You and Your Family (Boise, ID: Pacific Press, 1985), pp. 309-419. On the relationship between Rev 12 and 13 suggested above, see Kenneth A. Strand, "The Seven Heads: Do They Represent Roman Emperors?" in *Symposium*, p. 183, and Jon Paulien, "Eschatology and Adventist Self-Understanding," in *Lutheran and Adventists in Conversations: Report and Papers Presented 1994–1998* (Silver Spring, MD: General Conference of Seventh-day Adventists, 2000; and Geneva, Switzerland: Lutheran World Federation, 2000), pp. 237-253.

[7]This seems also to be the position taken by Grant R. Osborne, *Revelation* (Grand Rapids, MI: Baker, 2002), p. 453. Elisabeth Schüssler Fiorenza has suggested that 12:18–14:5 "expands upon the announcement of 12:17 that the dragon wages war with the rest of the woman's offspring" (*Revelation: Vision of a Just World* [Minneapolis, MN: Fortress, 1991], p. 82). But the fact that the prophetic period mentioned in 12:6, 14 is also mentioned in 13:5 (42 months x 30 = 1260) suggests that 13:1-8 is primarily a recapitulation and development of 12:6, 13-16. Hence 13:9–14:5 is an expansion of 12:17. However, it could be argued that chapter 13 is fundamentally about the end-time war. A careful reading of the text reveals that in some cases, the verbs are used in the past tense in order describe the actions of the two beasts in history. This idea has been suggested and developed by Jon Paulien, "Eschatology," pp. 237-253. He writes, "In each scene the Greek of Rev. 13 then moves from the description in the aorist tense to a mixture of present and future tenses (Rev. 13:8-10; 13:12-18), describing the actions of the two beasts in the context of the final attack of Rev. 12:17. So the two stages of history are clearly marked off by the Greek tenses signaling events prior to the dragon's war (aorist tense) and an elaboration of the events of the war itself (present and future tenses)" (pp. 243-244).

[8]Jürgen Roloff describes the connection between Rev 13 and 14:1 as follows: "Following the gloomier vision in chapter 13, which dealt with the unrestrained seizure of power by God's adversary and its creatures, now comes a counterpart that answers the question of the path and destiny of the salvation community in this situation that is so threatening to them. . . . The 144,000 are not the perfected martyrs, but rather the members of the earthly church. In their struggle against the totalitarian power of the world empire, embodied in the beast, they are not dependent upon themselves, but rather they are assembled around the lamb as the true ruler of the world to whom the future belongs. In a certain sense this vision, then, is also to be understood as a necessary continuation and a sharpening of 12:17: The descendants of the heavenly woman (i.e., the members of the church) are subjected on earth to the ruthless attacks of the adversary, but they are

The remnant coexists with the two beasts while the first is being healed. During that time the remnant proclaims the three angels' messages to all nations, tribes, languages, and peoples (14:6-12) in preparation for the return of the Lord described in the rest of the chapter (14:14-20).

We should now examine more closely the historical movement of Rev 12 and the personalities involved in that conflict.[9] Scholars generally agree that the woman clothed with the sun in 12:1 represents the people of God.[10] It is also acknowledged that the birth of the child is the fulfillment of the messianic prophecies of the Old Testament in the incarnation, life, ministry, death, and resurrection of Jesus.[11] The dragon is explicitly identified with Satan, who in the conflict unsuccessfully attempts to destroy the child.[12] The exaltation of Jesus to the throne of God testifies to the finality of His victory over evil powers. Realizing that he was defeated by the child, the dragon turns against the woman, i.e., the Christian community, God's instrument on earth for the proclamation of the redemptive work of the child. The woman is under attack for 1260 days and goes, so to speak, underground. At the end of that specific prophetic period, only the remnant of the woman is left, and it becomes the focus of the dragon's attack.[13]

---

not left alone. For even if the place at which their Lord exercises his dominion in the present age is heaven, he is still in their midst, even now, in a mysterious way" (*The Revelation of John: A Continental Commentary* [Minneapolis, MN: Fortress, 1993], pp. 169-170).

[9] See Paulien, "Eschatology," pp. 242-247, where he argues that Rev 12 and 13 are each an overview of three stages of Christian history.

[10] This is generally accepted by many scholars; see e.g., G. B. Caird, *A Commentary on the Revelation of St. John the Divine* (San Francisco, CA: Harper and Row, 1966), p. 149, who identifies the woman more specifically as the "messianic community" (he is followed by Schüssler Fiorenza, *Revelation*, p. 81); Robert W. Wall, *Revelation* (Peabody, MA: Hendrickson, 1991), p. 159, for whom the woman is "the faithful people of God" (cf. M. Eugene Boring, *Revelation* [Louisville, KY: Knox, 1989], p. 152; and Osborn, *Revelation*, p. 456; cf. Stephen S. Smalley, *The Revelation of John: A Commentary on the Greek Text of the Apocalypse* [Downers Grove, IL: InterVarsity, 2005], p. 315, for whom it designates "the heavenly counterpart of the true Israel"); and Roloff, *Revelation*, p. 145, who limits the symbol of the woman to "the end-time salvation community, a symbol of the church."

[11] The child is usually identified as the Messiah; see Osborne, *Revelation*, p. 457; Smalley, *Revelation*, pp. 319-120; and many others.

[12] It has been suggested that, according to Rev 12:4, the first object of attack of the dragon was the host of heaven, some of which he defeated (Osborne, *Revelation*, pp. 460-463; Smalley, *Revelation*, p. 318; Edmondo F. Lupieri, *A Commentary on the Apocalypse of John* [Grand Rapids, MI: Eerdmans, 1999], p. 192.). If that is the case, then the reference would be to the primordial war in heaven, explicitly mentioned in 12:7.

[13] Scholars disagree concerning the identity of the "offspring of the woman." For some they are the believing remnant in Israel; the 144,000—the remnant; the church on earth

In interpreting the book of Revelation, Adventists have used the historicist method of interpretation and consequently have found in Rev 12–14 a summary of the history of the Christian church. The term "historicism" is employed

> to describe a school of prophetic interpretation that conceives the fulfillment of the prophecies of Daniel and Revelation as covering the historical period from the time of the prophet to the establishment of the kingdom of God on earth. These prophecies were given in visionary cycles that recapitulate the content of the previous vision, adding new information or providing a slightly different perspective of the same historical period.[14]

Studies made on the history of this approach to prophetic interpretation have demonstrated that it was used by the early Church Fathers up to the fifth century A.D. Augustine introduced a significant shift in prophetic interpretation when he interpreted the kingdom of God as the Christian church, making the millennium a symbol of the Christian era.[15] Interestingly, the Reformation restored historicism as the method of prophetic interpretation and found in the apocalyptic prophecies predictions of the apostasy of the church.[16]

---

through the ages (for a list see Osborne, *Revelation*, pp. 484-485; Smalley, *Revelation*, p. 333). Since verses 13-16 describe the persecution of the woman and God's protection over her, the attack of the dragon against the offspring of the woman is the attack against the church at the end-time, called the remnant (see G. K. Beale, *The Book of Revelation: A Commentary on the Greek Text* [Grand Rapids, MI: Eerdmans, 1999], p. 678; Paulien, "Eschatology," p. 243; Stefanovic, *Revelation*, p. 394; Doukhan, *Secrets*, p. 112; David L. Barr, "Choosing Between Readings: Questions and Criteria," in *Reading the Book of Revelation: A Resource for Students*, David L. Barr, ed. [Atlanta, GA: Society of Biblical Literature, 2003], p. 164; cf. Lupieri, *Commentary*, p. 188).

[14]"Historicism," *AdvEnc*, vol. A-L, pp. 698-699.

[15]See Le Roy Edwin Froom, *The Prophetic Faith of Our Fathers*, vol. 1 (Washington, DC: Review and Herald, 1950), pp. 473-491.

[16]As a reaction against the Reformers' use of historicism, the Counter-Reformation developed the method of interpretation known as *preterism*. A Spanish Jesuit called Luis de Alcazar (d. 1613), argued that the prophecies of Revelation were fulfilled during the first six centuries of the Christian Era and that Nero was the antichrist (Froom, *Prophetic Faith*, vol. 2, pp. 505-506). It is interesting to observe that today *preterism* has been adopted by most Protestant scholars. According to them, Daniel was describing events that happened during the time of the Maccabees, and Revelation was dealing with the situation of the church during the time of John. Some more conservative scholars replaced historicism with *futurism* and applied the prophecies of Revelation mainly to events that will take place within a seven-year period just before the return of Christ. Adventists believe that

Concluding Essay: God's End-Time Remnant and the Christian Church

The history of the Christian church indicates that the persecution of the people of God was first brought about by pagan Rome and later by the apostasy of the church. It is no longer popular to speak about the apostasy of the church, but the fact that Paul predicted it implies that we should take it seriously. He said to the Ephesians: "I know that after my departure fierce wolves will come in among you, not sparing the flock; and from among your own selves will arise men speaking perverse things, to draw away the disciples after them" (Acts 20:29-30). In 2 Thess 2, Paul clearly states that the apostasy was not going to be limited to the church in Ephesus. In fact, he provides a chronology for it. He calls it "the rebellion, the apostasy" (*hē apostasia*), associates it with the "temple of God," and indicates that it will occur before the return of the Lord (2:3-4). According to Paul, the manifestation of this phenomenon was not yet a reality in his day because of the presence of a restraining power (2:6). The restraining force was commonly identified by the post-apostolic Church Fathers as "the civil order of the Roman Empire."[17] They concluded that the apostasy would appear after the fall of the Roman Empire.

During the Middle Ages the church united itself with the civil government and used force to impose its dogmas, persecuting those who rejected the traditions of the church. This age of persecution is described by Daniel as taking place for "a time, times, and half a time" (7:25), or 1260 days. According to Rev 12:6, this is the same time period during which the church hid itself. Together with many Christian interpreters, Adventists, employing the year-day principle,[18] have taken the 1260 days

---

historicism is supported by the Scriptures and that in using it, they are also restoring an important aspect of the Reformers' work.

[17] J. Terence Forestell, "The Letter to the Thessalonians," in *The Jerome Biblical Commentary*, vol. 2, Raymond E. Brown, Joseph A. Fitzmyer, and Roland E. Murphy, eds. (Englewood Cliffs, NJ: Prentice-Hall, 1968), p. 234.

[18] The year-day principle used by these writers to interpret the prophetic periods as indicating years rather than days is based on the fact that in the Scriptures, "day" can be used to designate a year. Ernst Jenni indicates that "day" is used for "year" in the Old Testament 876 times ("*Yôm* Day," *TLOT*, vol. 2, pp. 536-537). This has been confirmed by M. Saebo, "*Yôm*," *TDOT*, vol. 6, p. 21. For instance, a yearly sacrifice is called in the Hebrew Bible "a sacrifice of days" (1 Sam 20:6); a period of "a year and four months" is worded as "days and four months" (27:7); an old person is one "advanced in days," which obviously means "advanced in years" (1 Kgs 1:1). In the poetic books we find "days" and "years" used in synonymous parallelism (e.g., Job 10:5; 15:20; Ps 90:9-10).

An interesting case in which "days" is used for "years" is found in the Sabbatical law. The Lord said, "You shall count seven sabbaths of years, seven years seven times, and to you *the days* of the seven sabbaths of years shall be forty-nine years" (Lev 25:8). Here God

to be symbolic of the years extending from 538 to 1798.[19] This is a period characterized by apostasy and persecution. It is toward the end of this prophetic period that God raised up the Reformation to bring His church back to biblical truth.

The Reformation was in many ways a great success. The process of restoration was necessary because many false teachings had crept into the church.[20] God raised up individuals like Wycliffe, Huss, Jerome, and Luther, "the most powerful personality of the Reformation."[21]

---

is telling the Israelites to interpret the 49 days as 49 years. We also find a day standing for a year in the context of prophecies of judgment. This principle is established in Num 14:34 and Ezek 4:6. In Numbers, 40 days became 40 years, while in Ezekiel, 40 years are reduced to 40 days. However, in both cases we find the same wording concerning the principle involved: "Day for a year, day for a year I have given you." Another example is found in the first prophecy of judgment found in the Scriptures. God announced to the antediluvian world that its "days will be a hundred and twenty years" (Gen 6:3). There is here a clear connection between "day" and "year," indicating that one stands for the other. For the Hebrew mentality it was natural to use "day" and "year" interchangeably. God used this phenomenon in the apocalyptic visions of Daniel to designate long prophetic periods. The year-day principle was also used by Jewish writers during the intertestamental period, by those who lived in the Qumran community, possibly by Josephus, and by some Rabbinic writers (for an important discussion of the year-day principle, see William H. Shea, *Selected Studies on Prophetic Interpretation* [Silver Spring, MD: Biblical Research Institute, 1992], pp. 106-110). See also Roger T. Beckwith, "The Significance of the Calendar for Interpreting Essene Chronology and Eschatology," *RevQ* 10 (1980): 172-181; idem, "Daniel 9 and the Date of the Messiah's Coming in Essene, Hellenistic, Pharasaic, Zealot and Early Christian Computation," *RevQ* 10 (1980): 523, 524. See also, Brempong Owusu-Antwi, *The Chronology of Daniel 9:24-26* [Berrien Springs, MI: ATS Publications, 1995], pp. 225-226).

[19]See Froom, *Prophetic*, vol. 2, pp. 765-782; vol. 3, pp. 743-744. Some preferred 533–1793. The year 538 was usually chosen because this was the year when the Ostrogoths abandoned the siege of Rome, and the bishop of Rome, released from Arian control, was now free to exercise the prerogatives of the decree of Emperor Justinian issued in 533, which established the supremacy of the bishop of Rome over the churches of the East and West. Thus the Emperor increased tremendously the influence, power, and authority of the bishop. Exactly 1260 years later, in 1798, the armies of Napoleon placed the pope under the control of the French revolutionary government. In fact, the French army entered Rome, proclaimed the end of the political rule of the papacy, and took the pope prisoner to France where he died (see *AdvBibComm*, vol. 4, p. 834). Catholics recognize that the French Revolution brought with it "violent assaults against the papal spiritual and temporal power that seriously menaced the very existence of the office . . ." (J. F. Broderick, "Papacy: Modern Period (1789–1965)," in *New Catholic Encyclopedia*, vol. 10 [New York: McGraw-Hill, 1967], p. 965).

[20]See *Seventh-day Adventists Believe. . . : A Biblical Exposition of Fundamental Doctrines* (Washington, DC: Ministerial Association, 2005), p. 188.

[21]Ibid., p. 188.

Concluding Essay: God's End-Time Remnant and the Christian Church

The Reformation uncovered long-forgotten truths. Justification by faith, the great principle of the gospel, was rediscovered, as was a new appreciation for the once-for-all atoning sacrifice of Jesus Christ and its all-sufficient mediatorial priesthood. Many unbiblical teachings, such as prayers for the dead, veneration of saints and relics, celebration of the mass, worship of Mary, purgatory, penance, holy water, celibacy of the priesthood, the rosary, the inquisition, transubstantiation, extreme unction, and dependence upon tradition, were repudiated and abandoned.[22]

The Reformation did not advance as one would have expected. More biblical truth needed to be restored, but apparently the successors of the great Reformers felt comfortable with the truth their predecessors recovered and did not pursue a complete restoration. Religion slipped into formalism.[23] The more radical Reformers pushed their agenda further, seeking to take the Christian church back to apostolic times, but their success was limited. Yet the book of Revelation indicated that after the 1260 days, "a remnant" (Greek *loipos*) of the seed of the woman would still remain (Rev 12:17; cf. 11:13). Toward the close of the cosmic conflict, this remnant becomes the object of attack of the dragon and his allies (Rev 13:11-18) but finds refuge in the risen and glorified Lord (14:1-2). It is soon after the end of the 1260 days that God raised up the Adventist movement with a particular mission.

This brief overview of the apocalyptic significance of Rev 12–14 establishes that the remnant is indeed an end-time movement that was to appear after the fulfillment of the prophetic period of 1260 days. This indicates that *the end-time remnant is a historical entity*. There is a historical progression in the prophetic events narrated in Rev 12–14, moving from the time of the coming of the Messiah, through the period of the Christian church, and reaching to the time just before the coming of Christ. The prophecies deal with historical entities and movements that play particular roles within the flow of history.

Appropriation Based on the Biblical Characteristics of the Remnant

Adventist appropriation of the concept of the end-time remnant is grounded on the distinctive characteristics of the remnant people found

---

[22]Ibid., p. 188.
[23]See ibid., p. 189.

in Revelation.[24] Revelation specifically says that the remnant keep the commandments of God (12:17; 14:12), which would at least refer to the Decalogue, including the Sabbath commandment.[25] Also, they have "the testimony of Jesus," interpreted as the "spirit of prophecy" (19:10). Adventists have historically taken the "testimony of Jesus" to mean that within the end-time remnant, there would be a manifestation of the gift of prophecy and that it found expression in the ministry of Ellen G. White.[26] The phrase may also point to the content of that revelation as found in the Scriptures and particularly in the book of Revelation.[27] The other characteristics of the remnant include "having the faith of Jesus"— that is, following the teachings of Jesus based on a faith commitment to Him—and having "the patience of the saints," a willingness to remain loyal to the Lord at a time when the dragon is enraged against those who keep God's commandments (14:12; 12:17). These biblical characteristics of the remnant are also characteristics of the Adventist movement. The fact that it possesses certain characteristics means that *the remnant is a visible entity*. It is easily identifiable. Its concrete historical expression as the remnant people facilitates the fulfillment of its mission to the world. At the same time, the remnant's visibility contributes to making them the target of the wrath of the dragon and its associates.

The characteristics of the end-time remnant people of God listed in Revelation demonstrate that they are called to be and remain loyal to the Lord, committed to the truth they have been entrusted to proclaim. In that sense they are *a faithful remnant*. This collective identity does not signify that they are beyond the need for personal and collective spiritual growth and constant reformation. The Old Testament often points to the need for the remnant to experience cleansing. Although this is not emphasized in the book of Revelation, there are some indicators pointing to it. The fact that the book was written to encourage its audience to remain loyal to the Lord in the midst of serious attacks from the dragon suggests

---

[24]These marks are discussed by Gerhard Pfandl, "Identifying Marks of the End-Time Remnant in the Book of Revelation," in this volume.

[25]See Johannes Kovar, "The Remnant and God's Commandments," in this volume.

[26]See Gerhard Pfandl, "Identifying Marks of the End-Time Remnant in the Book of Revelation," in this volume. See also Pfandl, "The Remnant Church and the Spirit of Prophecy," in *Symposium on Revelation—Book II*, pp. 295-333; and Jean Zurcher, "Le témoignage de Jésus est l'esprit de la prophétie," in *Études sur l'Apocalypse*, vol. 1, pp. 230-250.

[27]See Rodríguez, "The 'Testimony of Jesus' in the Writings of Ellen G. White," and Lehmann, "The Remnant in the Book of Revelation," in this volume.

the possibility that some church members are running the risk of being shaken out of the church because of their lack of a firm commitment to the Savior (Rev 2:4-7, 10, 14-16).[28]

We also know that the remnant people of God will go through a testing period and that the end result will be a cleansed people. We read in Rev 7:14 (NIV): "These are they who have come out of the great tribulation; they have washed their robes and made them white in the blood of the Lamb."[29] They came out of the tribulation victorious because they put their trust in the redeeming blood of Christ, and it purified them and made them victorious (12:11). Persecution and oppression test the faith of God's people (2:10); there is always the risk of soiling one's clothes (3:4) or losing one's crown of victory (3:11). Only those who persevere to the end will be victorious and will form part of God's faithful remnant. If we associate the remnant with the message to Laodicea (3:14-22), we would then have to acknowledge that even the remnant contains members who are not totally faithful to the Lord. The Protestant conviction that *ecclesia semper reformanda* ("The church [is] always in [the] process of being reformed") also applies to the end-time remnant. One could say that as long as the message proclaimed by the remnant shines clearly, the historical, visible remnant is fulfilling its mission as a faithful remnant.[30] A time will come when God's cleansing process will come to an end, and those who do wrong will continue to do wrong, those who do right will continue to do right, and those who are holy will continue to be holy (22:11).

Appropriation Based on the Biblical Mission of the Remnant

The appropriation of the concept of the end-time remnant by Adventists is also based on the description of the mission of the remnant in the book of Revelation. That mission is described in Rev 14:6-14 under the symbol of three angels flying through the heavens proclaiming three closely-related messages. The purpose is to gather God's remnant scattered throughout the world. The proclamation of the three angels' messages takes place before the second coming of Christ (14:13-20) and is universal in scope. The basic content is the eternal gospel and includes

---

[28]The messages of each church are applicable in every age; see Lehmann, "The Remnant in the Book of Revelation," in this volume.

[29]On the connection between the sealing of God's people described in Rev 7 and Ezek 9, consult LaRondelle, "Remnant," pp. 870, 871.

[30]This is the basic definition of the remnant that Clifford Goldstein gives in *The Remnant* (Boise, ID: Pacific Press, 1994), pp. 78-79.

a call to a commitment to Christ that expresses itself in exclusive worship and submission to the will of God.[31] Since the message is global, one should conclude that the remnant is also a global movement.

The *message of the first angel* begins with the proclamation of the "eternal gospel" in the context of end-time events. This is the good news of salvation through Christ exclusively determined by God's grace. It is described as "eternal" to emphasize its permanent relevance and inalterability.[32] In the apostolic church acceptance of the gospel included not only believing in Christ but also worshiping the true God and rejecting idolatry (cf. Acts 14:15; 20:24). The call to fear God and give glory to Him takes place within the frame-work of the gospel and implies divine judgment. When confronted by God, humans are to fear Him by humbling themselves and recognizing His sovereignty and lordship over them. To glorify God is to exalt Him. The dragon and its instruments are not to be feared or glorified by humanity.

One of the motivations for this appeal is that "the hour of God's judgment has come." The reality of the judgment implies that the history of salvation is coming to an end and that God's eschatological judgment is reaching its consummation. Therefore, the human race should not submit to the authority of the dragon because the dragon itself and its instruments will experience God's executive judgment. The proper response of those who accept the gospel is to worship only the Creator of heaven and earth. The allusion to the Sabbath in this call is worth emphasizing because the Sabbath itself is a weekly reminder of the central biblical truth that God is indeed the Creator.[33]

The *message of the second angel* announces the fall of Babylon[34] and

---

[31]This has been carefully developed by Robert Badenas, "Vraie et fausse adoration dans les messages des trois anges (Apoc. 14:6-13)," in *Études sur l'Apocalypse*, vol. 1, pp. 144-167.

[32]See Beale, *Revelation*, p. 748.

[33]See Mathilde Frey, "Sabbath Theology in the Book of Revelation," in this volume.

[34]Scholars have interpreted the symbol of Babylon in Revelation in different ways. For a summary and evaluation of the different views, see LaRondelle, "Babylon: Anti-Christian Empire," in *Symposium in Revelation—Book II*, pp. 151-176. "Babylon" is commonly taken to be a designation for Rome. An idealistic interpretation was suggested by Ernest Lohmeyer, who found in it a symbol of satanic power and not a historical entity (*Die Offenbarung des Johannes* [Tübingen, 1953], pp. 138-147); a literal interpretation has been suggested by some Dispensationalists who believe that the old city of Babylon will be rebuilt (see Charles H. Dyer, "The Identity of Babylon in Rev 17–18," *BSac* 144 [1987]: 305-316, 434-449); it has also been identified with Jerusalem (Josephine Massyngberde Ford, *Revelation* [Garden City, NY: Doubleday, 1978], pp. 3-4); a symbolic-universal approach has been proposed by several scholars, including Paul Althaus (*Die Letzten Dinge* [Gütersloh,

the reasons for its fall. Here we find a typological connection between ancient Babylon and end-time Babylon.[35] In the Old Testament, Babylon was the archenemy of God and His people; in Revelation it represents God's eschatological archenemy. It is represented under the symbol of a city, possibly to emphasize its political power. But it is also represented under the symbol of a woman who is a prostitute (Rev 17). In Revelation one finds a faithful woman (12:1-2) and an unfaithful woman (17:1-4). In the Old Testament the symbol of an unfaithful wife is used to designate apostate Israel (Ezek 16:15-34; Jer 3:1-3, 8-9; Isa 1:21; Hos 2:2, 4). It would appear that in Jeremiah and Ezekiel, the figure of Jezebel is used as a model to depict the unfaithful people of God (e.g., Jer 4:30). This woman introduced a false system of worship in Israel and killed those who feared the Lord (cf. 1 Kgs 18–19). Revelation uses the figure of Jezebel as a symbol of apostasy and persecution. It is through the activities of Jezebel that a false system of worship was introduced into the church of Thyatira (Rev 2:20).

The prostitute/Babylon mentioned in Rev 17–19 has as its background the great Jezebel of the Old Testament who persecuted and killed the people of God (17:4, 6; 18:7).[36] The apostasy predicted by Paul is described in Revelation under the symbolism of Babylon/the harlot. The false religious system that was established in Israel becomes now a symbol of the false system that entered the Christian church. Adventists believe that this apostasy, which developed during the Middle Ages, will continue to the end and will reach universal dimensions. Only God's remnant will resist it. The application of the term "Babylon" to the union of church and state during the Middle Ages is something Adventists have in common with the Reformers.[37] According to Rev 17:5, the harlot/Babylon

---

1957], pp. 264-285). According to him the symbol of Babylon in Revelation refers to Rome, but the conflict between Babylon and the church takes different forms throughout history, making the antichrist everything that opposes Christ. Even the church, he comments, could become anti-Christian itself. He adds that the identification of the papacy with the antichrist by the Reformers was historically conditioned and should not be dogmatized.

[35]For an Adventist discussion on the typological connections between the Old Testament Babylon and mystical Babylon, see *AdvBibComm*, vol. 7, pp. 866-869; and LaRondelle, "Babylon," in *Symposium on Revelation—Book II*, pp. 151-176.

[36]See Paul B. Duff, *Who Rides the Beast? Prophetic Rivalry and the Rhetoric of Crisis in the Churches of the Apocalypse* (New York: Oxford, 2001), pp. 89-92.

[37]See Froom, *Prophetic Faith of Our Fathers*, vol. 2, pp. 531, 787. The earliest application of the symbol of Babylon to the Roman Catholic Church is found in the writings of the twelfth-century Waldenses and Albigenses. This was also taught by Luther, William Tyndale, Bishop Ridley, John Knox, and others. The same position was assumed by post-

is a "mother." Hence, Adventists believe that the title could be rightly applied to others. They watch with interest and great concern what is happening in the Protestant world with its tendency to reject the principle of *sola Scriptura*. Since the Reformation, many Protestants have come to reject some of the fundamental teachings of the Reformers and to question others. Rejection of Scriptural truth leads to apostasy. Although the term "Babylon" symbolizes all apostate religious organizations and their leadership, it especially designates the culmination of an eschatological process of apostasy in the Christian world. Then the beast and its image will form an alliance that unites religious and civil powers, culminating in the crisis described in Rev 13:15-17 and that will result in the final spiritual and literal fall of Babylon.[38] Adventists believe that it is their responsibility to call the attention of the Christian world to this upcoming tragedy and to restore the truth that was cast to the ground.

The *message of the third angel* is a warning against worshiping the beast, the image of the beast, and against receiving the mark of the beast. In strong terms and vivid images it announces the final defeat of evil powers and of those loyal to them. Adventists have historically identified the mark of the beast with the end-time universal enforcement of Sunday observance in the Christian world.[39] They do not believe that Sunday observance today constitutes the mark of the beast or that those who are Sundaykeepers have the mark of the beast.[40] The full manifestation of Babylon will take place when religious leaders use civil authority to impose religious ideas and practices and to oppose and even perse-

---

Reformation men like King James I, Joseph Mede, Sir Isaac Newton, John Wesley, and many others (see *Seventh-day Adventists Answer Questions on Doctrine* [Washington, DC: Review and Herald, 1952], pp. 198-199).

[38]Ellen G. White summarizes this idea: "Revelation 18 points to the time when, as a result of rejecting the threefold warning of Revelation 14:6-12, the church will have fully reached the condition foretold by the second angel, and the people of God still in Babylon will be called upon to separate from her communion" (*Great Controversy* [Mountain View, CA: Pacific Press, 1911], p. 390).

[39]The most recent Adventist discussion of the mark of the beast is the one by C. Mervyn Maxwell, "The Mark of the Beast," in *Symposium in Revelation—Book II*, pp. 41-66; but see also Richard Lehmann, "Le sceau de Dieu et la marque de la bête," in *Études sur l'Apocalypse*, vol. 1, pp. 187-198. See also, Anthony MacPherson, "The Mark of the Beast as a 'Sign Commandment' and 'Anti-Sabbath' in the Worship Crisis of Revelation 12-14," *AUSS* 43 (2005): 267-283.

[40]Adventists believe that "Sunday keeping is not yet the mark of the beast" (Ellen G. White, "Comments on Revelation," p. 977), and that "no one has yet received the mark of the beast" (Ellen G. White, *Evangelism* [Washington, DC: Review and Herald, 1946], p. 234).

cute those who do not submit to their beliefs and demands. However, Adventists recognize that the mark of the beast is obviously more than the observance of Sunday. In Rev 13:17, it is further defined as the name of the beast. The name in the Bible is an expression of the character of its bearer; therefore, to have the name/mark of the beast is to be totally identified with its purpose, intentions, and message.[41]

The people of God, on the other hand, will have the end-time seal of God on their foreheads (Rev 7:3), which is further defined as the name of the Lamb and the name of the Father "written on their foreheads" (14:1). Adventists have defined this seal in terms of Sabbath observance,[42] recognizing at the same time that it includes much more. Having the name of the Lamb and the Father does not simply mean that the remnant belongs to God, but also that they reflect in their lives the saving power of God and are firmly established in their loyalty to Him. The profession of faith in Christ would then express itself in complete loyalty and commitment to Christ and His law in the midst of great opposition from evil powers.

The mission of the remnant will contribute to the polarization of the human race. There will be only two groups: Those who are "called, chosen and faithful followers" of the Lamb (17:14) and the dwellers of the earth who worship the dragon and the beast (13:4). The first group could be called the *eschatological remnant*, also referred to as "saints," that is to say, those who belong to the Lord (13:10; 14:12) and "those who would not worship the image of the beast" (13:15). This remnant will be not only a *historical* entity *faithful* to the Lamb, but also a fully visible *eschatological remnant*.

We can conclude that the remnant in Revelation is fundamentally an end-time entity that appears on the scene of human history sometime

---

[41]Lehmann wrote, "To receive the mark of the beast is to adhere to certain values, to adore in a way that is totally opposed to the one proposed by God, to bear its name, that is to say, to be totally identified with it. It is more than a question of rest; it has to do with receiving its law, with honoring its will. The issue of Sabbath or Sunday is only the visible point of an immense iceberg of demonic values entirely opposed to those of God" ("Le sceau," p. 198; translation mine).

[42]Adventists found support for this position in the fact that the Sabbath is called in the Bible a sign of God's creative and sanctifying power (Exod 31:13, 17; Ezek 20:12, 20). The commandment itself "appears as a sign or seal of ownership and authority. God is identified as the Creator (Exod 20:11; 31:17), distinguishing Him from the other gods; and the sphere of ownership and authority is identified as 'heaven and earth' (chaps. 31:17; 20:11; Gen 2:1-3). These are ancient constituents of the seal, namely the identity of the owner and the sphere of ownership and authority" (Gerhard F. Hasel, "The Sabbath in the Pentateuch," in *The Sabbath in Scripture and History*, Kenneth A. Strand, ed. [Washington, DC: Review and Herald, 1982], p. 34).

after 1798. Adventists have found in that remnant their self-identity and mission. They argue that the historical moment indicated in Rev 12 coincides with the moment when the Adventist movement was raised. They also argue that the characteristics of the remnant mentioned in Revelation apply in a particular way to the life and message of the Adventist movement, and they believe that the mission of the remnant described in Revelation is being fulfilled by them. They acknowledge the imperfections of the remnant and trust in God's power to refine them as they fulfill their mission. This remnant is not exclusive in nature but open to all. It is fundamentally controlled by a sense of mission that should not allow for exclusiveness.[43]

---

[43]Occasionally the Adventist concept of the remnant has been considered by some to be offensive, exclusivist, and triumphalist (see Frank Hasel, "The Remnant in Contemporary Adventist Theology," in this volume). This opinion is based on a distorted understanding of the biblical data and of our understanding of it. In response to these charges, we can say that, first, the chapters found in this volume have shown that the application of the concept of the remnant to a specific group of individuals through whom God was fulfilling in a particular way His design for humanity is found throughout the Scriptures. On that basis the prophets and those who joined them in the preservation and practice of God's truth would have been considered offensive, exclusivist, and triumphalist. Of course, the same would have applied to Jesus and to the Christian community. But the biblical evidence indicates that the biblical remnant was not exclusivist (this has been shown in the articles of Tarsee Li, Leslie Pollard, Clinton Wahlen, and Richard Lehmann in this volume), and the same applies to the writings of Ellen G. White (see Rodríguez, "Remnant . . . White," in this volume).

Second, the Scripture makes clear that those who have formed part of God's remnant people very often came into view at critical spiritual moments in the life of the larger people of God. This usually happened in the context of apostasy and oppression. In that setting the role of the remnant was that of servanthood. They were called by God to serve others and to call others to His undivided service. In fact, at times they themselves had to go through a purifying experience, thus suggesting that they were also in constant need of God's grace (cf. Rev 3:14-22). Therefore, God's remnant people were called to humble service to Him who in His grace called them to His service.

Third, the existence of the remnant does not mean that salvation is exclusively theirs. It is true that the history of the concept of the remnant shows that it has been misused along exclusivist lines (See Leslie Pollard, "The Remnant in Non-Canonical Jewish Apocalyptic Works and in Qumran," in this volume). But the truth is that God's people are found everywhere. We will argue below that an Adventist remnant ecclesiology presupposes that God is actively involved in the salvation of people outside the remnant. His people are larger than the remnant. This should put to rest any charges of exclusivism in Adventist ecclesiology and soteriology.

Fourth, the biblical remnant has always had a message that was of relevance and importance to God's people at a particular historical moment. It often contained elements of judgment against the larger religious community, but its ultimate intent was to proclaim salvation. The real aim of the message of the remnant has always been salvific and may have included restoration of truth and rejection of apostasy. This is what we find in the biblical prophets, in Jesus, and in the apostolic church.

III. The Remnant and the Unity of the Church

A remnant ecclesiology that is genuinely Christian has to deal with the relationship between the remnant and the larger group from which they were constituted into a remnant. One of the central concerns in any ecclesiology, and particularly in a Protestant ecclesiology, is the need to address the reality of the fragmentation of the Christian church. Although many factors contributed to that breakup, it is unquestionable that the visible unity of the church was compromised by the introduction of radical theological and doctrinal diversity into it. From the perspective of apocalyptic thinking, the lack of unity prevalent in the Christian world should be interpreted as the presence of Babylonian elements within it. This condition needs to be addressed in an Adventist ecclesiology that by nature is expected to emphasize the universal unity of the church (cf. John 17). We say "by nature" because the possibility of ecclesiastical oneness is presupposed in the mission of the remnant people of God. Their end-time proclamation of the eternal gospel invites people from all nations, peoples, and tongues to be reunited to the Creator and Redeemer in a commitment of faith and in submission to His will (Rev 14:6-12). In other words, the remnant works to rectify the fragmentation of the Christian world in anticipation of Christ's soon return. We could then suggest that a remnant ecclesiology is in a sense a revolt against the fragmentation of the Christian world.

IV. The Remnant and the Universal Church

Adventist remnant ecclesiology operates on a conceptually and operationally bidirectional template. On the one hand, it has to justify

---

Fifth, we should keep in mind that exclusivism and triumphalism are not only dangers for the Adventist church: they are also a danger for any Christian community claiming to possess a message of universal value and relevance or that requires from those who will become members the acceptance of specific beliefs and practices, considered non-negotiable for the life of that particular religious community. Any religious community that claims to have a particular identity and mission (and which does not?!) could be open to charges of arrogance, triumphalism, and exclusivism. However, those claims by themselves do not make them that way. For a brief discussion of this concern in the context of ecumenism, see, G. Bloesch, *The Church: Sacrament, Worship, Ministry, Mission* (Downers Grove, IL: InterVarsity, 2002), pp. 255-256.

We as Adventists should do all we can to avoid giving wrong impressions that may provide, in the opinion of some, reason to raise those charges against us. But we should not allow those charges to undermine our self-identity and mission as God's remnant people.

and define its coexistence and relationship with other Christian ecclesial communities; on the other hand, it must constantly examine the nature and effectiveness of its existence and commitment to its unity with the Risen Lord. In other words, Adventist ecclesiology looks outward, seeking to establish a point of contact with the fragmented world of Christianity as well as with non-Christian religions, but at the same time it looks inward by attempting to nurture unity within itself while fulfilling its mission. In pursuing that double task, the Adventist movement reveals its distinctive identity which directly contributes to the global unity of the movement.

The Remnant and the Fullness of the Church

Possibly one of the most critical questions any ecclesiology faces is this: Where does the fullness of the church of Christ reside? Christians have given various answers to this important question. Roman Catholics usually hold that the fullness of the church resides in the Roman Catholic Church, particularly in the mutual communion of the pope and the bishops.[44] The Eastern Orthodox Churches have insisted that true orthodoxy has been preserved by them and that, therefore, they are the true church,[45] the expression of the fullness of the church of Christ. Protestants in general tend to believe that the fullness of the church is located in the different Christian communities in which the gospel and the sacraments are clearly understood and proclaimed. One of the goals of ecumenical dialogue is to achieve mutual recognition, inviting the party in dialogue to recognize the other as an expression of the fullness of the church of Christ.

Adventists differ from those ecclesiological opinions, affirming that *the fullness of the church of Christ does not reside in any particular ecclesiastical organization.* This is not a denial of the value of ecclesiastical organization, but rather an affirmation that the church is not by definition a hierarchical structure. This conviction is part of the outcome of an ecclesiology that is firmly rooted in the conviction that the church is constituted by those who have accepted Christ as Savior and Lord. This may appear to make irrelevant the existence of an end-time remnant movement with a particular mission to the world. Therefore, it is necessary to look more closely at what Adventists have stated concerning the nature of the church.

We have specifically dealt with the nature of the church in two of our

---

[44]Consult Veli-Matti Karkainen, *An Introduction to Ecclesiology: Ecumenical, Historical & Global Perspectives* (Downers Grove, IL: InterVarsity, 2002), p. 26-38.

[45]Ibid., pp. 17-25.

Fundamental Beliefs.[46] Adventists have understood the church to be "the community of believers who confess Jesus Christ as Lord and Savior."[47] Believers "join together for worship, for fellowship, for instruction in the Word, for the celebration of the Lord's Supper, for service to all mankind, and for the worldwide proclamation of the gospel."[48] Its authority is derived from Christ and from the written Word. As the body of Christ, the church is "a community of faith of which Christ Himself is the Head."[49] This understanding of the church does not exclude the usefulness of organizational structures, but it describes the church, to be sure, as much more than an institutional phenomenon. It is fundamentally a community of believers. This notion is further clarified by establishing a distinction between a "universal church" and "a remnant."[50] The distinction is extremely important for the formulation and comprehension of an Adventist ecclesiology. How do we understand this "universal church"? We have stated that it "is composed of all who truly believe in Christ." This definition is a practical rejection of denominationalism in that the church itself is described as transcending denominational borders. The "universal church" is not embodied in any particular Christian organization, but it is diffused throughout the Christian world. We could state that, in a sense, the "universal church" is a church in exile, in Babylon, scattered throughout the religious world.[51]

The Remnant and the Church

Once we define the *universal church* as being "composed of all who truly believe in Christ," we are basically claiming that it is invisible. At present its members are spread throughout the different Christian and even non-Christian communities, making it practically impossible to dif-

---

[46]For a list of the Seventh-day Adventist beliefs, see "Fundamental Beliefs of Seventh-day Adventists," in *Yearbook 2008: Seventh-day Adventist Church* (Silver Spring, MD: General Conference of Seventh-day Adventists, 2008), pp. 5-8. The two statements dealing with ecclesiology are Nos. 12 and 13 (p. 6).

[47]Ibid., p. 6.

[48]Ibid.

[49]Ibid.

[50]Ibid. The distinction reads as follows: "The universal church is composed of all who truly believe in Christ, but in the last days, a time of widespread apostasy, a remnant has been called out to keep the commandments of God and the faith of Jesus."

[51]Ellen G. White has commented, "Notwithstanding the spiritual darkness and alienation from God that exist in the churches which constitute Babylon, the great body of Christ's true followers are still to be found in their communion" (*Great Controversy*, p. 390).

ferentiate them from others within those communities. It exists under unusual circumstances, under the direct and exclusive leadership of the Spirit. The "universal church," as we are defining it here, is what Jesus was referring to when He said: "I have other sheep that are not of this sheep pen. I must bring them also" (John 10:16). In the book of Revelation, it is designated as "My [God's] people" who are still in Babylon.

The question of the invisible church has been debated by Catholics and Protestants.[52] It was seriously discussed during the Reformation when Luther rejected the Catholic ecclesiastical structure as the expression of the Church of Christ. It was then that the important question of the presence or identity of the "true church" (Latin, *vera ecclesia*) was raised. If it was no longer the Catholic Church, where was now the *vera ecclesia*? Protestants argued that the true church was invisible.[53] As already argued in this volume, the church is not by nature invisible.[54] However, there is an invisible dimension of the church. If the "universal church" transcends denominationalism, then it is invisible. This most

---

[52] For an Adventist discussion of the visible-invisible church, see Raoul Dederen, "The Church," in *Handbook of Seventh-day Adventist Theology*, Raoul Dederen, ed. (Hagerstown, MD: Review and Herald, 2000), pp. 545-546. He argues that "an invisible church would be as unthinkable to biblical thought as a Messiah without a community. The church is bodily, visible, tangible. It has a definite structure with differentiated parts or 'members.' It is actual, both local and universal. At the same time the church can be described as having an invisible dimension, which is not measurable by sinners, even when redeemed" (p. 546). See also, *Seventh-day Adventists Believe*, p. 171.

[53] For a discussion of this controversy between Protestants and Catholics, see Scott H. Hendrix, "In Quest of the *Vera Ecclesia*: The Crisis of Late Medieval Ecclesiology," *Viator* 7 (1976): 347-378. According to him, attempts at reform and renewal of the church before the year 1300 were commonly based on the model of the apostolic ideal or the "primitive church" (*ecclesia primitiva*). In the later Middle Ages, the main emphasis was on the church itself. Where was the true church? The Spiritual Franciscans and the Waldensians concluded that they were the true spiritual church. "Since this belief placed both groups in minority positions, they were forced to develop remnant ecclesiologies which located the *vera ecclesia* in the faithful few opposed to the apostate many" (p. 354). The *ecclesia primitiva* was now defined as a remnant (the *vera ecclesia*). The true church was now located in a remnant of faithful believers existing apart from the Roman ecclesiastical hierarchy (p. 360). Within that historical context, "Luther's Reformation is best explained as an ecclesiological response to the last great medieval crisis of the church's identity and authority" (p. 377). The Reformers' churches were considered to be "new manifestations of the true church over against the papacy and the Roman hierarchy" (ibid.). The Anabaptists and other radical Reformers also used the model of the *ecclesia primitiva*. The Reformation appears to have been a search for the *vera ecclesia*. See also Susan E. Schreiner, "Church," in *Oxford Encyclopedia of the Reformation*, vo. 1, Hans J. Hillerbrand, ed. (New York: Oxford University, 1996), pp. 323-327.

[54] See Hasel, "The Remnant in Contemporary Adventist Theology," in this volume.

unusual condition has been the result of the process of apostasy in the Christian world.

We also believe that "in the last days, a time of widespread apostasy, a remnant has been called out to keep the commandments of God and the faith of Jesus."[55] One of the theological implications of that statement is that *the remnant is the visible expression of the people of God, the church.* One could even suggest that *at the present time, the remnant is the visible church without being the totality of the expression of the church.*[56] This also means that the existence of this remnant is a reaffirmation of Christianity (the remnant people of God are part of something larger than themselves) and also a judgment against it in the sense that it finds in Christianity spiritual unfaithfulness. In other words, with respect to the Christian world, the remnant exists in the tension between a reaffirmation of it and calling it to repentance and reformation. The existence of an invisible "universal church" and a visible remnant introduces in Adventist ecclesiology a challenging and intriguing element related to their respective natures and spiritual relationship. If the two are part of the people of God, they must have some elements in common.

Common and Unique Elements

I will limit myself to a brief discussion of a few of the elements that the remnant and the "universal church" appear to have in common.

1. *A Common Future:* One of the aspects of the mission of the remnant as it relates to the church in exile is to call it out of Babylon (Rev 18:4). The imagery is taken from the experience of Israel during the exile. Like the people of God in the Old Testament, the church in exile has been scattered throughout the mystical "Babylonian empire." As we have already indicated, soon after the end of the 1260 years (Rev 12:17), God raised a visible, historical, and faithful end-time remnant to call the rest of His people out of Babylon. Hence, one of the most important functions of the visible expression of the church of Christ, the end-time remnant,

---

[55]"Fundamental Beliefs," *Yearbook*, p. 6.

[56]See Lehmann, "The Remnant in the Book of Revelation," in this volume. The expression "visible church" is used by Ellen G. White to designate the Adventist Church, God's end-time remnant people. She writes, "*Every member of the church* has an individual responsibility as a *member of the visible church*, and a worker in the vineyard of the Lord, and should do his utmost to preserve harmony, union, and love in the church. Mark the prayer of Christ, 'that they all may be one; as Thou, Father, art in Me, and I in Thee, that they also may be one in Us: that the world may believe that Thou hast sent Me'" (*Manuscript Releases*, vol. 12 [Silver Spring, MD: Ellen G. White Estate, 1993], p. 293; italics supplied).

is to pull the "universal church" of Christ out of its invisibility before the final polarization of the human race at the close of the cosmic conflict. At that point in history, we will later argue, the invisible church will merge into the visible eschatological remnant. Meanwhile, the people of God visibly exist in the eschatological remnant of Rev 12:17 and invisibly in the universal people of God who are still in Babylon (18:4).

2. *Openness to Truth:* The invisible universal church and the visible remnant also seem to have openness to biblical truth in common. One of the roles of the remnant is to restore biblical truths that have been rejected or ignored, thus strengthening the unity of the church with the Risen Lord. In that task, Scripture is the determining factor and the sole instrument of reformation. This requires that the remnant be open to new biblical truth or to truth that has been rejected or ignored. The proclamation of biblical truth to God's people in Babylon also presupposes that the universal invisible church is composed of those who, are open to biblical truth.[57] They are those living up to the light they have received and who after listening to the biblical truth that is being restored, willingly embrace it.[58]

---

[57]This is in fact a presupposition of the gospel commission recorded in Matt 28:18-20. The proclamation of the gospel is preceded by the work of the Spirit in the human heart attempting to prepare humans to give a positive response to the message of salvation. Concerning the commitment to truth of God's people in exile, Ellen G. White wrote, "Many in retired homes are God's hidden ones, serving Him according to the light they have received. These hidden ones greatly delight in the Word of God. His precepts are appreciated and treasured by them, and many are the works of love that they do for Christ's sake ("They Shall be Mine, Saith the Lord of Hosts," *ST* 30 [Nov 23, 1904]: p. 1).

[58]The idea of biblical truth was at the center of the Reformation, but today it seems to have disappeared from the forum of ecumenical dialogue. There is a tendency to consider the present disunity of Christianity as an expression of divine providence, and consequently, the question of truth has become irrelevant. For an exposition of this view, see Ephraim Radner, *Hope Among the Fragments: The Broken Church and Its Engagement of Scripture* (Grand Rapids, MI: Brazos, 2004), pp. 55-75. This approach makes the search for a remnant irrelevant (p. 73). The emphasis now is on an ecclesiology defined by communion that is becoming popular among Christian churches and is becoming a defining element in ecumenical dialogues. For a discussion of communion ecclesiology in ecumenical relations, see Lorelei F. Fuchs, *Koinonia and the Quest for an Ecumenical Ecclesiology* (Grand Rapids, MI: Eerdmans, 2007); for an Adventist discussion of communion ecclesiology and the underlying assumptions, see Tihomir Lazić, "Koinonia: A Critical Analysis and Comparison of the Concept of *Koinonia* within Joseph Ratzinger's, John Zizioulas's and Miroslav Volf's Version of 'Communion Ecclesiology' " (M.A. thesis, Newbold College in Partnership with the University of Wales, Lampeter, England, 2008). For a discussion of the significance of the Reformation in current ecumenical discussions, see Mark A. Noll and Carolyn Nystrom, *Is the Reformation Over? An Evangelical Assessment of Contemporary Roman Catholicism* (Grand Rapids, MI: Baker, 2005).

3. *Faithfulness to Christ:* Likewise, common to both the remnant and the universal church is their faithfulness to Christ. They are characterized by perseverance in the midst of a spiritual conflict that promotes a superficial religious commitment to Christ (Rev 14:12). Even among non-Christian religions, there are people who are faithful to the light they have received from God, are being transformed by the power of the Spirit in their hearts, and are part of God's children.[59] However, with respect to faithfulness to the Lord, there is a significant difference between the "universal church" and the remnant. Since the faithfulness of the remnant is manifested in a particular way in obedience to all God's commandments, their faithfulness is visible in a unique way. In the case of the "universal church," the faithfulness of believers is less visible because they do not yet have the fullness of God's truth being proclaimed by God's end-time remnant people.

4. *"A Remnant" in Babylon:* Some Adventists have suggested that the term "remnant" could also be used to designate the people of God who are still in Babylon.[60] If that were the case, then both the Adventist church and the universal church would be in some sense "remnant" peoples. It is true that in the Bible the term "remnant" is applied to the remnant of the nations that will join God's remnant people at the eschatological consummation.[61] We also found that Ellen G. White appears to use the

---

[59]Ellen G. White wrote, "Among earth's inhabitants, scattered in every land, there are those who have not bowed the knee to Baal. Like the stars of heaven, which appear only at night, these faithful ones will shine forth when darkness covers the earth and gross darkness the people. In heathen Africa, in the Catholic lands of Europe and of South America, in China, in India, in the islands of the sea, and in all the dark corners of the earth, God has in reserve a firmament of chosen ones that will yet shine forth amidst the darkness, revealing clearly to an apostate world the transforming power of obedience to His law. Even now they are appearing in every nation, among every tongue and people; and in the hour of deepest apostasy, when Satan's supreme effort is made to cause 'all, both small and great, rich and poor, free and bond,' to receive, under penalty of death, the sign of allegiance to a false rest day, these faithful ones, 'blameless and harmless, the sons of God, without rebuke,' will 'shine as lights in the world.' Revelation 13:16; Philippians 2:15. The darker the night, the more brilliantly will they shine" (*Prophets and Kings* [Mountain View, CA: Pacific Press, 1917], pp. 188-189).

[60]See the discussion in Hasel, "The Remnant in Contemporary Adventist Theology," in this volume, and *Questions on Doctrine*, p. 192.

[61]See Tarsee Li, "The Remnant in the Old Testament," in this volume. A good example is found in Zechariah. He describes an eschatological attempt to destroy God's people that will result in failure. But there is a remnant of the nations that will join God's people: "Then the survivors [*yātar*] from all the nations that have attacked Jerusalem will go up year after year to worship the King, the LORD Almighty, and to celebrate the Feast of Tabernacles" (14:16, NIV). The verb *yātar* is used here in the nifal formation meaning "what is left over," "those who survive," and belongs to the language and ideology of the "remnant." This

term "remnant" to refer to true believers outside the Adventist church.[62] If we were to accept that suggestion, it would have to be carefully nuanced. The universal church would be a "remnant" only in the sense that they are the few faithful ones who are still living in exile, in Babylon. At the present time they are not clearly identifiable as an ecclesiastical unit. *They are not yet part of the visible end-time faithful eschatological remnant of Rev 12:17.*[63] If the term "remnant" were to be used, it would have to be made clear that it does not carry with it the technical theological and eschatological meaning found in Rev 12:17. It simply means "a minority, a few." The reason for this suggestion is that the end-time remnant possesses specific marks that distinguish it from the "universal church" and make it an historical, visible entity with a clear identity. One of the most definitive differences between both groups is that even though they are both open to new light, the end-time remnant has been entrusted with a present truth that is relevant and indispensable for every human being, including those belonging to the "universal church."

The following diagram could be helpful in summarizing the nature of both the remnant and the universal church.

CHURCH OF CHRIST

God's End-Time Remnant People	Universal Church
Visible Entity	Invisible Entity
Specific Marks	Lacks Specific Marks
Keep the Commandments of God	In Babylon
Have the Testimony/Faith of Jesus	Christ's Other
Have the Patience of the Saints	Sheep
Specific Mission to Babylon	Called to come out of
Messages of the Three Angels	Babylon

---

remnant of the nations was not confused in the Old Testament with the remnant of the Israelites who left Babylon and returned to Jerusalem. In Isa 66:19-20, we read that it was God's intention to use the remnant of Israel to proclaim His "glory among the nations" to bring their brothers back from exile to Jerusalem. At the end the remnant of God's people in exile and from the nations will join God's remnant in Israel.

[62]See Rodríguez, "The Remnant People of God in the Writings of Ellen G. White," in this volume.

[63]Of course, Rev 12:17 is not the only place where the end-time remnant is mentioned. The concept permeates the book of Revelation; see Lehmann, "The Remnant in the Book of Revelation," in this volume.

V. The End-Time Remnant Fully Disclosed

The end-time remnant is a divine project in progress and will reach its ultimate expression shortly before the end of the cosmic conflict. Through their mission God is reaching out to His people around the world, gathering the fullness of His remnant (Rev 14:6) and calling God's people to come out of Babylon (18:4). It would appear that it is God's intention to merge the "universal church" into the end-time eschatological faithful remnant. That remnant is already here as a historical reality, but its fullness is coming into being and will be revealed when the rest of God's people will come out of Babylon, particularly at the close of the cosmic conflict. During the final days of earth's history, true Christians of every denominational background, as well as many from non-Christian religions who found in Christ their Savior, will find themselves involved in a common experience of marginalization and persecution (Rev 12:17). In that setting, "Adventists expect that their past experience and their understanding of the Scriptures will make an essential contribution to the understanding of other Christians as well as themselves." [64] At that moment the eschatological expectation of the visible unity and oneness of the fullness of the church of Christ will be a reality in ways that at the present time we can hardly anticipate. A people from every nation and people "will give voice to one great final Christian witness to the world."[65] Then the militant church will become the triumphant people of God. The existence of this glorious remnant before Christ's return in glory is of decisive importance.

At a time when the forces of evil will seek to unite the human race against God's government through deception (Rev 13:13-14; 16:13-14), the remnant stands on God's side.[66] They signal the fact that evil has not totally conquered the earth, that there are some through whom God is still active, that they are reclaiming the planet and anticipating the moment when it will be fully integrated into the harmony of the cosmic kingdom of God. Through them, together with those who throughout the ages were loyal to Him, the human race will be eternally preserved.

---

[64]Paulien, "Eschatology," p. 239.

[65]Ibid., p. 237.

[66]Referring to God's end-time remnant people, Ellen G. White comments, "Satan numbers the world as his subjects; he has gained control of the apostate churches; but here is a little company that are resisting his supremacy. If he could blot them from the earth, his triumph would be complete" (*Testimonies to the Church*, vol. 9 [Mountain View, CA: Pacific Press, 1948], p. 231).

VI. Conclusion

The existence of the remnant is an act of divine grace grounded in the fact that Jesus is the ultimate expression of the remnant as the true Faithful One through whom God saved and preserved humanity. This Christological understanding of the remnant shows that its identity is derived, supported, and preserved through Christ. His victory is indeed their victory. The long historical trajectory of the concept of the remnant as a designation of those through whom God is fulfilling in a special way His design for the human race implies that we can anticipate the existence of an end-time remnant. This is precisely what we find in the book of Revelation. The Adventist self-designation as God's remnant people is based on a historicist reading of Revelation, on the characteristics of that remnant recorded in Revelation, and on the mission of that remnant.

Adventist ecclesiology, developed from a remnant perspective, acknowledges that the church of Christ is larger than its expression in the remnant. There is a "universal church" "composed of all who truly believe in Christ"[67] (the "other sheep that are not of this sheep pen" [John 10:16]). This church is scattered throughout the religious world and cannot be identified with any particular ecclesiastical organization. In that sense it is the invisible church in exile, in Babylon. But the church is not by nature invisible. The end-time remnant people are the visible expression of the church of Christ, possessing certain specific characteristics and a particular mission to the world. Through them God is restoring fundamental biblical truths that will play a significant role in the final confrontation between the forces of evil and God. In the fulfillment of their mission, the remnant will be used by the Lord to pull the universal church out of its invisibility in preparation for the coming of the Lord in glory. At that moment the fullness of God's eschatological remnant will be a reality, and the oneness of the church will reach its deepest expression.

---

[67] "Fundamental Beliefs," p. 6.

APPENDIX

THE "TESTIMONY OF JESUS" IN THE WRITINGS OF ELLEN G. WHITE

Ángel Manuel Rodríguez
Director
Biblical Research Institute
Silver Spring, MD

Previous discussions in this book indicated that the phrase "testimony of Jesus" in Rev 12:17 played a significant role in defining the self-understanding of the Adventist church.[1] Our pioneers interpreted it in several ways,[2] but soon they found in it a reference to the manifestation of the gift of prophecy in the church, a mark of the remnant church.[3] Interestingly, although Ellen G. White uses the phrase in several ways, we do not find a clear statement from her indicating that her prophetic ministry was a fulfillment of Rev 12:17. She interpreted the "testimony of Jesus" as a rich and meaningful phrase. It is this richness of usage that we want to ex-

---

[1] See chapters by Frank Hasel and Gerhard Pfandl in this volume.

[2] See "Spirit of Prophecy,"*AduEnc,* vol. M-Z, p. 691.

[3] Apparently the first one who made a connection between Rev 12:17 and 19:10 and the manifestation of the gift of prophecy in the remnant church was James White, "The Gift—Their Object," *RH*, Feb 28, 1856, p. 172. Based on those two texts and Joel 2:28-32, he concluded, "No one, then, need marvel because the dragon's ire is stirred, on seeing the 'spirit of prophecy' revive in the church." See also R. F. Cottrell, "Spiritual Gifts," *RH*, Feb 23, 1858, p. 126; D. T. Bourdeau, "Spiritual Gifts," *RH*, Dec 2, 1862, p. 5; James White, "The Spirit of Prophecy," *RH*, Jan 25, 1870; George I. Butler, "Visions and Prophecy," *RH*, June 2, 1874, p. 1. Butler mentions Rev 12:17 and 19:10 and then writes, "The Spirit of prophecy is that manifestation of the gifts of the Spirit which enables one to prophesy, or if you please, have visions; for if there is a prophet among God's people, he will reveal himself through visions. Be it known to every reader of this Supplement, yea, to all who care to know it, that S. D. Adventists, as a body, firmly believe that there has been connected with this people, through their whole history, *one who has visions from the Lord.* . . . We firmly believe the visions of Mrs. White are a genuine manifestation of spiritual gifts." George I. Butler, "The Visions—How They Are Held Among Seventh-day Adventists," *RH* Supplement, Aug 14, 1883, p. 11. See also W. H. Littlejohn, "Seventh-day Adventists and the Testimony of Jesus," *RH* Supplement, Aug 14, 1883, p. 14; and Uriah Smith, "The Spirit of Prophecy and Our Relation to It," *G.C. Bulletin*, March 18, 1891, pp. 150-151.

plore. The vast majority of her statements dealing with this phrase were written between 1883 and 1911, and only a handful before that period.

I. Testimony of Jesus and the Remnant

Identifying Mark of the Remnant[4]

On several occasions Ellen White applies Rev 12:17 to "the remnant people of God,"[5] "a remnant,"[6] and the "true children of God."[7] Based on that specific passage, she concludes that the remnant is characterized by keeping the commandments of God and having the testimony of Jesus.[8] Since the dragon is angered against the people of God, they will endure trials and persecution. In fact, Ellen G. White explains her own trials as attacks of the enemy against her and sees herself in line with the many individuals who in their work of reform had to endure persecution.[9]

Message of the Remnant

For her the "testimony of Jesus" was not only a mark that identified the remnant; it was also part of the message they proclaimed. Already in 1849, she described the people of God as going to battle, crying, "The commandments of God and the testimony of Jesus."[10] She suggests that the testimony of Jesus, like the commandments, is primarily content-oriented, a truth for the present time.[11] The commandments of God and the testimony of Jesus are "a special light in this age of the world, a spe-

---

[4]See Rodríguez, "The Remnant in the Writings of Ellen G. White," in this volume.

[5]*The Desire of Ages* (Mountain View, CA: Pacific Press, 1898), p. 398.

[6]"The Seal of God," *ST,* Nov 1, 1899.

[7]"Building the Old Waste Places," *ST,* June 12, 1893. Most of the time she quotes Rev 14:12 to identify the marks of the remnant church.

[8]"Preparation for the Testing Time," *RH, April 22, 1989.*

[9]Letter 28, 1872, Battle Creek, MI, Feb 27, 1872, W. H. Ball, New Hampshire.

[10]*Manuscript Releases, vol. 5* (Silver Spring, MD: Ellen G. White Estate, 1993), p. 200. In this particular case she did not explain what she meant by the phrase "testimony of Jesus." She does not seem to be using it here to designate the manifestation of the spirit of prophecy in her ministry.

[11]See *Spiritual Gifts*, vol. 4b (Battle Creek, MI: Steam Press, 1864), p. 90, where she states, "The only safety now is to search for the truth as revealed in the word of God, as for hid treasure. The Sabbath question, and man not immortal, and the testimony of Jesus, are the great and important truths to be understood, which will prove as an anchor to hold God's people in these perilous times. But the mass despise the truths of God's word, and prefer fables."

cial message to give in the proclamation of the third angel's message."[12] They constitute "the last message of mercy to the world."[13] Therefore we should "proclaim the commandments of God and the testimony of Jesus Christ."[14] The two together constitute "the standard of present truth,"[15] "the one great platform of faith."[16] In conjunction with the third angel's message, they are "the burden of our work."[17]

In the New Testament the word-group to which "testimony" (*marturia*) belongs is associated with the idea of proclaiming a message. That is to say, the testimony is something that can and should be proclaimed: "When I came to you, brethren, I did not come proclaiming to you the

---

[12]"Ye Are the Light of the World," *PT*, Nov 4, 1886. Writing about the Adventist publishing house in California, she says that it "is to stand as a witness for Him amid the moral darkness of error, shedding its bright rays in the publication of truth to be sent to all parts of the world, heralding the third angel's message, the commandments of God, and the testimony of Jesus" (Manuscript 6, 1878, "Testimony to Oakland Church").

[13]"Genuine Faith Leads to Obedience," *ST*, March 31, 1890. In 1894 she writes, "The commandments of God and the testimony of Jesus is the message we have to bear to the world" (*Selected Messages*, Book 2 (Washington, DC: Review and Herald, 1958), p. 88. She once asked, "What is our message to the world? The commandments of God and the Testimony of Jesus Christ" (Manuscript 231, 1902, San Diego, CA, Sept 25, 1902, "Remarks/City Restaurants").

[14]*Selected Messages*, Book 2, p. 116. Cf. *Publishing Ministry* (Hagerstown, MD: Review and Herald, 1983), p. 281: "The third angel, flying in the midst of heaven and heralding the commandments of God and the testimony of Jesus, represents our work" (1889).

[15]"If ever there was a time when we should elevate the standard of present truth, it is now. Our watchword should be, 'The commandments of God and the testimony of Jesus Christ' " (Letter 13, 1990, Sunnyside, Cooranbong, New South Wales, Australia, Feb 1, 1900, H. W. Kellogg, Battle Creek, MI).

[16]*Testimonies for the Church*, vol. 3 (Mountain View, CA: Pacific Press, 1948), p. 446.

[17]*Colporteur Ministry* (Mountain View, CA: Pacific Press, 1953), p. 138. See also *PHO87: Special Testimony to the Oakland and Battle Creek Churches* (1897), p. 22. In 1904 Ellen G. White wrote, "Because of the ever-increasing opportunities for ministering to the temporal needs of all classes, there is danger that this work will eclipse the message that God has given us to bear in every city—the proclamation of the soon coming of Christ, the necessity of obedience to the commandments of God and the testimony of Jesus. This message is the burden of our work" (*Counsels on Health*, [Mountain View, CA: Pacific Press, 1923], p. 515). In a special way she states that "the commandments of God and the testimony of Jesus are united. They are to be clearly presented to the world" (*Testimonies to the Church*, vol. 8, p. 117). In 1862, she stated, "Separate the Sabbath from the message, and it loses its force, but the Sabbath connected the message of the third angel and the testimony of Jesus—the whole taken together—cannot be overthrown. They have a power and force which affects and convicts the unbeliever and infidel and brings them out with some strength to stand and live and grow and flourish" (Manuscript 3, 1862, "The Cause in Wisconsin").

testimony [*marturion*] of God in lofty words of wisdom" (1 Cor 2:1).[18] This appears to be the background for the particular usage of the phrase "testimony of Jesus" we have just described in the writings of Ellen G. White.

II. Specific Usage: A Message Proclaimed by Different People

Ellen G. White's broad understanding of the phrase "testimony of Jesus" becomes more evident when she associates it with the work of specific individuals and with Christians in general. An examination of these cases will help us to gain a better understanding of the way she employs the phrase.

Jesus, John, and Paul

When she associates the phrase "testimony of Jesus" with Jesus Himself, it designates Jesus' testimony or witnessing to divine truth. This testimony could be His teachings as recorded in the gospels[19] or more specifically the witness He bore to the perpetuity of the law.[20] John uses the phrase the "testimony of Jesus" to state the reason he was exiled to the island of Patmos (Rev 1:9). In this particular case Ellen G. White interpreted it as referring to "the testimony which he bore concerning Jesus."[21] The content of that testimony was received by John through divine revelation. While in Patmos, he received from Jesus "a more wonderful revelation of Himself to give to the world. The Lord was preparing John to endure hatred and scorn for the sake of the Word of God and the testimony of Jesus."[22]

---

[18]See, J. Beutler, "*Martyria* testimony, evidence," *EDNT,* vol. 2, p. 391.

[19]"Teach the Word," *RH,* Oct 22, 1903.

[20]*Upward Look* (Washington, DC: Review and Herald, 1982), p. 101.

[21]*Spiritual Gifts,* vol. 1 (Battle Creek, MI: Adventist Publishing House, 1858), p. 130. The statement says that after John was delivered from death, "many were convinced that God was with him, and that the testimony which he bore concerning Jesus was correct." On the following page (131), she quotes Rev 19:10 and 22:9, indicating that she was aware of the fact that in Revelation, the "testimony of Jesus" is identified as the prophetic gift. Yet she does not make any specific comments about the gift or its manifestation in her ministry. See also, "Thoughts on the First Epistle of John," *ST,* May 23, 1895. The following year (1896), she writes that John was banished to the Island of Patmos by men inspired by Satan "to persecute those who bore faithfully witness to God" ("Letter to Believers on the Pitcairn Island," *RH,* Aug 4, 1896). He testified about the death and resurrection of Jesus, that he was the eternal Word, and Kings of kings (" 'Not by Might, nor by Power,' " *RH,* May 16, 1899).

[22]Manuscript 106, Sept 22, 1897, "Christ and the Law."

Concerning the apostle Paul, Ellen White wrote that he suffered "for the word of God and the testimony of Jesus Christ."[23] He was "God's ambassador," and as such he "exalted Jesus Christ as the world's Redeemer. Grace . . . makes his voice heard sweet and clear, repeating the story of the cross, the matchless love of Jesus."[24] In fact, Paul "poured out his blood as a witness for the word of God and the testimony of Jesus Christ."[25] The phrase from Rev 1:9 is now used to explain why Paul was persecuted and finally killed. The emphasis is placed once more on the message contained in the "testimony of Jesus" and Paul's willingness to proclaim it at any cost.

The Reformers and Believers

Based on the Bible, Ellen G. White concluded that the "testimony of Jesus" provokes persecution. According to her, the Reformers were persecuted for the same reason John and Paul were persecuted. The "Waldenses laid down their lives upon the mountains of Piedmont 'for the word of God, and for the testimony of Jesus Christ,' similar witness to the truth had been borne by . . . the Albigenses"[26] and other Reformers.[27] One could say that they had the "testimony of Jesus" and were not afraid to proclaim it. Consequently, they suffered persecution. The phrase is not being used in the technical sense of a "prophetic gift," but it presupposes that the biblical message originated through the prophetic gift, through divine revelation.

The work of the Reformers is unfinished; therefore, others "like the reformers of past ages, will be called, even at the peril of all earthly good, to witness 'for the word of God, and for the testimony of Jesus Christ.'"[28] When describing the experience of those living in the last days, Ellen G. White uses Rev 12:17 rather than 1:9: "The power of the gospel is to come upon the companies who are raised up to bear witness to the commandments of God and the testimony of Jesus Christ."[29] Here the "testimony of Jesus," together with the commandments, is something to which believers testify or witness to others. Those who listen are gath-

---

[23]"Bible Examples of True Courtesy," *RH*, Sept 8, 1895.

[24]Ibid.

[25]*Acts of the Apostles* (Mountain View, CA: Pacific Press, 1911), p. 513.

[26]*The Great Controversy* (Mountain View, CA: Pacific Press, 1911), p. 271, also p. 78.

[27]"Christian Privileges and Duties," *ST,* Jan 4, 1883.

[28]Ibid., p. 1.

[29]*Manuscript Releases,* vol. 12, p. 225.

ered "from every nation, kindred, tongue, and people . . . a people who keep the commandments of God and have the testimony of Jesus. . . . [They are] to stand faithful and true, bearing their testimony in favor of the law."[30] There is no indication in these quotes that she is equating the "testimony of Jesus" with her prophetic gift.

III. Content of the Testimony of Jesus

As already suggested, when Ellen G. White discusses the "testimony of Jesus," she places the emphasis on its content rather than on the fact that it reached us through the ministry of the prophets. It is now pertinent to examine more closely the content of that "testimony." It is at this point that content and medium come together.

The Totality of Scripture

The combination of the message that comes through the gift of prophecy is well illustrated when she says that "it was Christ that spoke through the prophets [she quotes 1 Pet 1:10-11]. It is the voice of Christ that speaks to us through the Old Testament. 'The testimony of Jesus is the spirit of prophecy' (Rev 19:10)."[31] In this case one could say that the "testimony of Jesus" encompasses both the prophetic gift and the content of the revelation received through it, namely the Old Testament itself.[32] We have already shown that, according to Ellen G. White, the teachings of Jesus are also part of the "testimony of Jesus." This suggests that the phrase could designate the totality of Scripture.[33]

This helps to explain why in some cases Ellen G. White placed the "testimony of Jesus" in close proximity to "the Word of God," the Bible, without necessarily equating them: "We have the commandments of God

---

[30]Ibid., vol. 20, p. 221.

[31]*Patriarchs and Prophets* (Washington, DC: Review and Herald, 1958), pp. 366-367.

[32]Compare that with the following: "We have the commandments of God and the testimony of Jesus Christ, which is the spirit of prophecy. Priceless gems are to be found in the Word of God. Those who search this Word should keep the mind clear" (Letter 16, 1900, Sunnyside, Cooranbong, New South Wales, Australia, Jan 27, 1900, to F. E. Belden, Review and Herald, Battle Creek).

[33]The "testimony of Jesus" in conjunction with "the commandments of God" becomes for her the test by which truth is identified: "We have our test in the Bible— the commandments of God and the testimony of Jesus" (Manuscript 149, 1901, Battle Creek, MI, April 15, 1901, "Talk/An Appeal to our Ministers"). In reading her one gets the distinct impression that she is using the phrase in terms of Isa 8:20: "To the law and to the testimony! If they do not speak according to this word, they have no light of dawn."

and the testimony of Jesus Christ, which is the spirit of prophecy. Priceless gems are to be found in the word of God."[34] After encouraging believers to spend time in searching the Bible, she exhorted them to "let the commandments of God and the testimony of Jesus Christ be in your minds continually and let them crowd out worldly thoughts and cares. When you lie down and when you rise up, let them be your meditation."[35] Perhaps even clearer is the following statement: "It is essential that all who have the name of Christ have a personal knowledge of the word of God and the testimony of Jesus Christ. They should understand the Scriptures for themselves."[36] We get the impression that in this case, "the word of God" refers to the Old Testament, while "the testimony of Jesus" refers to the New Testament. The two together constitute "the Scriptures."[37] We should keep in mind that for her, the Bible was "the unerring word of prophecy,"[38] that is to say, we received it as a revelation from God through His prophets.

Jesus' Revelation to John

There is a case in which Ellen G. White uses the phrase "testimony of Jesus" in connection with John's revelations: "The conditions of again partaking of the fruit of the tree are plainly stated in the testimony of Jesus Christ to John: 'Blessed are they that do his commandments, that they may have right to the tree of life, and may enter in through the gates into the city.'"[39] In fact, she is calling the book of Revelation "the testimony of Jesus Christ to John."[40] She is only quoting one passage from that "testimony," but the reference is to the book. One has to wonder whether it was this particular meaning of the phrase that she had in mind when using it to designate a central aspect of the message to be proclaimed

---

[34] *Testimonies to Ministers and Gospel Workers* (Mountain View, CA: Pacific Press, 1923), p. 114.

[35] *Early Writings* (Washington, DC: Review and Herald, 1945) p. 58.

[36] "Address and Appeal, Setting Forth the Importance of Missionary Work," *RH,* Jan 2, 1879.

[37] She admonishes God's people to be "careful, attentive students of the prophecies of the Old and New Testaments" and then quotes Rev 1:9, where reference is made to the "word of God" and to "the testimony of Jesus" (Manuscript 33, April 6, 1897, "We Would See Jesus").

[38] *Selected Messages,* Book 2, p. 88.

[39] *Lift Him Up* (Hagerstown, MD: Review and Herald, 1988), p. 22; also in Manuscript 72, Aug 2, 1901, "The True Obedience to the Commandments of God."

[40] She uses the phrases "the testimony of Jesus" and "the testimony of Jesus Christ" interchangeably.

by the remnant. That will certainly be a distinguishable work of the remnant.

The Central Message of the Scriptures

Ellen G. White considers Rev 12:17 and 14:12 to be parallel passages. She seems occasionally to equate "the testimony of Jesus" in 12:17 with "the faith of Jesus" in 14:12. A few examples may suffice. In 1875 she wrote: "God is leading a people out from the world upon the exalted platform of eternal truth, the commandments of God and the faith of Jesus."[41] A few lines down she added: "God is leading out a people and establishing them upon the one great platform of faith, the commandments of God and the testimony of Jesus. He has given his people a straight chain of Bible truth, clear and connected."[42] It would appear that she is not making any distinction between the meaning of the two passages. In 1901 she wrote: "Very many will get up some test that is not given in the word of God. We have our test in the Bible,—the commandments of God and the testimony of Jesus Christ. 'Here are they that keep the commandments of God and have the faith of Jesus.' This is the true test . . ."[43]

This close association between the "testimony of Jesus" and the "faith of Jesus" enriched her understanding of the meaning of the "testimony of Jesus." In the writings of Ellen G. White, the "faith of Jesus" is used to refer to the teachings of Jesus (1857).[44] But during the 1888 discussions on righteousness by faith, she related "the faith of Jesus" to the doctrine of justification by faith.[45] At that time she asked the rhetorical question: "What constitutes the faith of Jesus, that belongs to the third angel's message?" Her answer was,

> Jesus becoming our sin-bearer that he might become our sin-pardoning Saviour. He was treated as we deserve to be treated. He came to

---

[41] *Testimonies to the Church,* vol. 3, p. 446. Notice that she refers to the two elements as "truths."

[42] Ibid., p. 447.

[43] "An Appeal to our Ministers," *General Conference Bulletin,* April 16, 1901, pr. 8. Cf. *Evangelism* (Washington, DC: Review and Herald, 1970), p. 197.

[44] *Manuscript Releases,* vol. 5, p. 290.

[45] We would say that she interpreted the "faith of Jesus" not only as a subjective genitive (the teachings of Jesus), but also as an objective genitive (the faith that we put on Jesus as our Savior). These usages are to some extent found by her in the phrase the "testimony of Jesus." Together with the commandments of God, the "testimony of Jesus/ the faith of Jesus" is our message.

our world and took our sins that we might take His righteousness. Faith in the ability of Jesus to save us amply and fully and entirely is the faith of Jesus.[46]

In 1889 she commented that while the first part of the message of the third angel—keeping the commandments—had been strongly emphasized, the last part—the faith of Jesus—had been proclaimed casually and was not comprehended by the people.[47] That same year she spelled out clearly the meaning of the sentence "keep the commandments of God and the faith of Jesus" in terms of law and gospel.[48] It is this emphasis on the gospel and obedience to the law that makes the message of the remnant peculiar.[49]

Ellen G. White's understanding of the "faith of Jesus" spilled over into the phrase the "testimony of Jesus." Once, after quoting Rev 14:12, she wrote, "Who are these? God's denominated people—those who on this earth have witnessed to their loyalty. Who are they? Those who have kept the commandments of God and the testimony of Jesus Christ; those who have owned the Crucified One as their Saviour."[50] The question is repeated twice. The first answer identifies them as those who are loyal to God—"those who have kept the commandments of God." The second answer seems to explain the "testimony of Jesus" in terms of owning Christ as our Savior.

In another statement she seems to equate "salvation" and the "testimony of Jesus:" "The work that the Lord has given us at this time is to present to the people the true light in regard to the testing questions of obedience and salvation,—the commandments of God and the testimony of Jesus Christ."[51] One wonders if by the "testimony of Jesus" she meant here the teachings of Jesus and of the New Testament according to which there is salvation only by faith in Christ. This would be a very particular usage of the expression. However, she would probably argue that even in this case, the phrase designates the Scriptures, because all of it testifies concerning Christ's saving power.

---

[46]*Manuscript Releases*, vol. 12, p. 193.

[47]Ibid., vol. 8, p. 271.

[48]*RH*, Nov 27, 1889, pr. 17.

[49]She never lost sight of the fact that the "faith of Jesus" was also a way of referring to the teachings of our Lord, the light He brought to the world; see, "Thoughts on the First Epistle of John," *ST*, May 23, 1895, pr. 4; *Gospel Workers* (Washington, DC: Review and Herald, 1948), p. 162.

[50]"Ellen G. White Comments: Revelation," *AdvBibComm*, vol. 7, p. 981.

[51]*Counsels to Writers and Editors* (Nashville, TN: Southern, 1946), p. 151.

IV. "The Testimony of Jesus" and Opposition to Her Prophetic Ministry

There are four documents in the writings of Ellen G. White where she comes very close to applying the phrase "testimony of Jesus" to her own prophetic ministry. This would be understandable not only because that was the prevailing view among the pioneers, but also because the book of Revelation itself interprets it in terms of the gift of prophecy.[52] The statements we will discuss are found in her unpublished writings, namely some of her letters and manuscripts. In these documents she was addressing the case of individuals who were attacking her person and prophetic ministry.

Letter 20, 1860

The first statement is found in a letter she wrote to believers in Mansville. Between 1859 and 1862, some church members in Mansville questioned the manifestation of the gift of prophecy in the ministry of Ellen G. White. She sent them a letter, encouraging them to retain their faith in the gift. Concerning the origin of the visions, she commented that there were only two possibilities; namely, they were from God or from Satan. She then argued that, based on the fact that the visions had always had a positive influence on the church and in the lives of believers they had to be from the Lord. Besides, she argued, the fact that those who rejected them sooner or later departed from other biblical truths indicated, that in their rejection of the visions, they were not being led by the Lord. Then she added:

> Just as soon as you begin to crush or smother the gifts of the church or to slight them, just so soon the blessing of God leaves that church. Here is where the war is coming against the remnant because they keep the commandments of God and have the testimony of Jesus. I am sorry that this war is often started among brethren. They do not wait for the dragon host to make this war, but they fall under the temptations of Satan and commence the war themselves.[53]

This is one of the earliest usages of the phrase "the testimony of Jesus" in the writings of Ellen G. White, and it deserves some comment. First, the

---

[52]See Gerhard Pfandl, "Identifying Marks of the Remnant in the Book of Revelation," in this volume.

[53]"Dear Friends in Mansville and Vicinity," Letter 20, 1860.

context makes clear that she was not attempting to exegete Rev 12:17 or to establish the meaning of the full phrase "keep the commandments of God and have the testimony of Jesus." Second, nowhere in the letter does she explicitly equate the manifestation of the gift of prophecy in her ministry with the historical fulfillment of the phrase "the testimony of Jesus" in Rev 12:17. One could argue that since she was defending her prophetic call, there is an implicit identification of the two. Nevertheless, the implication is not obvious. Third, in the letter she identified the attack against the manifestation of the gift of prophecy in her ministry as an attack against the biblical truth of the permanency of the spiritual gifts in the church. This is a biblical teaching that, according to her, Adventists should never abandon. She explicitly said in the same letter, "There has been great labor, much perseverance, and a steady pressing through conflicts and untold trials to maintain the position we now occupy of bearing a decided testimony in favor of the gifts God has placed in the church, and is this position to be readily yielded? No, no."[54] It would appear that she was defending not simply her prophetic role but a biblical teaching that was under serious attack. Finally, she apparently considered an attack against any biblical teaching as a manifestation of the wrath of the dragon against the end-time people of God, identified by her as those "who keep the commandments of God and have the testimony of Jesus." Notice that she not only mentions "the testimony of Jesus," she also refers to "the commandments of God." The two together are the fundamental characteristics of the end-time remnant. That seems to be the reason she quoted the phrase.

Manuscript 22, 1885

The second statement we will examine is found in a manuscript dated November 30, 1885.[55] It describes her experience with Miles Grant, a first-day Adventist minister who was publicly defaming her through personal attacks, undermining her prophetic gift and attacking the law of God. In the manuscript she indicates that she had decided not to answer his attacks but chosen instead to leave the situation in the hands of the Lord. According to her, a person who has rejected the law of God, the very foundation of morality, is not to be trusted. She quotes Rev 12:17 to show that "this raid made against those who keep the commandments of God will not cease until probation closes."[56] In other words, she was interpret-

---

[54]Ibid., p. 2.
[55]Manuscript 22, Cir. Nov 30, 1885, "Regarding Miles Grant in Italy."
[56]Ibid.

ing this incident in the light of the cosmic conflict and Satan's opposition to God and His truth.

After quoting Rev 12:17, she writes, "The testimony of Jesus is the Spirit of prophecy. To whom does this apply?"[57] One would expect her to apply it to her prophetic ministry, but that is not what she did. In fact, she did not clearly answer the question! One could assume that she is expecting the reader to answer it, saying, "It applies to Ellen G. White." But we should be careful not to assume something that is not clearly indicated by the context. The truth is that she is not clear, making it difficult for us to give a final answer to her question. Perhaps what is important in our discussion is that this was an excellent opportunity for her to clearly indicate that "the testimony of Jesus" was to be identified with her prophetic gift, yet she stopped short of drawing that conclusion. It would be inappropriate for us to draw that conclusion by ourselves, particularly in the light of her understanding of the phrase in the rest of her writings.

Based on the context of her statement, I will venture a possible way of interpreting what she was attempting to communicate. After quoting Rev 12:17, she immediately wrote, "Men will be tested upon the truth. Satan will not let one go from his ranks without he makes a desperate resistance. . . . If these souls will flee to Jesus and make earnest prayer to God to know the truth, if they will go to God and their Bibles, they will ascertain the truth as it is in Jesus." She was dealing with revealed truth. It is at that point that she makes the statement "the testimony of Jesus is the Spirit of prophecy." I will suggest that with that statement she was referring to the content of that revelation and not so much to the process through which it was revealed. But what about the questions she asked? I will suggest that when she asked, "To whom does this apply?" she was asking for the identity of the one who had always opposed "the testimony of Jesus" and "the commandments of God." If that were the case, then she answered the question because she immediately identified him as Satan. She described his attacks against God's revealed truth in heaven and on earth (the testimony of Jesus) and against God's revealed will (the law).

Letter 17, 1887

The third statement we should examine is found in a letter Ellen G. White wrote on September 6, 1887.[58] It was written to a pastor to whom

---

[57]Ibid.
[58]Letter 17, Battle Creek, MI, Sept 6, 1887, to Brother and Sister Andrews.

she had delivered a message from the Lord, a testimony. He was questioning the testimony, but it was particularly his wife who at the camp-meeting had been planting doubts in the minds of others. In doing this, Ellen G. White wrote, his wife was making of none effect God's message to His people. After briefly describing what this person was doing, she commented, "Satan's work is to make war against the commandments of God and the testimony of Jesus Christ; and if the temptations were not harbored and expressed, then the seed of doubt would not be sown."[59]

Since that statement is made in the context of a defense of her prophetic ministry, it would be logical to conclude that in attacking Ellen G. White's testimonies, this lady was fulfilling the prophecy according to which Satan was to make war against the "testimony of Jesus." In that case, Rev 12:17 would be referring to White's prophetic ministry. But the context seems to point to a different conclusion. If we simply read the statement the way she wrote it, all she seems to be saying is that Satan is at war against God's people, identified by her as those who keep the commandments of God and the testimony of Jesus. In that war he uses human instrumentalities to accomplish his purposes. One of the ways he does that is by tempting them to sow seeds of doubt. If they fall into temptation, he would use them to attack the faith of God's people. In this case the phrase "against the commandments of God and the testimony of Jesus" would be referring to the message that God had entrusted to His end-time people.

Manuscript 40, 1887

The final statement we will discuss is found in a manuscript from 1887.[60] In it Ellen G. White addresses the dangers of doubting, criticizing, and finding fault. She unambiguously states that "it is the work of Satan to encourage doubt and unbelief"[61] and adds, "Those who are continually looking for something to find fault with, something to strengthen unbelief, either in the testimony of God's Spirit or of His word, will soon find themselves so completely under the power of doubt and unbelief that nothing will seem sure to them."[62] She illustrates her message with references to the rejection of Jesus in Nazareth, where those listening to Him rejected His claim to be the Messiah. They found fault with Him and even

---

[59]Ibid.
[60]Manuscript 40, 1887, "Peril of Doubt and Unbelief."
[61]Ibid.
[62]Ibid.

tried to kill Him. In the Old Testament the Israelites found fault with Elijah and rejected his message. The reproof of wrong by Jesus and Elijah resulted in opposition by many. She brings the lesson home, saying, "The spirit of enmity which has in every age been manifested against the reprover of wrong is seen in greater degree as we near the close of time."[63] According to her, such individuals are opposing the work of God. Then, we find the statement that is of particular interest to us:

> The prophet is looking down to the last church when he declares that the dragon makes war with the remnant who keep the commandments of God and have the testimony of Jesus Christ. The testimony of Jesus is the Spirit of Prophecy. The same hatred that was manifested against the work of Christ has been manifested against the work of reproof the servants of God have been called to bear by those whose sins have been reproved.[64]

In this case "the testimony of Jesus" is the message He gave through the prophets and through Himself. This message brought opposition and hatred to Jesus by those reproved by Him. She placed herself among the servants of God who experienced hatred from those who were reproved because of their sins. She has been called to reprove sin and, consequently, together with the remnant will be the object of the dragon's hatred.[65] This remnant is again identified as those who keep the commandments of God and the testimony of Jesus.

---

[63] Ibid.

[64] Ibid.

[65] In one of her statements quoted above, Ellen G. White refers to her testimony as "the testimony of God's Spirit." But she also mentions "the testimony of God's word," by which she was designating the Scripture. There are people, she said, who find fault with both. She was not equating "the testimony of Jesus," mentioned in Rev 12:17, with her prophetic gift. In fact, she never refers to the testimonies she delivered as "the testimony of Jesus" but as the "testimony of God's Spirit." She knew that her prophetic gift, the testimony of the Spirit through her, was going to be a particular object of attack by the enemy: "The very last deception of Satan will be to make of none effect the testimony of the Spirit of God. 'Where there is no vision, the people perish' (Prov 29:18). Satan will work ingeniously, in different ways and through different agencies, to unsettle the confidence of God's remnant people in the true testimony. He will bring in spurious visions, to mislead and mingle the false with the true, and so disgust people that they will regard everything that bears the name of visions, as a species of fanaticism; but honest souls, by contrasting false and true, will be enabled to distinguish between them" (*Selected Messages*, Book 2, p. 78). See also *Selected Messages*, Book 3, p. 83; *Testimonies for the Church*, vol. 3, pp. 253-254, 257; ibid., vol. 5, p. 674; *Manuscript Releases*, vol. 10, p. 81; and ibid., vol. 21, p. 101.

Appendix: The "Testimony of Jesus" in the Writings of Ellen G. White

Those four statements are not as clear as we would like them to be, but in them Ellen G. White certainly came very close to applying to her prophetic ministry the phrase "the testimony of Jesus." What is surprising is that in none of them she explicitly makes the connection. For some reason she shied away from saying it. Although the statements are difficult to interpret, it would appear that she was simply indicating that Rev 12:17 was describing the identity of God's end-time remnant and the biblical message they were to proclaim. The attacks against the messages she delivered were understood by her as expressions of the wrath of the dragon against the remnant and their message.

V. Ellen G. White and the Spirit of Prophecy

We should emphasize that Ellen G. White was persuaded that she had received the prophetic gift from the Lord, that she was the messenger of the Lord. While she was reluctant to refer to it as "the testimony of Jesus," she applied the phrase "Spirit of Prophecy" to her writings. That phrase was interpreted by her as referring to the prophetic gift. She speaks about her messages as "directions given through the Spirit of prophecy."[66] This is the same gift of prophecy that biblical writers received and through which they predicted the coming of the Savior.[67] In 1907 she wrote,

> A wealth of moral influence has been brought to us in the last half century. Through His Holy Spirit the voice of God has come to us continually in warning and instruction to confirm the faith of the believers in the Spirit of Prophecy. Repeatedly the word has come, Write the things that I have given you.[68]

She writes about people who rejected testimonies given to them and "who have more confidence in themselves than in the spirit of prophecy."[69] It is intriguing that she would consider her ministry to be a manifestation of "the Spirit of prophecy," refer to the messages she writes as "testimonies,"[70] and yet avoid applying to herself the phrase "the testimony of Jesus," which, according to Rev 19:10, is defined as "the

---

[66] *Testimonies for the Church*, vol. 8, p. 298.
[67] "The Sending Out of the Seventy," *ST*, Dec 10, 1894.
[68] *Selected Messages*, Book 1, p. 41.
[69] *Testimonies for the Church*, vol. 4, p. 330.
[70] See, e.g., *Testimonies for the Church*, vol. 5, pp. 672-691.

Spirit of prophecy." Her use of the phrase "the testimony of Jesus" helps to understand why she did it.

VI. Conclusion

Our study has revealed that, in the writings of Ellen G. White, the phrase "testimony of Jesus" refers to the gift of prophecy. Her usage of that phrase presupposes the definition of it found in Rev 19:10. However, we have shown that she uses the phrase primarily to designate the end-product of that gift, namely Scripture, the message it contains, and the message of the book of Revelation.[71] Although the "testimony of Jesus" refers to all biblical truth, it designates in a very particular way the central truth of the Bible, namely the message of salvation by faith in Christ. The proclamation of the biblical truth found in the Old Testament and taught by Jesus and His apostles resulted in the persecution and even deaths of some of Christ's followers. The end-time remnant has been called by God to accept, appropriate, and proclaim that biblical truth. In fact, the combination of the testimony of Jesus and obedience to the commandments of God are identifying marks of the remnant (Rev 12:17).

As far as I can ascertain, Ellen G. White never clearly or explicitly interpreted Rev 12:17 as pointing to her prophetic ministry within the remnant.[72] Her usage of the phrase "testimony of Jesus" would not exclude

---

[71] In the book, *The Great Controversy*, Rev 12:17 is only quoted once (p. 592), at the end of her discussion on the law of God, the commandments of God. After reading the biblical passage, one would logically expect her to discuss in the following chapter "the testimony of Jesus." But the title of that chapter is "The Scripture a Safeguard."

[72] The following quotation shows up in the Ellen G. White CD-ROM when doing a search for "testimony of Jesus": " 'And the dragon was wroth with the woman, and went to make war with the remnant of her seed, which keep the commandments of God, and have the testimony of Jesus Christ.' This prophecy points out clearly that the remnant church will acknowledge God in His law and will have the prophetic gift. Obedience to the law of God, and the spirit of prophecy has always distinguished the true people of God, and the test is usually given on present manifestations" (*Loma Linda Messages*, 33). I became suspicious of the statement for two reasons. First, the style of writing is not that of Ellen G. White, and second, its content is out of line with what she writes elsewhere on the subject. I decided to consult the White Estate. Timothy L. Poirier, Vice-Director/Archivist of the White Estate, confirmed my suspicion. He wrote: "As question has been raised concerning the authorship of pages 33-38 in 'Loma Linda Messages,' entitled 'Established Prosperity,' I can tell you that it is not the work of Ellen White. This seems evident not only from the vocabulary and style of the article itself, but also from the fact that Ellen White's writings are quoted in various places to support the point of the author. Furthermore, on one of the original copies of the collection in our file, the name of J. A. Burden has been added on the title page in handwriting that appears to be W.

the manifestation of the prophetic gift in her life and experience, but she chose not to make a clear or explicit connection between the two. This appears to me to be something she intentionally decided to do. The reason for this decision is not stated in her writings. We could venture two closely related reasons.

First, she always placed the authority of Scripture above any other source of information, including her own prophetic ministry. The Protestant principle *sola scriptura* controlled her theology to the extent that she may have decided to limit the meaning of the phrase "testimony of Jesus" to Scripture as the supreme authoritative end-product of the prophetic gift. She firmly believed that the biblical message God's remnant people are to proclaim today is to be grounded exclusively in the Bible. Second, she perhaps refrained from using the phrase "the testimony of Jesus" to designate her own prophetic ministry to avoid possible misunderstandings of her role inside and outside of the church. This may have been an expression of Christian modesty. In any case, she never denied that the Lord called her to the prophetic ministry. She was a messenger of God.

C. White's. By way of background, 'Loma Linda Messages' is also known as the Burden Collection, since it represents materials Elder Burden compiled to narrate the history of God's leading in the purchase and establishment of Loma Linda. As such, the collection not only includes communications from Ellen White but also many letters from other church leaders, minutes and actions from committees, and in this instance, either an article or sermon apparently prepared by Elder Burden himself" (E-mail from Tim Poirier to Ángel M. Rodríguez, Oct 20, 2005).

Scriptural Index

OLD TESTAMENT

Genesis
Reference	Page
1:1–2:3	129
1:31–2:3	132
2:1-3	130
3:15	86, 99, 105, 203
4:1-15	26
6:3	208
6:9	29
7:23	26
12:3	32
18:19	32
18:23-32	29
21:12	80
45:7	30

Exodus
Reference	Page
15:12	105
16:25	135
19:4	105
19:6	95, 98
20:1	136
20:2	101
20:5	136
20:5-6	101
20:8-11	134, 136
20:10	135
20:11	101, 119, 122
24:12	115
25:1	129
25:16	118
25–31	129
30:6	118
30:11, 17, 22	129
30:34	129
31:1, 12	29
31:12-17	129, 130
39:43	132

Leviticus
Reference	Page
11:44	99
20:7	99

Numbers
Reference	Page
12:7	154
14:34	208
24:17-19	64
33:55	26

Deuteronomy
Reference	Page
3:1-4	36
7:9	154
10:1-5	118
21:15	80
22:13	80
24:3	80
32:11	105

Judges
Reference	Page
3:1	26

Ruth
Reference	Page
1:3, 5	31
4:14-17	31

1 Samuel
Reference	Page
20:6	207
26:23	154

1 Kings
Reference	Page
17:1-7	104
18–19	213
19	27
19:14, 18	105
19:17-18	33
19:18	64
19:18	105

2 Kings
Reference	Page
5:2-3	33
17:18	31
25:11	31

1 Chronicles
Reference	Page
1–9	36

2 Chronicles
Reference	Page
30:6	35
30:7-8	39
34:9	39

Ezra
Reference	Page
1:2-5	36
1:4	35
1:5	36
2:1-70	36
3:11-13	38
5:1-2	36
9:8	35
9:13-14	39
9:13-15	35
10:2	151

Nehemiah
Reference	Page
1:8-10	36
7:5-65	36
7:72	25

Job
Reference	Page
10:5	207
14:19	151

Psalms
Reference	Page
9:18	151
36:9	151
37:9	151
90:9-10	207
91:10	47
146:6	136

Proverbs
Reference	Page
12:17	154

Isaiah
Reference	Page
1:4	64
1:9	185
1:21	213
6:13	64
10:20	186
10:20-21	38
10:20-23	35
10:22	81
10:22-23	81
11:6-9	34
11:10-13	35
11:11, 16	35
14:1-2	37
14:22	64
15:18	154
16:14	65
51:9-10	105
53	97
57:4	46
58:13	135
58:13-14	191
65:8	33

66:18-20	32	**Haggai**		**Luke**		
		1:12	35	3:1-18	66	
Jeremiah		1:12-13	36	4:18	75	
2:21	46	1:14	35	6:5	135	
3:1-3, 8-9	213	2:2	35	6:35	74	
4:30	213	2:19	36	16:8	74	
5:1	154			24:1	134	
23:2-3	74	**Zechariah**				
31:7	38	2:7	35	**John**		
31:7-9	34	3	95	1:19-28	66	
31:27	46	8:6	37	2:12, 24	103	
51:34	105	8:11-12	37	6:44, 65	155	
		13:8-9	37	8:44	100	
Joel		14:16	37	10:16	74, 220	
2:11, 31	135	14:16-19	32	13:34	115	
2:31-32	26			14:21-24	101	
2:32	37	**Malachi**		15:20	101	
		1:2-3	80	16:13	155	
Ezekiel		3:16-4:3	28			
4:6	208	3:16-18	64	**Acts**		
6:8-10	34	4:5	135	18:27	155	
11:14-21	34			20:7	134	
14:21-22	34			20:29-30	207	
16:15-34	213	**NEW TESTAMENT**				
29:3	105			**Romans**		
32:2	105	**Matthew**		2:8	155	
		3:1-12	66	2:16	157	
Daniel		3:8	66	7:8-13	140	
4:13, 17, 23	47	4:4, 7	101	8:32	155	
7	123	5:9	74	9:6-13	78, 79	
7:21-22	45	7:23	125	9:13	80	
7:21	124	8:12	74	9:27	81	
7:25	124, 125, 207	9:13	99	11:1-6	83	
		12:8	135	11:4	83	
Hosea		13:24-30	72, 74	11:5	99	
2:1	81	13:47-50	72	11:26	84	
2:2, 4	213	13:41	125	13:9	115	
2:18-23	186	15:3, 6	140			
		16:18	74	**1 Corinthians**		
Amos		19:17	140	2:1	230	
4:1-3	25	22:11-14	71	2:12	155	
5:14-15	30	22:14	30, 74, 75	12:8-10	144	
5:15	29	24:12	125	12:28	96, 144	
5:18-20	135	25:1-13	71	15:22-28	202	
		26:31	74	16:2	134	
Micah		26:39	203			
7:2, 7	151	28:18-20	222	**2 Corinthians**		
				10:1	94	
Habakkuk		**Mark**				
2:4	154	2:27-28	135	**Ephesians**		
		6:6-13	68	1:4	98	
Zephaniah		9:42	75	2:8	155	
1:14	135	10:19	140	2:20	96	
3:12-13	64	12:28-31	115	3:5	96	
3:19-20	75	16:2	134	4:11	144	

Scriptural Index

Philippians		3:11	211	13:11-17	93
1:29	155	3:14-22	211	13:11-18	204
4:5	94	3:21	90	13:12-15	157
		5:3	119	13:13	105
1 Thessalonians		5:9-10	98	13:13-14	225
1:3	151	5:10	95	13:13-18	196
2:15	96	6:2, 5, 8	92	13–14	120
		6:9	96, 149	13:15	101, 103, 215
2 Thessalonians		6:17	93	13:15-17	214
2:3	125	7:3	96, 215	13:16	103
2:7-8	125	7:14	97, 211	13:17	215
2:13	155	7:15-17	93	14:1	215
3:5	151	8:13	88	14:1-3	60
		9:16-17	92	14:1-5	92, 140
1 Timothy		9:19–15:5	118	14:3	97
2:5	202	9:20	88	14:4	93
		9:20-21	119, 120	14:5	93
Titus		10:6	120	14:6	136
1:1	155	10:10-11	96	14:6-12	131, 157, 173
		11:3	103	14:6-14	211
Hebrew		11:4	95	14:7	119, 122, 136, 157
2:14-15	202	11:5-6	105		
3:2	202	11:8	97	14:9-11	157
11:6	101	11:9	118	14:12	96, 100, 116, 125, 136, 140, 150, 152, 153, 156, 187, 189, 215, 234
12:2-3	151	11:13	88, 96		
		11:15-19	117, 118		
1 Peter		11:19	117		
1:10	96	12	106		
1:16	99	12:5	203	14:13-20	211
2:9	98	12:6	104, 204, 207	15:1-4	60
23:23	152	12:7	124	15:1-8	117
		12:9	105	15:3	105
2 Peter		12:10-12	90	15:5	117, 118
1:1	155	12:11	60, 90, 107, 211	16:13	93
				16:13-14	225
Jude		12:12	60, 88, 93	16:17	130
1:3	156	12:13-16	204	17:1	131
		12–14	140, 157, 203	17:1-6	93, 131
Revelation		12:14-16	105	17:8	97
1:1	96, 102	12:15	105	17:10	88
1:2	141, 149	12:17	21, 60, 87, 88, 93, 100, 113, 116, 124, 125, 136, 139, 141, 149, 152, 156, 161, 164, 171, 173, 187, 189, 203, 221, 227, 231, 234	17:14	215
1:5-6	98			18:4	106, 157, 221, 222
1:6	95			18:4-5	100
1:9	88, 141, 149, 230			19:2	97
				19:5	97
1:10	133, 135			19:8	97
2–3	90			19:10	88, 96, 102, 144, 232
2:4-7	211				
2:10	211			19:21	88
2:14	88	13:1	100	20:4	88, 141, 149, 150
2:14-16	211	13:1-10	204		
2:20	213	13:4	100, 215	20:5	88
2:24	88	13:5-6	100	20:6	98
2:27-29	60	13:7	124, 152	20:10	93
3:2	88	13:8	97	20:12	97
3:4	211	13:10	152, 153, 215		

20:13	97	21–22	90	22:9-10	100
20:15	97	21:27	97	22:10	103
21:3-4	93	22:6	96	22:14	116, 140
21:6	130	22:8-9	102, 144	22:18-19	103
21:9–22:5	130	22:9	102, 145		

Thematic Index

1 Enoch, 44–46
  remnant will be protected, 44
  seed theology, 46
  work of the Elect One, 45
4 Ezra, 49, 51
  remnant are the "few", 49
  two ages, 49
144,000, 91, 93, 98
  and the Remnant, 91
  totality of the end-time people of God, 98
1260-day period, 157

Abraham, 32, 79, 92, 184
Abraham's descendants, 29
Abyssinian churches, 175
Adoration, 98
Adventism, 20
  apocalyptic movement, 20
  reform movement, 20
Adventist, 21, 203
  appropriation of the remnant motif, 203
  ecclesiology, 21
Adventist church, 104, 108–109, 112
  prophetic movement, 109
  the "remnant church", 108
Adventist ecclesiology, 17, 40, 201, 217, 226
  a remnant perspective, 226
  universal unity of the church, 217
  need, 17
Adventist movement, 18, 21, 40, 216
  mission, 21
  relevance, 18
  vitality, 18
Adventists, 18, 20, 40, 162, 172
  and other Christian churches, 172
  body of beliefs, 18
  called themselves "the remnant", 162
  historical and faithful remnant, 40
  lifestyle, 18
  restoring truths, 20
  visible end-time remnant, 172
  worldview, 18
Adventist self-understanding, 164
Albigenses, 231
Anabaptists, 175
Anointed one, 53
Anomia, 125
Antichrist, 125
Apocalyptic interpretation, 109
Apocalyptic writings, 43
Apocrypha, 48
Apostasy, 27, 44, 90, 105, 157, 175, 185, 189, 199, 206–208, 213, 221
Apostates, 59
Ark of the covenant, 117–118, 125
Authority, 219
Authority of Scripture, 243

Babylon, 31, 35, 92–93, 97, 100, 103–104, 106, 110, 112, 131, 157, 185, 195, 213–214
  a city, 213
  a harlot, 131, 213
  all apostate religious organizations, 214
  a "mother", 214
  archenemy of God and His people, 213
  a somber woman, 106
  a woman, 213
  culmination of a process of apostasy, 214
  union of church and state, 213
Babylonian captivity, 39–40
Baptism, 107
Beast, 104
Behemoth, 52
Bible prophecy, 108
Blood, 92, 98, 109
Book of Life, 97
  and the Remnant, 97
Buddhism, 169

Characteristics of the remnant, 209
  found in Revelation, 209
  have the testimony of Jesus, 210
  keep the commandments of God, 210
  the faith of Jesus, 210
  the patience of the saints, 210
Character of God, 182
Children of God, 79
Chosen people, 59
Christ, 98–99, 202
  absolutely faithful to God, 202
  God's instrument for salvation, 202
  human nature, 202
  overcome the forces of evil, 202
  posterity of the woman, 99
  Servant of the Lord, 202
  the truest "remnant", 202
Christ as, 20
  mediator, 20
Christian church, 90, 190, 203
Christians, 173
Christological hymn, 90
Christ's character, 91
Christ's endurance, 152
Christ's righteousness, 196
Church, 18–19, 21, 171, 176, 180, 219–220
  a community of believers, 219
  a prophetic minority, 171
  authority, 19
  community of believers, 19, 219
  inclusive, 180
  invisible dimension, 220
  mission, 18
  more than an institutional, 219
  mystery, 18

nature, 18
not essentially invisible, 180
of the predestined, 176
origin, 19
unity, 18
universal, 21
Church and state, 180
Church of Christ, 85, 224
  end-time remnant, 224
  universal church, 224
Church of Sardis, 88
Cleansing, 199, 210–211
Commandments, 56, 58, 89
Commandments of God, 51, 96–97, 100, 190
  in Revelation, 100
Communion ecclesiology, 222
Concept of the remnant, 85
Conflict, 102
Conscience, 174, 180
Cosmic conflict, 20, 22, 126, 157, 182, 187, 198, 203, 209, 222, 225
Covenant, 47, 54, 78, 80
Covenantal remnant, 79
Covenant community, 178
Covenant loyalty, 53
Covenantors, 59
Covenant promises, 27, 58, 84, 198
Creator, 136

Damascus document, 58
Damascus rule, 57
Day of the Lord, 28
Day of Yahweh, 30
Decalogue, 100, 118, 122, 141, 191
Deliverance, 30, 51, 53, 91
Demonic hosts, 153
Demonic spirits, 103
Divine election, 31, 176
Divine grace, 226
Divine intention, 202
Divine mercy, 46
Divine plan, 174
Dragon, 89, 100, 105–106, 192, 204
  against the remnant, 204
  apostate Christendom, 193
  Babylon, 105
  gain the support of civil powers, 193
  ineffective, 106
  seek to divide, 192

symbol of Egypt, 105
Dragon's wrath, 107

Eastern Orthodox Churches, 218
Easter Sunday, 134
Ecclesiastical oneness, 217
Ecclesiastical organization, 171, 218
Ecclesiology, ix
Echō, 148
  to have or to hold, 149
Ecumenical dialogue, 218
Ecumenical movement, 170
Election, 67, 78–80, 176–177
Election of Israel, 48, 77
Elijah, 33, 64, 83, 86, 94, 104, 240
Ellen G. White, 104, 162, 165, 198, 241
  inclusive nature of the remnant, 198
  received the prophetic gift, 241
Emperor's day, 134
End-time remnant, 87, 139, 141, 167, 184
  essential characteristics of, 140
  keeping the Sabbath, 141
  Keep the commandments of God, 140
Enemy, 60
Entolē, 113, 116
Eschatological community, 55, 84
Eschatological day of the Lord, 135
Eschatological deliverance, 51
Eschatological generation, 49
Eschatological judgment, 50
Eschatological promise, 34, 92
Eschatological remnant, 26, 33, 35, 37–38, 40, 47, 87, 91, 96, 99, 105, 112, 179, 186–187, 194, 203, 215, 222
  essential characteristics, 188
  inclusive, 40
  in the writings of Ellen G. White, 187
  suffers persecution, 105
  visible community, 33
Eschatological salvation, 77
Eschatological war, 56
Eschatology, 26, 37, 43, 49

Esther, 195
Eternal gospel, 157, 163, 179, 211
Exclusiveness, 46, 71
Exclusivism, 173, 217
Experience of the Remnant, 193

Faith, 109, 155, 171, 192, 196, 211, 234
Faithfulness, 39, 89, 179, 223
Faithful remnant, 26, 28–29, 30, 34, 38, 40, 72, 78–79, 81, 84, 86, 95, 100, 184, 193, 210
  keep the commandments of God, 100
  qualities, 30
  tension, 40
  unfaithfulness, 29
Faithful woman, 213
Faith in Christ, 78
Faith of Israel, 43
  teachings of Jesus, 234
Faith of Jesus, 96, 101, 156, 234
  content of the Christian faith, 156
  faith in the Word of God, 101
  justification by faith, 234
  teachings of Jesus, 234
Fall of spiritual Babylon, 157
False doctrines, 192
False prophet, 93, 103
Fanaticism, 194
Fear God, 131, 140, 212
Final remnant, 171
Flesh, 79
Forgiveness, 107, 185
Formalism, 209
Fulfillment of prophecy, 35, 40
Fullness of the Church, 218
Future, 221
Future of humanity, 46
  a remnant, 46
Futurism, 206

Generation, 86
Gentiles, 49, 54, 58, 78, 81, 84, 93, 186
George I. Butler, 161
German Pietists, 175
Gift of prophecy, 237
God, 196
  gather the remnant church, 196

Thematic Index

Godly remnant, 60
God's commandments, 116
  end-time remnant, 172
  faithfulness, 84
  faithful remnant, 96
  freedom, 80, 81
  grace, 30, 97, 112
  judgment, 46, 158
  mercy, 190
  people, 239
  remnant people, 126
  saving purpose, 182
  sovereignty, 29
  worship, 94
Gomorrah, 82
Goodly remnant, 185
Gospel, 20, 176, 199
Gospel message, 190
Grace, 27, 29, 79, 83, 99, 112
  remnant of, 29
Grace of God, 109
Gratitude, 97, 193
Great multitude, 91
Great tribulation, 92

Hate, 80
Hermeneutics, 109
Historical remnant, 26, 29, 35, 78, 86, 99, 110, 184
Historical writings, 37
Historicist method, 206
  used by the early Church, 206
Historicist methodology, 160
Holiness, 98–99
Holy remnant, 24, 96, 99, 102
Holy Spirit, 147, 155, 176, 179
Hope, 29, 59, 76, 82, 94, 107, 151, 162, 192
Humility, 112, 164
Hupomonē, 150–151
  steadfast endurance, 151

Idolaters, 59
Inclusive, 60
Inclusiveness, 37, 47
Inclusive remnant, 60
Intertestamental literature, 60
Intertestamental period, 43
Invisible church, 32, 165, 175, 177, 220
  apologetic device of the Reformers, 175
  the totality of the elect, 177
Invisible remnant, 170
Islam, 166

Israel, 76–80, 93, 104, 213
  of faith, 76, 79, 179

James White, 162
Jesus, 69, 72, 178
  and Israel, 69
  and Remnant Theology, 72
  and the Remnant, 69
  true Shepherd, 178
Jewish apocalyptic literature, 43
  apostasy, 44
  divine judgment, 44
Jewish apocalyptic works, 53
Jews, 84, 186
Jezebel, 94, 104, 213
  symbol of apostasy, 213
  unfaithful people of God, 213
John, 88–89
  and the Remnant, 88
  emblematic of a remnant, 89
John the Baptist, 66
Joseph Bates, 161
Josephus, 67
Joshua, 95
Jubilees, 47–48
  faithful remnant, 48
  God's elect, 48
  nationalistic remnant, 47
  nationalistic view, 48
  remnant people, 47
Judgment, 33, 44–45, 47, 50, 53, 68, 71, 76, 82, 97, 100, 157, 212

Kenosis, 107
Kingdom, 76
Kingdom of God, 108
Kingdom of priests, 98
  and the Remnant, 98
Kingdom of the dragon, 108

Lamb, 93, 98
Land, 50, 52
Landmarks, 192
Laodicea, 90, 211
Law, 235
  and gospel, 235
  in Daniel, 124
  of God, 199
Leviathan, 52
Life, 201
Light, 173, 179, 222
Liturgy, 18

Loipos, 87
Lord's day, 133, 135
  the seventh-day Sabbath, 135
Love, 193
Love commandment, 115
Love of Christ, 111
Loyalty, 59, 89, 194, 215
Lutherans, 176

Mark of the beast, 214
Martin Luther, 175
Marturia, 143, 229
Martyrdom, 107
Martyrs, 88
Mercy, 56, 65
Message of the first angel, 212
Message of the second angel, 212
  the fall of Babylon, 212
Message of the third angel, 214
Messiah, 50, 84, 183, 186, 209, 239
Messiahs, 58
Messianic age, 49
Messianic kingdom, 52
Messianism, 55
Methodists, 175
Michael, 106
Middle Ages, 207, 213
  Daniel, 207
Militant church, 225
Millerite movement, 160
Millerite Revivalists, 175
Misconceptions, 164
Mission, 31, 41, 68, 94, 179, 190–191, 203, 210–211, 215, 225
  of the Remnant, 190, 211
  prepare the world for the coming of the Lord, 191
  purpose, 211
  restoration, 68
  the two witnesses, 94
  three angels' messages, 211
  to the nations, 41
  universal in scope, 211
Mohammed, 166
Moses, 94
Muslims, 166
mystery, 22
Mystery of God, 94

Name, 94
  of God, 94
  of the beast, 215

Naomi, 31
Nationalism, 60
Nations, 32, 37, 41
Nehemiah, 36
New covenant, 34
New Jerusalem, 90, 130
Noah, 28, 46, 49
Noah's mission, 31
Non-Christian, 219
Non-Christian religions, 166, 223, 225
Number seven, 127, 132–133
  number of completeness and fullness, 133
  symbolic value, 132

Old Testament, 32
  remnant, 32
Oligos, 88
Open remnant, 84
Opposition, 192
  to the Remnant, 192
Oppression, 187
Orthodoxy, 155, 218
Overcomers as remnant, 89

Palestinian sectarianism, 57
Patience, 89, 150
Pauline remnant, 81
  expansive, 81
  inclusive, 81
Paul's remnant conception, 81
Paul's remnant theology, 82
People of God, 174
People of promise, 78
Persecution, 51, 105, 187, 207–208, 213, 228, 231, 242
  by pagan Rome, 207
  by the apostasy of the church, 207
Perseverance, 223
Perth declaration, 109
Philo, 63
Post-exilic community, 35, 36, 38
Predestination, 97, 177
Pre-exilic prophets, 34
Preterism, 206
Priestly people, 95
Priests, 98
Proleptic remnant, 171
Promise, 29, 38, 105
Prophecy, 109
Prophetic gift, 161, 231
Prophetic movement, 163

Prophetic period, 209
Prophets, 102, 182, 198
Protection, 52–53
Protestant, 211
Protestant Bohemians, 186
Protestant ecclesiology, 217
Purified remnant, 38
Puritans, 175

Qumran, 43, 55–56
  covenantors, 55–56
  documents, 54
  eschatological remnant, 55
  remnant community, 60
  sectarian, 54
  special status, 56
Qumranites, 58
  remnant from the remnant, 58
  separated remnant, 58
Qumran texts, 55
Qur'an, 167

Radical reformers, 209
Reformation, 175, 185, 206, 208, 220, 222
  restored historicism, 206
Reformed theology, 176
Reformers, 157, 231
Remnant, 21, 23, 27, 32, 34, 39, 43, 44, 47, 48, 51, 53–54, 61, 79, 85, 90, 91, 96, 98–101, 104, 106–108, 110, 113, 136, 150, 157, 159–160, 163–167, 169–172, 182–184, 186, 190, 193, 196–197, 199, 201–202, 205, 210, 212, 217, 221, 223
  accept Christ as their Savior, 197
  according to grace, 79
  a global movement, 212
  among non-Christian religions, 169
  among unbelievers, 197
  a movement for social justice, 171
  and God's commandments, 113
  and the Commandments of God, 100
  and the Universal Church, 217
  and the visible church, 110
  an inclusive group, 183

  announces the good news of salvation, 100
  a religious entity, 172
  as a community, 110
  a sign of hope, 201
  as mediators, 98
  authentic posterity of the woman, 101
  a visible entity, 111, 210
  characterized by faithfulness, 91
  closeness to Jesus, 91
  come out of Babylon, 196
  defective elements, 193
  dragon's wrath, 107
  ecclesiastical entity, 111
  emerges victorious, 108
  exclusive, 39
  faithful community, 27
  faithful generation, 110
  future reality, 171
  glorify God, 96
  has nothing to fear, 107
  have the patience of the saints, 150
  identifiable, 27, 111
  in *1 Enoch*, 44
  in *2 Baruch*, 51
  in Adventist contemporary theology, 159
  in Babylon, 223
  in church history, 186
  inclusive, 39
  in Jubilees, 47
  in Qumran Literature, 54
  in Revelation 12, 100
  in the book of Revelation, 85
  in the Gospels, 61
  in the New Testament, 186
  in the Old Testament, 184
  in the post-Old Testament period, 61
  in the writings of Ellen G. White, 182
  invisible entity, 170
  invisible group, 165
  Jewish Apocalyptic, 43
  joined Christ, 203
  keep the commandments of God, 136
  listen to God's Word, 197
  Non-Christians, 166
  nucleus of God's people, 202
  object of the wrath of evil powers, 199

Thematic Index

Old Testament, 27
open to biblical truth, 197
other Christians, 160, 164
post-exilic community, 34
proclaiming the message, 157
proclaims the final call, 106
proclaims the three angels' messages, 205
Qumran, 43
Qumran documents, 54
reformers, 190
remnant groups, 111
resisted, 90
restore biblical truth, 199
simplest definition, 23
specific community, 32
survives, 53, 99
survivors, 201
sustained by the grace of God, 99
total reliance on Scripture, 104
visible Christian movement, 163
visible expression of the people of God, 221
visible or invisible, 160
within Islam, 167
Remnant church, 110
Remnant communities, 33
  identifiable, 33
Remnant ecclesiology, 217
Remnant groups, 41
Remnant idea, 50, 60
Remnant language, 84
Remnant motif, 23–24, 37, 39, 50, 85
  ancient Near East, 24
  eschatological emphasis, 24
  Hebrew roots, 25
  negative sense, 25
  Old Testament, 24
  origin, 24
  post-exilic, 39
  post-exilic writings, 39
  Yahwistic faith, 24
Remnant of all ages, 97
Remnant of Israel, 59
Remnant of Joseph, 30
Remnant of the seed, 96
Remnant people, 153, 196
  keep the faith of Jesus, 153
  threatened with death, 196
  unable to defend themselves, 196

Remnant people of God, 181
  writings of Ellen. G. White, 181
Remnant self-consciousness, 57, 60
Remnant terminology, 85, 87
Remnant theology, 52, 57, 78
Repentance, 30, 66, 221
Restoration, 65, 67
Returnees, 36
Revelation, 128, 131
  concentric structure, 131
  sevenfold division of the book, 128
Reward, 90
Righteous, 49
Righteousness, 29
Righteous remnant, 44
Roman Catholic Church, 218
Ruth, 31

Sabbatarian Adventists, 159
Sabbath, 122, 131–132, 167, 187–188, 191, 212
Sabbath allusion, 136
Sabbath theology, 127, 135
  book of revelation, 127
  Philo, 127
Sacraments, 218
Salvation, 41, 44, 53–54, 56, 58, 78, 91, 93, 99, 107, 157, 177, 185, 192, 198, 202, 235
  only by faith in Christ, 235
Sanctuary, 39, 129–130, 132, 187
Satanic deceptions, 157, 191
Scripture, 60, 179, 222, 243
  end-product of the prophetic gift, 243
  instrument of reformation, 222
Scriptures, 96
Seal of God, 93, 215
Secret election, 176
Sectarianism, 60
Seed, 63, 74, 82
Seed of the woman, 60
Seed theology, 46, 60
  remnant idea, 46
Self-criticism, 173
Self-identity, 34, 40
Selfishness, 193
Serpent, 105
Servants, 96
  and the Remnant, 96

Seven churches, 91, 152
Shaking, 194
Signs, 50
Sin, 50, 193, 202, 240
Sincere believers, 199
  come out of Babylon, 199
  in Babylon, 199
  join God's eschatological remnant, 199
Sincere Christians, 110
Sodom, 82
Sola Scriptura, 214
Sons of darkness, 57, 60
Sons of light, 57, 60
Spirit, 67
Spirit of prophecy, 102, 104, 144, 148
  prophetic gift, 148
Spiritual Babylon, 40
Suffering servant, 97
Sunday, 133, 214
Survival, 38
Survivors, 34, 82, 86, 88, 94

Tablets of stone, 125
Targumim, 146
Temple, 36, 38, 59, 117–118
Ten Commandments, 115, 125, 140
Ten Commandments in Revelation, 119
  allusions to, 119
Tent of the testimony, 117
Testimony of Jesus, 88, 98, 102, 141, 144, 227–228, 230–232
  and the Remnant, 102
  a special light, 228
  a special message, 228
  content-oriented, 228
  in the writings of Ellen G. White, 227
  Jesus' Revelation to John, 233
  Jesus' testimony or witnessing to divine truth, 230
  possible explanations, 141
  prophetic gift and the content, 232
  provokes persecution, 231
  six times in the book of Revelation, 141
  subjective genitive, 144
  the totality of Scripture, 232
  truth for the present time, 228

Thematic Index

Word of God, 144
The Christian community, 205
The faith of Jesus, 188
  have faith in Jesus, 188
  teachings of Jesus, 188
The Lord's day, 135
  the seventh-day Sabbath, 135
Theodicy, 49, 50
The true and faithful remnant, 202
Three angels, 101
Three angels' messages, 131, 163
Thyatira, 213
Time of trouble, 196
Times of distress, 52
Torah, 56
Tribulation, 211
Tribulations, 88
Triumphalism, 173, 217
True believers, 32, 178
Truth, 20, 155, 173, 178, 187, 189, 222, 238
Two-age eschatology, 50
Two witnesses, 94–96
  and the remnant, 94
  attacked by the beast, 94
  give testimony, 94

Old and New Testaments, 95

Unfaithful woman, 213
Unholy trinity, 157
Unity, 190, 218
  based on biblical truth, 190
Unity of the church, 179
Universal church, 108, 175, 178, 219
  a church in exile, 219
  all who truly believe in Christ, 175, 219
  and the remnant, 175
  diffused throughout the Christian world, 219
  it is invisible, 219
  transcending denominational borders, 219
Universal election, 59
Universalism, 44
Uriah Smith, 162

Vengeance of God, 51
Victorious remnant, 97
Victory of Christ, 107
Vindication, 45, 53
Violence, 94, 103
Visible church, 170, 221

Visible unity, 225

Waldenses, 175, 186, 231
Wickedness, 50, 57
Wilderness, 57
Woman, 95, 104, 205
  and the Remnant, 104
  faithfulness to the Holy Scriptures, 95
  in the wilderness, 95
  people of God, 104
  represents the people of God, 205
  Word of God, 88, 96, 98, 104, 112
Work, 79, 99
Work of deception, 157
Works, 54, 97
Worship, 94, 97–100, 102, 105, 118, 131, 152, 157, 175, 184, 215
Wrath, 91, 93, 99, 195, 237

Yahweh, 59
Year-day principle, 207

Zerubbabel, 95, 185